W9-CFO-298

The Southern Subculture of Drinking and Driving

CURRENT ISSUES IN CRIMINAL JUSTICE
VOLUME 17
GARLAND REFERENCE LIBRARY OF SOCIAL SCIENCE
VOLUME 1107

CURRENT ISSUES IN CRIMINAL JUSTICE

FRANK P. WILLIAMS III AND MARILYN D. MCSHANE

Series Editors

THE SOUTHERN SUBCULTURE OF DRINKING AND DRIVING
A GENERALIZED DEVIANCE MODEL FOR THE SOUTHERN WHITE MALE

JULIAN B. ROEBUCK
KOMANDURI S. MURTY

GARLAND PUBLISHING, INC.
NEW YORK AND LONDON
1996

Library of Congress Cataloging-in-Publication Data

Roebuck, Julian B.
    The Southern subculture of drinking and driving : a generalized deviance
model for the Southern white male / by Julian B. Roebuck, Komanduri S.
Murty.
        p.   cm. — (Garland reference library of social science ; v. 1107)
(Current issues in criminal justice ; v. 17)
    Includes bibliographical references and index.
    ISBN 0-8153-2376-X (alk. paper)
    1. Drinking and traffic accidents—Social aspects—Southern States.
2. Drunk driving—Social aspects—Southern States.   3. Alcoholism—Treatment—Southern States.   I. Murty, Komanduri Srinivasa.   II. Title.
III. Series.   IV. Series: Garland reference library of social science. Current
issues in criminal justice; 17.
HE5620.D7R63   1996
363.12'51—dc20   95-53726
                                                                                          CIP

Printed on acid-free, 250-year-life paper
Manufactured in the United States of America

To our respective wives and children:

Elizabeth, Marybeth, Lance, Julian and Mary Elizabeth

Andal, Vandana and Chandana

CONTENTS

Series Editors' Foreword

Volumes in the Current Issues in Criminal Justice series focus on scholarship, original thought and research, and readability. This one is no different. Julian B. Roebuck and Komanduri S. Murty have produced a volume that will be of vital interest to those who study and create policy on drunken driving — one of the more enduring social problems of the past two decades.

The volume has two major components that make it unique in the drunken driving literature. First, Roebuck and Murty focus on drunken drivers themselves and, through the use of a large dataset, add to our knowledge of that group of people by describing their characteristics. Second, and perhaps more important, Roebuck and Murty delve into the phenomenology of the drunken driver through a lengthy interview process. Thus, we begin to understand what drinking and driving means to those who do it and the cultural circumstances under which it occurs. The results of their inquiry yield lessons for most of our attempts at controlling this social problem, particularly so for those who subscribe to deterrence and rational theories of human behavior.

Roebuck and Murty's work is an excellent example of original scholarship being brought to bear on a contemporary issue. Indeed, we believe that this volume has important implications for policy makers who carefully read what the authors have to say.

Frank P. Williams III
Marilyn D. McShane

Preface

Drinking and driving is institutionalized in American society, and the majority of the general driving population, at one time or another, drives after drinking. Yet social control of the drinking driver persists as an important policy issue in the United States because some drinking drivers pose a potential threat to public safety. Since the 1960s researchers have developed several categories of drinking drivers. However, no extant typology for different segments of the population adequately encompasses the characteristics and patterns of these motorists' offenses. The purpose of this study is to further develop drunk-driving offender subtypes that will serve heuristic, treatment and control policy needs within the southern working-class subcultural context. To this end we analyze a sample of drunk-driving offenders attending 65 DUI (driving under the influence of alcohol) clinics throughout the state of Georgia. Unlike other DUI subtype studies, this work employs a particular arrest history analysis anchored in the generality of deviance and subcultural-interaction theory grounded in ethnographic analysis.

Guided by the generality of deviance theory, we first classify at the normative level four subgroups of DUI offenders based on arrest history analysis : (1) First-time DUI Offenders (social drinkers); (2) DUI Recidivists (alcoholics); (3) DUI and Other Traffic Offenders (problem drinkers and bad drivers); (4) Mixed Multiple Offenders (problem drinkers and "criminals on the road"). Second, at the structural, sociodemographic and social psychological levels we examine each subgroup's personal characteristics, drinking type, drinking-related perceptions of self and others, and drinking history. Third, at the subcultural-interaction level, we utilize the ethnographic data obtained from personal interviews with a subsample of 311 white male DUIs to reconstruct their social reality along the following six dimensions: self-concept and identities, life-history and personal relationship problems, life-style, world view, drinking and driving patterns and attitudes, and reactions to the criminal justice system and the DUI label. We reason here that one must go to the social actors themselves to find out who they are, what they do, and why they do what they do in relationship to drinking and driving.

The manuscript is organized into six chapters. In Chapter 1 we introduce the emergence of drunk driving and the drinking driver as a social problem utilizing the constructivist approach. We review the research literature on DUI offender subtypes, detail our theoretical frame of reference and methodology, and define the data sources in Chapter 2. In Chapter 3 we classify 2,786 Georgia DUI offenders into four arrest history subgroups, and then examine the sociodemographics and social psychological characteristics of each. In Chapter 4, the core of the study, we analyze the four DUI subgroups along all eight study dimensions on the basis of a subsample of 311 white males. That is, in addition to the above two dimensions (sociodemographics and social psychological characteristics), we utilize personal interviews to obtain data on the remaining six dimensions. In Chapter 5, we sketch the available DUI deterrence, treatment and mechanical control measures. Finally, in Chapter 6, Summary and Conclusions, we indicate how the generality of deviance and subcultural-interaction theory explicate the deviant and/or criminal behavior of the multiple DUI offenders under study, suggest treatment and control measures for each, and provide study implications.

In conclusion, we found that the recidivistic DUI offenders in subtypes 2, 3, and 4 possess a deviant southern working-class culture, whose carriers feel they are criminalized and controlled by middle-class morality. We hope that future researchers will find our arrest history and ethnographic DUI subtype analysis useful as a generalized deviance model for the southern working-class white male. We trust that a more refined analysis along these lines will follow for different segments of the drunk-driving population.

We acknowledge the theoretical suggestions of Frank P. Williams III and the help of other Garland Publishing reviewers of the manuscript. We extend our appreciation to Estella C. Funnyé, Administrative Assistant, Clark Atlanta University for proofreading the manuscript, and to Krishna Suryadevara, a graduate student at Clark Atlanta University for her assistance in data processing and the typing of the manuscript. We also thank Mary Teets of the Federal Highway Administration, the Scientific Communications Branch of National Institute of Alcohol Abuse and Alcoholism, Betty Hanacek of Metropolitan Atlanta Council on Alcohol and Drugs, and Douglas Espinosa of the Security Guild International for furnishing us with national licensed driver statistics and information on deterrence and treatment measures. Finally, we are most grateful to our study subjects for their input during the personal interviews, without which the study would not have been possible.

This book is coauthored and represents coequal efforts in all respects.

THE SOUTHERN SUBCULTURE
OF DRINKING AND DRIVING

I. DRUNK DRIVING AS A SOCIAL PROBLEM

Drunk Driving and the Drunk Driver

Drunk driving entails the intersection of two social problems, alcohol abuse and traffic safety and is defined as irresponsible, antisocial, and illegal behavior by the general public and the law. Though there are several approaches to this phenomenon (for example, the legal, moral, economic, epidemiological, actuarial, and social psychological), any plausible analysis of this issue must include a combination of sociocultural and individual factors (Waller, 1985; Thurman, Jackson, and Zhao, 1993). This serious traffic violation and/or crime, depending on jurisdictional definition, encompasses either one or both of two components: (1) driving a motor vehicle while intoxicated as determined by a police officer's field test for intoxication, and/or, a BAC[1] level at or beyond limits set by state law (usually 0.08% - 0.10%); and, (2) the commission of a traffic law violation (generally a strict liability offense) while intoxicated. Driving while intoxicated, though at times difficult to ascertain, is considered to be (at law) a self-induced physical impairment that puts oneself and others at risk. Therefore, the drunk driver is assumed to intentionally drive when intoxicated whether or not he commits any other violation, or is consciously aware of his intoxicated condition (Gusfield, 1981; Jacobs, 1989). Although drunk-driving laws and the definition of the drunk driver vary somewhat from state to state, the sequential unfolding of events involved in a typical drunk-driving arrest generally include several basic types of evidence that may be relevant in prosecuting the charge: the intoxicated driver's role in a traffic accident, irregular or illegal driving before a police stop, drunken comportment after the stop, behavioral

3

impairment on the field sobriety tests, and blood-alcohol levels that exceed the legal limit (Snortum, Riva, and Berger, 1990).

The drunk driver is generally defined in the literature as a DUI (Driving Under the Influence), DWI (Driving While Intoxicated or Driving While Impaired), DWIA (Driving While Intoxicated by Alcohol), or DUIL (Driving Under the Influence of Liquor). We use the term DUI throughout this work in a generic sense for all these designations and view such offenders as   social types[2].   Drugs other than alcohol are excluded from the analyses.

Although there is an awareness of the drunk driver's inevitability given the consumption of alcohol and motor vehicle driving in our society (both legal), there is an increasing public demand for reducing the number of drunk drivers.   During the last decade, several researchers have documented the costs of drunk driving in terms of injuries, deaths, and property damage (Gould and McKenzie, 1990). Though recent research suggests (Lund and Wolfe, 1991) that the incidence of drunk driving has decreased over the past five years, approximately one and one half million drunk-driving arrests are made annually in the United States -- more arrests than for any other offense for which national data are compiled (Greenfeld, 1988; Federal Bureau of Investigation, 1992). For national trends in DUI Arrests, see Appendix A.

Though alcohol, the intoxicating agent of the drunk driver, occupies an important and acceptable place in the social life of the United States, it is simultaneously associated with many problems; for example, alcohol abuse, alcoholism, crime (particularly assault, sex offenses, and homicide), violent behavior, suicide, cirrhosis of the liver, traffic accidents, domestic difficulties, etcetera (Gould and Gould, 1992).   The use of alcohol particularly impinges on highway safety in that millions of Americans drive after drinking, some of whom are drunk drivers at one time or another. Though drunk driving is not the paramount cause of ordinary traffic accidents, drivers with BAC levels exceeding .08 increase the probability of becoming involved in traffic accidents. Furthermore, the more severe the accident, the higher probability that it is alcohol related. There is certainly a relationship between drunk driving and traffic accidents, but the preciseness of this relationship has not been determined because of the interference of other causal factors and a number of methodological measurement problems (Borkenstein et al., 1974; Jacobs, 1989:27-41; Kennedy et al., 1994). More than a decade ago, Gusfield (1976, 1981) claimed that the drunk-driving problem has been constantly exaggerated through and by faulty press releases and distorted research studies (usually because of poor research design and other methodological errors). He referred to this exaggeration as "a social construction of the drunk-driving problem." That is, various social actors (including drinking drivers, law enforcement personnel, journalists, the media, legislators, and researchers) create/ construct this highway social problem.[3]

Drunk Driving as a Public Issue

The Highway Safety Act of 1966 mobilized public attention on, and provided resources for, combating drunken driving by federalizing the issue through the National Highway Safety Bureau [the forerunner of the National Highway Traffic Safety Administration (NHTSA)]; and, by authorizing and publishing the U.S. Department of Transportation's crucial 1968 report, *Alcohol and Highway Safety*. This report underlined the necessity for counter measures to the drunken driving problem (U. S. Department of Transportation, 1968). The association of this problem with traffic casualties in the United States and elsewhere in the western world has led both government agencies and the private sector to concentrate on drunk-driving prevention as a nationwide priority (Surgeon General's Report, 1979; Light, 1994). In addition to the activities of legislative bodies, government policy makers, the media, private industry, and health care professionals, a number of grassroots organizations [for example, Remove Intoxicated Drivers (RID) founded in New York in 1978, Mothers Against Drunk Driving (MADD) in 1980, and Students Against Drunk Driving (SADD)] have emerged across the country. The efforts of all these agencies have constructed drunk driving as a social problem--along with a militant public agenda to alleviate this condition. This was accomplished not only through successful attempts to change drunk-driving laws but also through attempts to alter moral beliefs about drinking and driving. Jacobs (1989) and Ross (1992) note that the 1980s marked a decade of legal (at the federal and state levels) and extralegal efforts to reduce drunk driving through and by changes in the law, and attempts to alter moral beliefs, views, and community standards related to drinking and driving (Grasmick, Bursik, Jr., and Arneklev, 1993). These efforts have included general educational programs on drunk driving, the treatment of drunk drivers, and a proliferation of drunk-driving schools made mandatory for DUI offenders prior to or following conviction (in order to retain drivers' licenses or have them returned following revocation).

The passage of stiffer laws against drunk driving has been the focal point of these endeavors (Sheingold, 1974; Weed, 1987; Hingson and Howland, 1990; Kingsnorth, Alvis, and Gavia, 1993). States continue to vie with each other in an attempt to reduce drunk driving by: reducing legal BAC levels of intoxication; intensifying law enforcement procedures (tougher criminal sanctioning, stiffer fines, extended sentences, mandatory jail terms, stringent license suspensions and revocations); the restriction of plea bargaining; increasing police vigilance in drunk-driving arrests; special drunk driving patrols, and night-time road blocks at which all drivers are stopped and checked for signs of intoxication. In short, a "temperance movement" is developing with regard to drinking and driving; that is, absolutely no driving after drinking is to be permitted.

To date, drunk-driving control strategies from within and without the criminal justice system (education, prevention, deterrence, the extension of civil liability laws and insurance surcharges, incapacitation, opportunity blocking, and rehabilitation) have proved of meager long-term value (Zimring, 1978, 1982; Jacobs, 1989:102-190; Moskowitz,1989; Nichols, 1990; Morse and Elliott, 1990, 1992; Elliott and Morse, 1993). Ross et al. (1990:163-164) explain this failure of long-standing deterrence on the basis that drivers who perceive a severe punishment if caught, but a near zero chance of being caught, are being rational in ignoring the threat. Furthermore, Ross and Foley (1987) noted reluctance within the criminal justice system to impose ever-increasing harsher mandatory sentences for drunk driving. Other studies have yielded mixed results concerning the deterrent effect of legal sanctions. Some researchers claim that deterrent strategies utilizing the moral factor have been more effective than legal sanctions (Grasmick, Bursik, Jr., and Arneklev, 1993). The validity of these moral factor studies is subject to criticism because they are based on interviews with general population groups within hypothetical situations instead of on interviews with actual drunk-driving recidivists. These studies further suffer from the difficulty of separating the deterrent effects of legal sanctions and the so-called moral factor (for example, shame and embarrassment), because legal sanctions entail moral sanctions. Moreover, many researchers point out that the failure of DUI control and treatment measures may inhere in the absence of well-delineated drunk-driving subtypes (Murty and Roebuck, 1991).

Drinking Norms, Sociability, and The Booze Factor

There is an overlap between two separate legal and socially acceptable behaviors, drinking and driving. Moderate (non-intoxicated) drinking is not illegal. Approximately one-third of the U.S. male population report total abstention; 44% drink an average of fewer than three drinks per week; about 37 percent drink about two drinks per day; 19 percent average three or more drinks per day (U.S. Department of Health and Human Services, 1993: 1-30). Therefore, the drinking practices among most Americans render them unlikely to drive drunk. Approximately 79 percent of the population have drinking habits that preclude the probability of their driving under the influence of alcohol on a regular basis. They either do not drink and drive or probably drink within legal BAC limits or drive very carefully after drinking or are fortunate enough not to be caught. Another 15 percent of all drivers are heavy social drinkers who may be on the road at times with illegal BACs.

About 10 percent of all drivers are problem drinkers who may frequently be on the road with illegal BACs (U.S. Department of Health and Human Services, 1993:1-30; U.S. Department of Transportation, 1992:24-36, 1993:1-6).

Though drinking and driving patterns may vary from state to state and region to region, drinking and driving is an important aspect of recreational lifestyle among many males in the United States. Male patrons travel to myriads of bars, taverns, cocktail lounges, country clubs, night clubs, and other drinking establishments via personal automobiles, their preferred mode of transportation. Some drinking places are not accessible by public transportation. Society provides different kinds of drinking establishments, from posh cocktail lounges to dives, to meet the style and needs of different social classes. Research literature on bars reveals that drinking places are time-out unserious settings wherein sociability and play constitute the most general standing behavior pattern. This is the case despite variation in drinking places with respect to ecological location, use, characteristics of patrons, decor, goods and services, and history (See Cavan, 1966; Roebuck and Frese, 1976; Donnelly, 1978; Gusfield, Rasmussen and Kotarba, 1984; Roebuck 1986; Snow and Landrum, 1986; Snow and Wells-Parker, 1986; Wieczorek, Miller and Nochajski, 1992; Scribner, MacKinnon and Dwyer, 1994). Regular participation in bar culture supposedly requires the patron to maintain driving competency while at the same time consuming several alcoholic drinks during each and every drinking episode--usually varying from one to three or more hours. Most regular bar patrons consider themselves to be competent drinkers and drivers, and their drinking companions mutually support such claims. For many of them, the automobile represents more than a means of transportation--it is a status symbol and an indication of one's personal taste and persona. For many bar patrons, drinking is a convivial, social ritual which promotes camaraderie among boon drinking companions and inheres in the masculine role--and frequently results in driving when intoxicated. Unfortunately, we do not have enough studies on intoxicated drivers from different segments of the population; i.e., by region, state, and social class.

Alcohol-Related Traffic Crashes and Intoxicated Drivers

In 1993, 6.6 percent of all traffic crashes (400,000) were classified as alcohol related. However, 43.5 percent of all fatal crashes (15,536) and of all traffic deaths (17,461) were found to be alcohol related. These traffic deaths represent an average of one alcohol-related fatality every 30 minutes. About 2 in every 5 Americans will be involved in an alcohol-related crash at some time in their lives. The National Highway Traffic Safety Administration (NHTSA) defines a fatal traffic crash as being alcohol related if either driver or a nonoccupant (e.g., pedestrian) had a blood alcohol concentration (BAC) of .01 grams per deciliter (g/dl) or greater in a police-reported traffic crash. Persons with a BAC of .10 g/dl or greater involved in fatal crashes are considered to be intoxicated. This is the legal limit of intoxication in most states. More than 1.6 million drivers were arrested in 1992 in the United States for driving under the influence of alcohol or narcotics, comprising an arrest rate of 1 for every 108 licensed drivers. In 1993, 35 percent of all traffic fatalities occurred in crashes in which at least one driver or nonoccupant had a BAC of .10 g/dl or higher. More than two-thirds of the 13,984 people killed in such crashes were themselves intoxicated. The remaining one-third were passengers, nonintoxicated drivers, or nonintoxicated nonoccupants. Thirty-three percent of all fatal crashes during the week were alcohol related, compared to 56.9 percent on weekends. For all crashes, the alcohol involvement rate was 4 percent during the week and 12 percent during the weekend (U. S. Department of Transportation, 1993).

The highest intoxication rates in fatal crashes were recorded for drivers 21 to 24 years old (30.7 percent), followed by ages 25 to 34 (28.5 percent) and 35 to 44 (23.6 percent). Intoxication rates were highest for motorcycle operators (32.9 percent) and lowest for drivers of large trucks (1.7 percent). The intoxication rate for drivers of light trucks was higher than that for passenger car drivers (24.9 percent and 20.7 percent, respectively). Safety belts were used by only about 16 percent of the fatally injured intoxicated drivers, compared to 26.4 percent of fatally injured impaired drivers and 41.5 percent of fatally injured sober drivers.   Fatally injured drivers with BAC levels of .10 g/dl or greater were about 6 times as likely to have a prior conviction for driving while intoxicated compared to fatally injured sober drivers (13.1 percent and 2.0 percent, respectively).   More than one-third of all pedestrians 16 years of age or older killed in traffic crashes were intoxicated. By age group, the percentages ranged from a low of 10.6 for pedestrians 65 years and older to a high of 53.2 percent for those 25 to 34 years old.   All states and the District of Columbia now have 21-year-old minimum drinking age laws. NHTSA estimates that these laws have reduced traffic fatalities involving drivers 18 to 20 years old by 13 percent and have saved an estimated 13,968 lives since 1975 (U.S. Department of Transportation, 1993).

Some researchers claim that drinking even moderately deteriorates one's ability to drive and contributes to highway fatalities.   Seasoned drinkers, they claim, can handle themselves better at the same blood-alcohol level than novices, but, nonetheless experienced drinkers are typically far too overconfident about their ability to drive safely while intoxicated. Because alcohol tends to dull anxiety and tension, drunk drivers frequently think they perform better than they actually do. Many are surprised when their reduced driving skill after drinking is demonstrated to them. Their problem then becomes not only a deterioration in mechanical ability, but false perception as well. These researchers further point out that at about the .03 percent blood-alcohol level, some very inexperienced drinkers display a decline in the ability to perform a wide range of mechanical tasks.   The Federal Aviation Administration (FAA) sets a .04 percent BAC as an alcohol-influenced condition and prohibits pilots from flying at this level of intoxication. This may be translated into slightly less than two ounces of distilled spirits (two drinks) within an hour for a 150-pound male. However, at the .04 percent level, for most people there appears to be no measurable increase in the likelihood of having a highway accident, but at the .06 percent level, the risk doubles (slightly more than two typical mixed drinks, or two beers, or two glasses of wine (Goode, 1994:143-144).

In conclusion, this overall sketch of drinking and driving as a social problem in the United States indicates to us the need for more particularistic studies of drunk drivers within specific subcultural regions. As James B. Jacobs demonstrates in his theoretically relevant book *Drunk Driving: An American Dilemma* (1989:53), little research has focused on the characteristics of drunk drivers, their patterns of offending, and their social meanings of drinking and driving within different population segments, that is, by region and state. In this endeavor, we focus on the southern subculture of drinking and driving with special reference to white working-class males.

II. DUI SUBGROUP STUDIES, FRAME OF REFERENCE, AND METHODOLOGY

Several researchers specify the necessity of delineating drunk-driving subtypes because of the probable interaction effect between offender characteristics and differential sanctions, deterrence, and control measures. That is, one type of drunk driver, for example, the first offender, may require a different regimen from that of the recidivist (Morse and Elliott, 1992). In this chapter, we review the relevant literature on drunk driver subgroups, present our theoretical frame of reference, and detail the methodology.

Who Is the Drunk Driver?

Not all individuals who drink, drive after drinking, or drink when driving get arrested for DUI; and, not all DUI arrestees recidivate (Perrine, 1990). However, some drinkers become DUIs, and some DUI offenders continue to drive recklessly and dangerously despite previous arrests, convictions, probations, incarcerations, license revocations, accidents, attendance at DUI schools and/or alcohol treatments. For this reason, Jacobs (1989) suggests that drunk drivers be placed on a continuum of deviancy, dangerousness and culpability--ranging from ordinary DWI traffic violators to aggravated, deviant, DWI offenders. "Ordinary DWI offenders" are presumably conventional non-recidivists who otherwise are law abiding. He considers persistent, recidivistic drunk drivers a much greater threat to the community than ordinary DWI violators and recommends that this deviant type of offender be identified and treated and/or controlled in a different manner from ordinary DWIs.

13

According to Jacobs, in this endeavor researchers and control agents must focus on: (1) the characteristics (personal, sociodemographic, and social psychological) of different types of drunk drivers; and, (2) their patterns of offending. (Many of the pertinent questions he poses in these two areas can best be obtained from ethnographic data, which is reflected later in our interview schedule.)

Though many researchers have identified demographic and psychological characteristics among different DUI subpopulations, a definitive profile of the drunk driver remains incomplete (Simpson, 1985; Perrine, 1990). Researchers do find that a large number of sampled DUI arrestees are problem drinkers (Ehrlich and Selzer, 1967; Waller, 1967; Selzer, 1971; Yoder and Moore, 1973; Vingilis, 1983; Borkenstein, 1980, 1985; Snowden, Nelson, and Campbell, 1986; Jacobs, 1989; Perrine, 1990; Smart et al., 1991).

Studies focusing on the personality traits of drunk drivers yield mixed results (Perrine, 1970; Zelhart, 1972; Zelhart, Schurr, and Brown, 1975; Marlatt and Rohsenow, 1980; Donovan and Marlatt, 1982; Donovan et al., 1983, 1986; Scoles, Fine, and Steer, 1984; Snowden, Nelson, and Campbell, 1986; Donovan, 1993; Reynolds, Kunce and Cope, 1991; Stacy, Newcomb, and Bentler, 1991). Though first-time DUIs are reported to have fewer personality aberrations than multiple DUI offenders (Donovan, Marlatt, and Salzberg, 1983; Cox, 1987; Stacy, Widerman, and Marlatt, 1990; Reynolds et al., 1991), no specific drunk-driving personality type (personality structural characteristics apart from behavioral patterns) has been found, even after comparing personality types of subsets within the DUI population (Sutker, Brantley, and Allain, 1980; Donovan and Marlatt, 1982; Donovan et al., 1985, 1986; Donovan, 1989). On the other hand, several studies indicate that DUIs as a group tend to be impulsive, thrill-seeking, and non-conforming offenders, who possess a set of risk-taking characteristics (Zuckerman, 1979, 1989; Joksch, 1985; Jonah and Dawson, 1987; Stacy, Newcomb, and Bentler, 1991; Donovan, Umlauf, and Salzberg, 1991; Donovan, 1993). Johnson and White (1989) report the existence of a risky driver who speeds, follows too closely, wears no seat belt, and drives while intoxicated.

Wilson and Jonah (1985) found that drinkers who admitted driving when intoxicated used seat belts less, and reported being less likely to restrain from drinking at a party before driving than drinkers who did not report drinking and driving. Several other researchers report associations between drunk driving and other deviant behaviors; for example, drug use, aggressive behavior, thrill seeking, proneness to peer pressure, and other forms of illegal behavior (Wilson and Jonah, 1985; Farrow, 1987; Barnes and Welte, 1988; Farrow and Brissing, 1990). The implication of these personality findings is that DUIs are high-risk drivers who are in need of treatment for problems with alcohol.

Donovan, Marlatt and Salzberg (1983) found that personality factors and an alcohol consumption rate might interact, as a moderating effect, to influence drinking problems including DUI. Stacy, Newcomb and Bentler (1991) also found, on the basis of longitudinal study data, that there was a moderating or interactive effect of personality and alcohol consumptions on drinking problems, and the problems of driving when intoxicated. Greater alcohol consumption provided more frequent or extensive behavioral cues for people who scored low on a social conformity scale to engage in problematic or risky behaviors (including DUI) than those who scored high on such a scale.

Therefore, though a definitive DUI personality type has not been identified, the findings suggest that multiple DUIs in an individual's arrest history may be just one among several manifestations of a generalized deviant pattern. Furthermore, the ingesting of alcohol by persons low on self-control may more readily provoke them to engage in drinking and driving than is the case of those possessing high self-control. Additionally, some other researchers report stressful life-events as experienced by DUI arrestees immediately prior to the instant DUI arrest (Veneziano, Veneziano, and Fichter, 1993). [The authors found no such stressful life-events among their study subjects.]

The Portrait of Incarcerated Drunk Drivers

On June 30, 1989 there were an estimated 395,000 adults confined in the nation's 3,312 local jails and of these, an estimated 30,147 (13.8%) were serving sentences after conviction for DUI. Nearly 2 percent of those in jail were unconvicted inmates charged with DUI. Among convicted or unconvicted persons in jail for DUI, males predominated (90.1%), and the racial distribution was more similar to the adult general population (87.2% white, 8.2% black, and 4.6% other) than was the case for those jailed for offenses other than DUI (52.9% white, 45% black, and 2.1% other). The median age of the DUI jail inmates was 32 years, about 5 years older than the median age of those jailed for other crimes. About 47 percent had completed high school; approximately 20 percent had eight years or less of education. Almost 70 percent of DUI inmates were not living with a spouse at the time of their arrest. Nearly 35 percent had never been married, 35 percent were divorced or separated, and 2 percent were widowed. Twenty-two percent were unemployed; 69 percent were full-time employed; 9 percent part-time employed. Fifty-two percent of those jailed for DUI had previous DUI convictions. About 86 percent of DUI offenders had been previously convicted of a crime, including DUI, and had been sentenced to probation, jail, or prison--a greater proportion than that of those in jail for other crimes (76%). Nearly half (45%) of those in jail for DUI had a criminal justice status at the time of their arrest: probation (33%), parole (5%), bail/pretrial release (5%), or other release (3%). About four out of five jailed DUI offenders reported that they had been drinking with others, mostly in a bar/tavern/inn or a friend's house, prior to their arrest (Cohen, 1992). Statistics on arrestees, studies of DUIs in treatment programs, roadside surveys (Jacobs, 1989), and individual studies (Wilson and Jonah, 1985; Kingsnorth, Alvis, and Gavia, 1993) generally affirm this portrait.

DUI Criminal Justice Processing and Heterogeneity

When incarcerated, DUIs are frequently confined in special jail areas and enrolled in alcohol treatment and traffic safety educational programs, where they are generally considered to be offenders without criminal intent (National Institute of Justice, 1984; Greenfeld, 1988). Many are released on probation status that requires attendance at DUI schools, but receive little attention for non-alcohol related problems. The complete arrest records of those arrested on DUI charges are not usually analyzed, but when examined show other charges not directly related to alcohol (Waller, 1967; Willett, 1964; Landrum, Windham, Roebuck, 1981; Argeriou, McCarty, and Blacker, 1985; Wells-Parker, Cosby, and Landrum, 1986; Miller and Windle, 1990; Lucker et al., 1991; Gould and Gould, 1992; Keane, Maxim, and Teevan, 1993; Wells-Parker et al., 1993). Many drunk-driving studies limit arrest tabulations to DUI and other traffic charges, a misleading practice, which creates an artificial DUI offender category. Therefore, the popular (and legal) image of a specialized DUI offender persists, despite the fact that a number of studies have found that drunk drivers do not comprise a homogeneous group, but rather a number of subgroups varying in offender characteristics, drinking type, and criminal history (Zimring and Hawkins, 1973; Selzer, Vinokur, and Wilson, 1977; Steer, Fine, and Scoles, 1979; Sutker, Brantley, and Allain, 1980; Donovan and Marlatt, 1982; McCord, 1984; Argeriou, McCarty, and Blacker, 1985; Donovan et al., 1985; Wells-Parker, Cosby, and Landrum, 1986; Snowden, Nelson, and Campbell, 1986; Metzger and Platt, 1987; Beerman, Smith, and Hall, 1988; Laurence, Snortum, and Zimring, 1988; Homel, 1988; Nichols and Ross, 1990; Morse and Elliott, 1990, 1992; Gould and Gould, 1992).

This DUI diversity suggests to some that not only might there be an interaction effect between offender characteristics and the type of sanction employed (contributing to a differential sanction efficacy), but that the lack of attention given to factors other than alcohol problems among DUIs may explain the long-term failure rate of drunk-driver intervention programs (Donovan and Marlatt, 1982; Morse and Elliott, 1992; Gould and Gould, 1992; Nochajski et al., 1993). Additionally, several studies not only suggest that DUI prevention efforts need to be directed at specific subgroups but also that such prevention programs may require more than deterrence and alcohol programs (Nochajski et al., 1993; Wieczorek, Mirand, and Callahan, 1994). Many DUI studies do differentiate between first-time and multiple DUI offenders (Donelson, Beirness, and Mayhew, 1985; Donovan, Marlatt, and Salzberg, 1983; Perrine, Peck and Fell, 1989; Vingilis, 1983).

Subgroup Studies

Over the last two-and-one-half decades, several researchers have attempted to differentiate among drinking drivers by means of multidimensional conceptualizations and typologies. According to Perrine (1990) the "spectrum" of drinking drivers can be grouped into three subpopulations: (1) the "Quick" or the one who has never been arrested for alcohol-related problems; (2) the "Caught" or the one who is apprehended and convicted of DUI; and, (3) the "Dead" or the one who is fatally injured and has positive blood alcohol concentrations (BACs). From an extensive literature review he observed that the Caught had significantly more prior DUI convictions, more prior reckless-driving convictions, and more prior moving convictions than the Dead; that 1.5 times more of the Caught than the Quick consumed five or more drinks on specific drinking occasions; that approximately 50 percent of legally impaired drivers with BAC levels of 0.10 or higher would pass field sobriety tests because of their high alcohol tolerance level and therefore would not be part of DUI statistics.

Steer, Fine, and Scoles (1979) classified 1,500 male DUI arrestees into seven types based on their self-reported quantity and frequency of drinking, scores on an impairment index and on the neuroticism scale of the Eysenck Personality Inventory, and BAC at the time of arrest. In a subsample of 350 men, five characteristics differentiated significantly among the seven types: race, prior arrest for DUI, previous treatment for alcoholism, use of psychotropic drugs, and father's use of alcohol.

Donovan and Marlatt (1982) studied personality subtypes among 172 males who were arrested for DUIs. Cluster analysis of driving attitude, personality, and hostility measures yielded five subtypes. Two subtypes were found to have particularly high levels of risk-enhancing traits. The first of these subtypes was characterized by the highest levels of driving-related aggression, competitive speed, sensation-seeking behavior, assaultiveness, irritability and indirect and verbal hostility. The second subtype was characterized by the highest levels of depression and resentment, as well as the lowest levels of assertiveness, emotional adjustment and perceived control. The five DUI subtypes were compared to an additional set of demographics, current drinking, and driving risk variables to determine subtype validity. The analyses disclosed that the first two subtypes comprised individuals of lower social position, heavier drinkers, and high crash involvement risks when compared with the three other subtypes. Results indicated that the individuals with the highest overall level of driving risk in this study were those who drink heavily on a given occasion and those who had a high level of hostility.

Arstein-Kerslake and Peck (1985) analyzed a sample of first-time and multiple DUI offenders, in assessing the role of driver record, criminal record, and psychometric measures in predicting DUI recidivism and alcohol treatment program compliance. In addition, the data from a subsample of these DUI offenders were examined by cluster analyses to develop a "DUI offender typology." The analysis resulted in the identification of nine categories: (1) Negligent Operator; (2) Pre-DUI Alcoholic, I; (3) DUI Alcoholic; (4) Pre-DUI Alcoholic II; (5) "Life Crisis" Problem Drinker; (6) Deceptive Problem Drinker; (7) White-Collar Controlled Problem Drinker; (8) Blue-Collar Controlled Problem Drinker; and (9) Social-Normative Problem Drinker. They also found that members of certain categories might shift into other categories over a period of time; some might cease to be members of the DUI-offender population; while, still others might become new members of the DUI-offender population. These findings are highly significant because they designate process, and different drinking life stages. And as some researchers have known for some time drinkers shift from one category to another over a life-span without a known contributory cause other than age (Cahalan, Cisin, and Crossley, 1970).

Wells-Parker, Cosby and Landrum (1986) devised a typology of 353 offenders who were referred to a probation and rehabilitation program in Mississippi. They classified their study sample into five subgroups: the low (overall) offense group, the mixed (offense) group, the traffic (moving violation) group, the public drunkenness group, and the license offense (equipment and licensing violations) group. They found significant statistical relationships between the subgroups on BAC levels, Mortimer-Filkins scores, drinking status and subsequent 24-month accident and DUI recidivism rates. The public drunkenness and license groups had the highest percentage of problem drinkers, and the public drunkenness group, by far, had the highest rate of subsequent crashes. The license group and the public drunkenness group had the highest recidivism rates. The low offense, mixed, and traffic groups were younger and had comparatively lower proportions of problem drinkers and lower recidivism rates. They found as did Steer, Fine and Scoles (1979) and Donovan and Marlatt (1982) that their subjects varied in problem-drinker severity, age, and the extent to which their driving records reflected a general disregard for traffic laws.

Wilson and Jonah (1985) studied a sample of 2,000 Canadian drinking drivers, and classified a subset of 1,420 respondents into three categories: (1) drinkers who reported that they have not driven after drinking any alcohol within the past month ("nondrink-drive"), 52 percent; (2) drinkers who reported that they drove after drinking on one or more occasions but had not driven impaired ("drink-drive"), 35 percent; and, (3) drinkers who admitted that they drove on one or more occasion when they thought they might have been legally impaired ("driving while impaired"), 13 percent. Impaired drivers, as a group, differed from the "drink-drive" drivers along the following dimensions: drinking habits, driving behavior, peer influence, and attitudes toward drinking-driving. On the other hand, "drink-drive" drivers were found to be similar on the above dimensions to those who rarely or never drive after drinking. The impaired drivers appeared to be a small and socially deviant group, distinct from the larger group of average, occasional drinkers. This study, like others, posits that the tendency to drive while impaired may be just one manifestation of a broader constellation of high-risk behaviors. The alcohol consumption rate was found to be the single most powerful predictor of impaired driving. The study concluded that situational factors that increase the opportunity to drink and drive seem to control, to a considerable degree, the decision to drive after consuming moderate amounts of alcohol, whereas peer influence and such internal factors as attitude, perception, and behavior seem to play a vital role in predicting impaired driving. [This degree of differentiation among drinking drivers, as Perrine (1990) has commented on, implies a necessary differentiation in countermeasures in order to facilitate deterrence across the spectrum of drinking drivers.]

In a successive study, these investigators (Jonah and Wilson, 1986) categorized their study sample into three groups: (1) respondents who reported that they did not believe they had driven while legally impaired within the past 30 days (N=34); (2) respondents who admitted that they had done so (N=93); and, (3) respondents who were convicted of DUI (N=53). Despite the small sample size, the results showed that convicted DUI offenders had more prior accidents and convictions, drank a greater quantity of alcohol on a given occasion, showed more symptoms of problem drinking, and scored higher on measures of assaultiveness and depression. Both the admitted-impaired drivers and the convicted DUI drivers were more externally controlled, resentful, verbally hostile, impulsive, and self-deprecative. Thus, these results support the conclusions of Donovan and Marlatt (1982) and other researchers that impaired drivers are a deviant group characterized by low impulse control, personal maladjustment and a tendency toward heavy alcohol consumption associated with negative consequences of drinking. The study also suggests that convicted DUI drivers represent a deviant subgroup of all impaired drivers because they have been selected by the police on the basis of their high-risk behavior which is more visible; that is, involving a crash or reckless deviant driving.

The foregoing subgroup studies are somewhat consistent in terms of classification structure and the resulting subgroups but do not utilize complete   arrest-history analysis for their typologies.

Multiple-Offender Drunk Driving Subgroups: The presence of charges other than DUI in the arrest records of DUI offenders has suggested to some the necessity of a criminal history dimension in delineating DUI subgroups (Gould and Gould, 1992).   Furthermore, the frequency, nature, and diversity of these additional charges make obvious the requirement of arrest history analysis for constructing DUI subtypes (Argeriou et al., 1985; Beerman et al., 1988; Nochajski et al., 1993).

Research has identified various relevant characteristics among drunk drivers, for example, race, sex, age, prior driving record, and prior criminal history, and determined their correlations with multiple DWI offending (Gould, 1989; Stewart and Gruenewald, 1986; Argeriou, McCarty and Blacker, 1985).   These study findings suggest a higher risk of multiple DUI offending among those with a history of other criminal activities than among those DUIs without such a record (Gould, 1989; Stewart and Gruenewald, 1986).   Several studies based on convicted or incarcerated drunk driving samples have examined several aspects of the relationship between DUI offending, BAC levels, and criminal arrests.   Much of this research has dealt with only comparisons of one DUI subgroup to the general population, or with investigation of the criminal activity of just one DUI subgroup (Pollack, 1969; Yoder and Moore, 1973; Zelhart, Schurr, and Brown, 1975; Argeriou, McCarty, and Blacker, 1985).

The fact that the majority of arrested drunk drivers had other criminal arrest charges in their arrest records was first reported by Waller (1967).   Since then other researchers (including Pollack, 1969; Yoder and Moore, 1973; Zelhart, Schurr, and Brown, 1975) have confirmed his findings.   More recently, Argeriou, McCarty, and Blacker (1985), Gould (1989), and Gould and Gould (1992) have also confirmed these earlier findings and have helped to establish a relationship between a history of drunk driving and prior criminal arrests. Each of these studies found a statistically significant difference in rates of criminality between a sample of licensed drivers and a sample of DUI offenders (Tashima and Peck, 1986).

Other research has suggested that within the multiple offender category there is an identifiable group that is at higher risk for involvement in other types of criminal behavior (Gould, 1989; Stewart and Gruenewald, 1986; Argeriou, McCarty, and Blacker, 1985). These studies indicate that any efforts at deterring drunk drivers must take into account subgroups of DUI offender types (Gould, 1989; Stewart and Gruenewald, 1986; Gould and Gould, 1992). According to Gould and Gould (1992), the development of these DUI subgroups must include the DUI's life history patterns of deviant behavior along with his or her arrest and conviction record (only one facet, they find, of a generalized deviant career). Argeriou, McCarty, and Blacker (1985) noted an early pattern of criminal behavior and DUI arrests among DUI arrestees, however the nature of this relationship has not been spelled out. In a broader and more general sense, a significant relationship has been established between alcohol consumption and aggressive behavior, violent behavior, sex offenses, violent and property crime, anti-social behavior in general, and explosive shifts in mood and emotion (Wolfgang and Ferracuti, 1982; Roizen and Schneberk, 1977; Nathen and Lisman, 1976; Gould and Gould, 1992; and Jung, 1994).

The Generality of Deviance Thesis

The generality of deviance thesis herein is based on a social control theory incorporating the classical school of criminology's view of the role of choice and a positivistic view of the role of causation in explaining criminal behavior (Gottfredson and Hirschi, 1990). People who lack self-control tend to be impulsive, insensitive, physical and concrete (rather than abstract), risk-taking, shortsighted, and nonverbal; and, therefore are likely to engage in criminal and analogous deviant acts. These traits are identifiable in childhood, rise to a peak in late adolescence and decline sharply thereafter, but persist throughout life. The major cause of this low self-control is purported to be an ineffective child-rearing (dearth of discipline and affection in the individual's home) and his or her failure to bond with conventional people, associations, and institutions. People of this type when exposed to weak external social controls are likely to become generalized deviants who commit a wide variety of deviant and criminal acts with no inclination to pursue a specific criminal act or a pattern of deviant and/or criminal behavior to the exclusion of others (See Gottfredson and Hirschi, 1990; Akers, 1994). [Many clinical psychologists, with some justifications, would call such persons sociopaths, though sociologists would strongly disagree. Moreover, many clinical psychologists would claim a biosocial base for what they refer to as "low impulse control" or "low self-control" in sociologists' terminology. (See H. J. Eysenck, "Crime and Personality," in D. J. Miller, D. E. Blackman, and A. J. Chapman (Eds.) *Personality Theory, Moral Development, and Criminal Behavior*, Lexington, MA: Lexington Books, 1984.) Thus, criminality results from the individual's tendency or propensity to seek short-term, immediate pleasure without concentrated effort; that is, in the absence of social bonds.] Findings supporting this theory have been found for populations involved in adolescent and young adult deviance (Osgood et al., 1988; Donovan, 1993; Caspi et al., 1994); for career criminals (Blumstein, Cohen, and Farrington, 1988); and for recidivistic felons (Petersilia, Greenwood, and Lavin, 1977; Gould and Gould, 1992).

The research findings of Nagin and Paternoster (1994) were derived from a model of crime designed to link rational choice and social control theory, predicting an interaction between risk perception and present orientation. That is, individuals who are self-centered and present oriented invest less in conventional attachments and commitments than do individuals who are more future oriented and less self-centered, and therefore are more likely to risk criminal activity. The latter, due to their greater investment in "personal capital" (individuals who are more future oriented and less self-centered) are more likely to be deterred from committing criminal acts by the perceived risk of damage to their investment. To test this theory, they utilized a sample of university students faced with three offense scenarios: drunk driving, larceny, and sexual assault. In response to the scenario described, respondents were asked to estimate the probability that they would commit the act specified in the scenario and the chance that their commission of the crime would result in their arrest and their being publicly exposed without arrest. From a battery of questions all respondents were measured for present orientation, self-centeredness, and self-control. The future-oriented subjects were more likely to be deterred by the perceived risk than were the present-oriented subjects. [Though interesting and possibly significant, the authors of this book are leery of such behavioral modals based on non-offender attitudes and perceptions.]

Keane, Maxim, and Teevan (1993) in a secondary analysis of data from a roadside traffic survey examined (via interviews) the relationship between self-control variables and driving when intoxicated. Using several indicators of self-control (wearing seat belts, probability of being stopped by police, responses to others who discouraged them from driving when intoxicated, the number of drinks they had consumed in the past seven days, self-perception of intoxication, BAC levels, and response to life-style questions), they found the existence of a relationship (for both men and women) between low self-control and driving under the influence of alcohol.

Finally, Caspi et al. (1994) in their seminal and highly significant cross-national studies of personality and crime, in New Zealand and Pittsburgh, found support for Gottfredson and Hirschi's (1990) proposition that the lack of "self-control" predisposes some people to engage in criminal behavior across different countries, genders, races, and methods. *Moreover, they suggest an additional significant and necessary personality dimension to that of lack of self-control, namely negative emotionality which accompanies weak constraint (difficulty in impulse control) in the commission of antisocial acts.* Negative emotionality is defined as a tendency to experience aversive affective states, comprising a combination of aggression, alienation, and stress reaction. This position follows that of H. J. Eysenck, who claims that many criminals suffer from low impulse control on the basis of a classical conditioning behavioral modal; that is, many criminals do not condition well because of an impaired nervous system. (See Curt R. Bartol, "Chapter Two: Origins of Criminal Behavior," *Criminal Behavior: A Psychosocial Approach*, Third Edition, pp. 26-57, Englewood Cliffs, NJ: Prentice Hall, 1991.)

Generality of Deviance As Reflected in Arrest History Analysis

T. C. Willett (1964) identified a dangerous, deviant, drunk-driving offender type in a seminal study of offenders convicted of serious driving offense charges (including DUI) in the London metropolitan area. He found that they: (a) had an arrest history on other offenses as well; (b) led risky and deviant working-class life-styles; (c) drank and drove frequently; and, (d) drove as they lived--recklessly, unlawfully, and deviantly. In sum, Willett found them to be "criminals on the road," which contradicted the then-popular stereotype of these offenders as being otherwise law-abiding citizens. In a later study Willett (1973) compared 181 serious driving offenders in England with 163 non-offenders. The offender categories follow: (a) Causing death by dangerous driving (N=13); (b) Dangerous driving (N=38); (c) Drunken driving (N=46); (d) Failing to stop after, or to report, an accident (N=13); (g) Driving while uninsured (N=35). Ninety-five of these offenders were convicted of more than one of these seven offenses, and many of them were also driving under the influence of alcohol, though they were not charged with this offense.   Offenders were categorized according to their most serious conviction charge. He compared these seven subgroups with one another, and then with the controlled non-offender group on sociodemographic characteristics and personality inventory traits (Catell 16 Personality Factor Inventory). The criminal records revealed that one-half of the sample had been convicted at least three times either for motoring or non-motoring offenses; 63 percent had three or more motoring convictions; 27 percent had been incarcerated in prison or a juvenile institution. He found that serious motoring offenders differed from general driving population control groups, and corresponded more closely to offenders convicted of criminal offenses against property and person. The offenders, in comparison to general population control groups, were more frequently younger males with low educational and occupational status, having higher proportions with criminal records for both motoring and non-motoring offenses, and displaying more evidence of social pathology such as unstable employment and heavy drinking. The personality inventory showed that the serious Traffic Offenders were more aggressive, self-confident but less intelligent, and less sensitive to guilt feelings than the controls. As drivers the offenders were more experienced in terms of mileage driven per year than the controls and more confident of their driving ability. Arrest, conviction, court procedures, sentencing, and punishment did not change these offenders' attitudes toward driving or to the instant offense. They did not feel remorse, and did not consider themselves to be stigmatized. Moreover, they did not define themselves as criminals. Neither the police, the courts, nor the public stigmatized them, or looked upon them as criminals. To these offenders the criminal justice process wherein they were involved was a ritualistic inconvenience. Willett defined the recidivists among these offenders as a deviant driving group of criminals, "Criminals on the Road." He concluded that the public, the police, and the courts should be more concerned with sorting out serious dangerous drivers from less serious DUI arrestees (Personal written correspondence with Willett dated January 4, 1993).

He viewed his "criminals" as a deviant type, that is, those who lacked self-control and tended to be impulsive, insensitive, risk-taking, shortsighted and nonverbal. Therefore, they would be more likely to engage in a variety of deviant and criminal acts than people with adequate self-control. Though "dated," this benchmark study remains highly significant, but it has not received proper attention in the literature.

Milton Argeriou et al. (1985) examined the arrest histories of 1,406 randomly selected DUI offenders in Massachusetts, obtained from probation records in the Office of the Commission of Probation, Commonwealth of Massachusetts, in order to delineate arrest history subgroups. They defined and utilized the arrest history charges by arrest as primary behavioral data. They found that arrest histories were the most demonstrably important dimension in discriminating among DUI offender subgroups; though, they did not deny the usefulness of other dimensions (including personality and demographic characteristics). The arrest histories revealed that half (51.2%) had been arraigned for criminal offenses other than or in addition to traffic and DUI charges, and that one-fourth (27.7%) had been previously arraigned for DUI. Among those with prior DUI arrests 68 percent also had prior criminal arrests. A three-year follow-up study disclosed that 63 percent of those rearrested for DUI had prior criminal arrests. The sample was classified into eight subgroups of offenders on the basis of the presence or absence of criminal, traffic, and DUI offenses: (a) Criminal offenses only (11.3%); (b) Criminal and traffic (21.1%); (c) Criminal and prior DUI (3.2%); (d) Criminal, traffic and prior DUI (15.6%); (e) Traffic only (16.4%);(f) Prior DUI only (3.2%); (g) Traffic and prior DUI (5.8%); and, (h) No prior offenses (23.5%). This classification showed that DUI recidivism varied significantly among the subgroups. The more extensive the history of prior criminal arrests, the greater the rate of recidivism. Individuals with no previous arrests (Category H) exhibited the lowest rate of recidivism. Those with only criminal, traffic or prior DUI arrests (Categories A, E, and F) had a higher rate of recidivism. Those with criminal and traffic, criminal and prior DUI, or prior DUI and traffic (Categories B, C, G) had even higher recidivism rates. Those exhibiting all three types of previous arrests had the highest recidivism rate (Category D)--almost three times larger than that of individuals with no previous arrest. This mixed multiple category comprised the most dangerous deviant DUI type. Finally, Argeriou et al. identified an early and repeated relationship between criminal behavior and DUI arrests.

Kathy A. Beerman, Margaret M. Smith, and Roberta L. Hall (1988) examined 397 Benton County, Oregon DUI Offenders' complete arrest histories (both DUI and non-DUI) for a 12.5 year period (January 1, 1973 through July 24, 1985) in order to identify biographical variables, arrest circumstances, and recidivism that differentiated between drinking drivers on the basis of their total number of DUI offenses. They define a DUI recidivist as a driver who received more than one citation for drinking and driving within the study period. Recidivists (N=174) were subgrouped by the total number of DUI arrests recorded into three categories: those with two DUI arrests (N=96), those with three DUI arrests (N=43), and those with four DUI arrests or more (N=35). Their analysis shows that non-recidivists and recidivists differ significantly in terms of their criminal histories and BAC levels but that they do not differ in age, sex, race, occupation, etcetera. Furthermore, an increasing number of DUI arrests in an individual's arrest history is associated with a higher percentage of prior criminal offenses and with higher BAC levels at time of instant arrest. Both minor offenses (disorderly conduct, harassment, public intoxication, minor "in possession," destruction of property, resisting arrest, criminal trespass, criminal mischief, disturbing the peace, shoplifting and false pretense), and major offenses (theft, forgery, assault, parole violations, auto theft, bad checks, homicide, arson, illegal alien, possession of controlled substance violations, and assault with a deadly weapon) were included. They conclude that drivers having multiple DUI arrests also have had prior convictions for other criminal offenses, serious drinking problems, and difficulty in conforming to the norms of society; that is, they comprise a generalized deviant group.

Larry A. Gould and Kristin Herke Gould (1992) tested the degree to which the generality of deviance theory might apply to DUI offenders. To this end, a random sample was selected from the population of 14,356 persons charged with DUI in Louisiana in 1985. The sample of 723 was divided into two groups: (1) those DUIs arrested for the first time on any charge, N=227, and (2) DUIs for whom the instant arrest charge was on a second or subsequent arrest (on any charge), N=496. These two groups were found to be representative of the licensed population of the state in race; similar in age, similar in the number of years between the issuance of the first driver's license and the arrest in 1985, and similar in average educational level, socioeconomic status, and marital status. The specific hypotheses tested were: (1) that the first-time DUI arrestee group is less likely to have a prior criminal record than is the group of multiple-DUI offenders; (2) that the multiple offender group is likely to have a higher overall average BAC level (for all DUI arrests) than that of the first-time offender subgroup, (3) that for offenders in either group, the greater the prior criminal activity, the higher the BAC level at the time of the instant arrest. The data were also expected to lead to the identification of high-risk offenders in both the single and multiple offender groups. The hypotheses were based on the generality of deviance theory which would predict that the person with two or more DUI arrests (indicators of weaker levels of internal self- and external social control) would be more likely to have participated in, and been arrested for, other offenses than would a first-time DUI offender--who should hypothetically, represent a subgroup with higher levels of self- and/or social control.

Their sophisticated statistical findings based in part on a refined risk matrix showed that, except for the hypothesized differences, the two groups were similar in background and makeup. Multiple DUI offenders were more likely to have committed criminal acts than first-time offenders; more likely to have been arrested for acts of violence; more likely to have been involved in accidents; had a higher BAC at the time of the instant arrest; had an overall higher arrest BAC level for all offenses; had a higher risk matrix; tended to consume more alcohol than first-time offenders; comprised more career criminals than did first-time offenders; and were more frequently immersed in the drinking subculture than were first-timers. The multiple offenders also showed a higher consumption of alcohol in a single drinking episode. These findings support the major hypothesis that was grounded in the generality of deviance theory, in that the multiple offenders evinced a pattern of weaker self- and/or social controls (as measured by their indicators) than did first-time offenders. They concluded that the DUI offender (particularly the multiple DUI) should be evaluated prior to sentencing and placement in any treatment program on the basis of one's entire criminal history, pattern of life-time deviancy, and the circumstances of the instant arrest. Unfortunately the Goulds did not comment on treatment procedures, but such was not their research purpose. In addition to an excellent piece of drunk-driving subgroup analysis, they provide a valuable review of the literature on drunk-driving subgroups. Most significantly the study provides strong support for the generality of deviance theory.

The 1988 National Health Interview Survey

Though not specifically geared toward the development of DUI subgroups, the kind of data solicited from research respondents during this survey is essential to the construction of any DUI subtypes. For this reason, and because some of our interview questions were modeled upon this survey's interview schedule (as will be seen later) we examine briefly this 1988 interview survey which solicited questions from respondents about "driving after drinking too much." The 1988 National Health Interview Survey, a stratified multi-stage probability sample of the U.S. population, includes a detailed Alcohol Survey funded and structured by the National Institute on Alcohol Abuse and Alcoholism (U.S. Department of Health and Human Services, National Institute of Alcohol Abuse and Alcoholism, 1990, 90-1656). The Alcohol Survey collected data from over 43,000 individuals on drinking patterns, symptoms of alcoholism, family history of problem drinking or alcoholism along with standard socioeconomic and demographic data. Each respondent was considered a "current drinker" if he or she had "driven a car after having too much to drink" in the past year (that is, as defined and determined by the respondent). Additionally, questions were asked subsequent to the question on drinking and driving, such as, if he or she had "done things when drinking that would have caused you to be hurt," and "done things when drinking that would have caused others to be hurt." This 1988 Alcohol Survey provided the most useful guide for obtaining ethnographic data on DUIs via interview that we found in the literature.

Literature Summary

The literature discloses the heterogeneity of the drunk-driving population, the need for the further development of subtypes among this offender group for heuristic as well as treatment and control purposes, and the suitability of arrest-history and ethnographic analyses as an added dimension. (On the latter point, see Pruis, 1984.) These findings and suggestions appear to be anchored in the generality of deviance theory as enhanced by Caspi et al.'s "low impulse control component" in explicating deviant behavior (including drunk driving). Extant studies suggest that the most deviant drunk-driving-convicted offender is a young white male with a multiple arrest history, including criminal charges other than for DUI, who leads a risky and deviant life-style, drinks and drives frequently and recklessly, thereby posing a significant threat to roadway users. In brief, he is a generalized deviant. Convicted DUI offenders, as a group, are likely to have significantly more prior DUI convictions, more prior reckless-driving convictions, and more moving convictions than the alcohol-positive fatally injured drivers and are likely to consume significantly greater amounts of alcohol as the usual amount than do first-time DUI offenders. Further, the need for additional primary data with reference to DUI characteristics and patterns of offending by different population groups was made clear. We therefore concluded to meet this requirement via ethnographic interviews.

FRAME OF REFERENCE

Though some researchers have developed subgroups of drunk drivers on the basis of a number of characteristics and drinking types, there is no established typology of these offenders employing a comprehensive arrest history analysis in conjunction with sociodemographic, social psychological, and ethnographic data. This study, in an effort in this direction, provides a subgroup classification inclusive of all of these study dimensions. Based on the generality of deviance and subcultural-interaction theory, this study, unlike other DUI subgroup classifications, relies heavily on the extensive use of ethnographic data.

First, in order to establish arrest patterns at the normative level, we identify four subgroups among a sample of 2,786 convicted DUI offenders on the basis of individual arrest history charges; that is, all arrests by criminal charge. Then we tentatively interpret these arrest history subgroups in terms of number of arrests and types of charges. Second, at the structural, sociodemographic, and social psychological levels we examine personal characteristics, drinking type, drinking-related perceptions of self and others, and drinking history for each subgroup. Findings at this level are expected to support those at the first level. Third, at the subcultural-interaction level we analyze biographical and ethnographic data on a sub-sample of 311 DUIs (by offender subgroup) along the following additional dimensions: self-concept and identities, life history and personal relationship problems, life-style, world view, drinking and driving patterns and attitudes, and reactions to the criminal justice system and the DUI label. Here we try to get inside the head of the respondents in order to find out who they are and their social reality of drinking and driving.

Regarding the first level, we utilize each arrest history (arrest by criminal charges from first through last arrest) as our unit of analysis in the identification of DUI subgroups. More than one arrest for any offense indicates a pattern of crime given the assumptions of the relatively low probability of being arrested for DUI in the first place (Bankston et al., 1986), that engaging in one form of criminal behavior increases the likelihood of engaging in another (Gould and Gould, 1992), and that the longer the arrest history, the more deviant the offender. Furthermore, other researchers (including Argeriou et al., 1985; Beerman, Smith and Hall, 1988; Gould and Gould, 1992) have found that primary behavioral data and patterns of offending inhere in arrest histories; and, that arrest charges are the most significant dimension in discriminating among drunk-driving subgroups. Furthermore, we assume, along with some others, that legal offense categories specify behavioral categories to some degree, and that when classifying convicted offenders, it is first necessary to order behavioral categories within the confines of legal categories (see Willett, 1964; Roebuck, 1967; Willett, 1973; Clinard and Meier, 1979; Argeriou et al., 1985; Beerman, Smith and Hall, 1988; Gould and Gould, 1992).

Adopting the generality of deviance proposition (Osgood, et al., 1988; Gottfredson and Hirschi, 1990; Caspi et al., 1994), we assume that DUI arrestees with a record of multiple arrests (two or more) would have a criminal pattern; and, in comparison with first-time DUI offenders (without a criminal pattern) would evince a more deviant and/or criminal lifestyle, would engage in deviant and/or criminal activities earlier on in life, would display more impulsivity, insensitivity, risk-taking behavior and shortsightedness, and would possess less verbal ability. On the other hand first-time offenders would be less self-centered, more affiliated with conventional institutions, more self-controlled, and future oriented. We expected driving while intoxicated to be but one manifestation of impulsive and risk-taking behavior among DUIs with multiple arrests (on any charge). We also expected multiple offenders to operate in a personal and social environment of weaker behavioral controls than that of first-timers--thereby permitting them wider latitudes of all sorts of deviant behavior.

We did not assume that first-time DUI offenders would be uniformly different from multiple offenders, because every DUI offender is a first-time offender at one point. However, in this study (dealing with males of the same race, of the same age group, and from the same geographical area), we expected that, as a group, those with multiple arrests would, in general, represent a more deviant and criminal population than those with only one arrest (See Gould and Gould, 1992; McCord, 1984). We consider all offenders in this study to be deviants as well as criminals in a normative sense, because they had been convicted of an unacceptable violation of a major social and legal norm that elicits strong negative reactions by social control agents, as well as by the general public. Furthermore, the DUI label had been successfully attached to them by members of the criminal justice system as well as by some other citizens.

Second, at the structural, sociodemographic, and social psychological levels, we follow the leads of James B. Jacobs in his book *Drunk Driving; An American Dilemma* (1989) and T .C. Willett in his book *Criminals on the Road: A Study of Serious Motoring Offenses and Those Who Commit Them* (1964). Data from both sources include (and call for) ethnographic as well as personality and structural variables. At this juncture we focus on the characteristics of drunk drivers and their drinking patterns and drinking type. To reiterate, there is, as yet, no definitive profile of the drunk driver, nor do we know when and under what circumstances he or she drinks and drives. Who is the culpable, high-risk drunk driver, who warrants the strongest controls? Who are the DUIs who drive when aware of their intoxication? Who are the DUIs who intentionally become intoxicated while driving? Who are the DUI recidivists who continue to violate DUI laws despite warnings and previous sanctions? We anticipated finding problem-drinking multiple offenders with criminal arrests other than DUI as well as less serious and culpable DUIs--perhaps social drinkers.

The third, subcultural-interaction, level of analysis is two-fold. First, we are concerned with the DUIs' self concepts, how they identify and present themselves to others, and how they are defined and reacted to in their own regional, cultural, and social milieus. Social actors' self and audience definitions are crucial to personas and performances. Do they have particular cultural identities? Do they have deviant identities? That is, do they view their deviance as tangential to major life themes, or is deviance a central theme around which they identify themselves and organize their lives? In brief, is deviance a crucial, conscious identity, or do they deny a deviant identity and lifestyle? Here we rely on Erving Goffman's[4] paradigm of social, personal, and self-identities, stigma, and "presentation of self in everyday life" (Goffman, 1959, 1963).

Next we investigate their life histories, everyday lives, social meanings (particularly of drinking and driving), joint actions, and deviance within an interactionist framework. How do they and fellow rule breakers interact at the micro level to shape the direction and outcome of their legitimate and illegitimate activities? How do they perceive the world and their place in this entity? How do they justify their deviance, criminality and way of life? What are the symbolic meanings behind their behaviors? Here we rely on Herbert Blumer's social interactionist organizational theory that specifies a network of social relations including two different kinds of networks. First, social organization may be viewed as an association, a network of relations among those persons who form some sort of social group. Associations vary from peer group relations to corporations. They may be small or large, formal or informal, of brief duration or enduring. Second, social organization may be viewed as a transaction; that is, a network of relations among those involved in a common activity, whether or not they belong to the same association. Transactions vary from brief encounters to complex, rigid, and highly coordinated operations. Viewing social organization in terms of associations emphasizes the structure of joint activities such as the DUIs' drinking and driving, hunting and fishing, and honky-tonk activities. Associations and transactions are interrelated, two aspects of the same social response. Associations are dynamic; their members participate in transactions. Transactions involve associations of different kinds. Each form of organization complements the other. Although enmeshed, association can be separated from transaction for purposes of analysis. We examine the DUIs' significant associations and transactions; for example, peer group and joint activities (drinking and driving patterns, hunting and fishing activities, honky-tonk behaviors, cross-sex encounters, story telling, etcetera,) from the actors' perspectives, in order to find out what kind of world they live in, what they do, and why they perform as they do. We assume that the DUIs' associations with deviant peers and engaging in deviancy and law-breaking are related reciprocally; that is, their associations with deviant peers lead to increasing deviancy via the reinforcing environment offered by their peer groups; and, that engaging in deviancy lead to increases in associations with deviant peers (See Thornberry et al., 1994).

Whether one focuses on associations or transactions, the social organizational level of analysis utilizes two concepts: position and role (See Mead, 1934; Blumer, 1962, 1969, 1975; Best and Luckenbill, 1994). Position in this case refers to a category of membership whose occupier is supposed to act in a certain way; for example, how the leader of a peer group should act in a honky-tonk? Role refers to a pattern of action expected of a person in a particular situation; position and role are inseparable in a literal sense.

At this level we are particularly interested in how the DUIs' define themselves and how their ideology is tied in with drinking and driving practices, life-style, and reactions to the criminal justice system and the DUI label. On the basis of our cursory knowledge of the larger sample of 2,786 DUIs as gleaned from their drunk-driving school records (and our prior experience with working-class southerners in other research projects), we assumed the existence of specific subcultural themes in the lives of these men would help us in this endeavor.

Subcultural Influences

We define subculture for the purposes at hand as a body of shared knowledge within a larger culture that contains three major elements: first, a specialized vocabulary or argot composed of special words and idiomatic expressions connoting particular social meanings and identifying important persons, objects, or events in the world; second, social and cultural background expectations; third, a cognitive perspective or framework for interpreting their activities and life-style. This ideology has a history developed by carriers (peers, colleagues, and team players) over time. It has its own value system specifying what is desirable, which has been translated into behavioral expectations. Subculture carriers evaluate one another's performances in terms of these norms and support worthy peers for who they are and what they do; *the subculture provides security, and offers a structural base for interaction.* (For a theoretical discussion of deviant subculture development see Best and Luckenbill, 1994:24-25, 32-42.)

Specifically, we anticipated certain values, norms, behavioral prescriptions and cultural patterns among these men similar to those of lower-class males in segregated urban neighborhoods as postulated by Wolfgang and Ferracuti (1982). This subculture of violence theory holds that a set of ideas (values, norms, and behavioral expectations) exists among lower-class males in segregated urban neighborhoods which generate violent behavior. For example, such ideas formulate an ideology that prescribes, supports, and reinforces the quick resort to physical combat as a measure of daring, courage, or defense of status as a form of cultural expression. Therefore, in certain situations a male is expected or required to resort to violence as a means of maintaining status and settling disputes. This subculture reportedly has arisen in the past for specific historical reasons (traceable in part from the south) and is transmitted from one generation to another as a set of ideas. In brief, we expected to find a working-class southern subculture of violence transmitted over time through and by family and peer socialization. *Unlike other southern culture of violence studies, we focus on social-class differentiation in value systems within this region.* (For an analysis of a southern subculture of violence see Cash, 1941; Hackney, 1969; Gastil, 1971; Loftin and Hill, 1974; Gastil, 1975; Curtis, 1975; Doerner, 1978, 1979; Whyatt-Brown, 1982; Roebuck and Hickson, 1984; Vold and Bernard, 1986: 216-218; McWhiney,1988.)

Historians of southern mores contend that violence is an aspect of southern life that has distinguished this region from the rest of the country. Southern white males' penchant for violence has been the perceived, pre-modern social necessity for men of all ranks to preserve white manhood and personal status in the fraternity of his respective male tribe, family, neighborhood, and peer groups--rather than some vague frontier spirit or slavery. More than 100,000 Confederate soldiers died not to preserve slavery because less than one-fifth of them owned slaves. They gave their lives to preserve what they considered to be honor (local ethical rules). Historically the southern male' status depends on his race, family background, honor, physical courage, physical prowess, the proclivity to redress personal wrongs, the use of firearms, and loyalty to one's family and in-group--all buttressed by violence and revenge toward outsiders and perceived enemies. White southerners are generally reared in patriarchal homes that encourage male egocentrism and violent self-expression within a doting female, permissive atmosphere of childhood that accepts childhood aggression toward peers.   Shame is experienced and feared more frequently than guilt.   One's reputation is one's honor or lack of honor. One feels recreant not necessarily for a particular wrongdoing but for unworthiness in the eyes of others and therefore in one's own. Though personal physical violence is used to preserve a man's self-estimation, property, family, and in-group from perceived injury and disgrace within all classes, the working class commits a greater share of violent offenses. Members of the southern middle and upper classes are less prone to unlawful violence but at times let working-class members do their violence for them. White, young, single, menially employed, irregular workers, are those most likely to commit violent offenses, especially on a Saturday night.   Historically southern official criminal practices have ensured the dependence of local justice on the basis of neighborhood opinion. This consensus was (and in the authors' opinion) has been usually determined by the middle and upper classes (Whyatt-Brown, 1982).

Specifically, we expected to encounter some of the lower-class focal macho concerns found by Walter B. Miller (1958) in his studies of male juvenile delinquents.   For example, toughness (physical prowess, skill, masculinity, fearlessness, bravery, daring); smartness (ability to outsmart, dupe, "con"); excitement (thrill, risk, danger, change, activity); fate (being lucky or unlucky); trouble (law and other norm violating behavior); and autonomy (freedom from external constraint, freedom from authority, and independence).   These focal concerns operate according to Miller, as motivational factors in delinquency and crime.

We concluded that the primary data at this subcultural-interaction level could best be obtained from the research subjects' themselves, that is, through and by   personal interviews.   Therefore, we solicited their self-constructed social reality in the form of first-hand accounts, reactions, appearances, and expressed feelings as communicated to us during the personal interview encounters. Social reality here refers to the meanings (definitions, conceptions, and typifications) that these DUI social actors created and assigned to things they told us about in their milieu: their joint activities, negotiations, and behaviors, and human relationships that made social life possible. We viewed DUI respondents as active agents who behave on the basis of their "socially created" reason, choice, judgments, and intentions.

In summary, though we envisioned a separable three-step analysis as outlined above, there was inescapable overlapping from one step to another. Such imbrication was supportive of the other levels involved. We conjectured that such a three-step breakdown would enable us to classify the study sample into heuristically valuable subtypes--subtypes that would prove useful to other DUI subgroup researchers as well as to society's treatment and control agents.

METHODOLOGY

Data Sources

The data for this study were derived from three sources: (a) the 1989 Georgia DUI study data set on 2,786 DUI convicted offenders (Murty, 1989); (b) the official arrest histories of these DUI Offenders as obtained from the Georgia Department of Public Safety (DPS) and the Georgia Crime Information Center (GCIC); and, (c) the authors' personal interviews with a sub-sample of 311 DUI Offenders. For the description of each of these sources, see Appendix B.

The DUI Offender Under the Georgia Criminal Justice System

During the three-year period (1986-89) of the Georgia DUI study, a DUI offender was defined as one who drove, operated, or was in actual physical control of a vehicle under the influence of alcohol, a controlled substance, or both to a degree that rendered him or her incapable of safe driving; that is, as determined by the arresting officer's field test and/or a BAC level of .12 or over (this BAC level is currently reduced to .08). The driver's license of any person convicted of violating the Georgia criminal code (Section 40-6-391) could be suspended up to one year for a first DUI conviction, up to three years for a second DUI conviction, and up to five years for a third DUI conviction. However, any convicted DUI offender had to complete an appropriate alcohol course (Level I for first DUI conviction, and Level II for second or more DUI convictions) at a certified Georgia DUI school within 120 days from the date of conviction and pay a $25 reinstatement fee in order to have their licenses reinstated. Although DUI offenders could be sentenced to jail anywhere from 10 days to one year, the judge could suspend such jail sentences at his/her discretion. The law provided that first and second DUI convictions would constitute a misdemeanor and that third and subsequent convictions would constitute a high and aggravated misdemeanor. The offense for driving with a revoked license was (and is) a felony (paraphrased from the Official Code of Georgia Annotated, 1989). The current Georgia DUI law provides for stiffer penalties than in 1989.

All DUI arrestees in this study spent a minimum of 24 hours in jail following arrest at which time their driver's licenses were automatically revoked. All appeared before a magistrate for a court hearing. In the interim some were released on bail and others (a minority) remained confined until arraignment. At arraignment most pleaded guilty or nolo contendere (no contest), and received suspended jail sentences for varying periods pending completion of a designated alcohol course at a DUI school. Some were required to perform several hours of community services in addition to jail time. The remaining were found guilty following a court trial and received similar penalties. All were required to attend a state certified DUI school for a 16- or 24-hour period in order to have their driver's licenses reinstated.

Arrest History Analysis

We examined each DUI's pattern of offending as disclosed in their complete arrest history; that is, each arrest by criminal charge (charges) from first through last arrest by date and place of arrest. In case of multiple charges, we selected the major offense as determined by the Georgia criminal code in terms of the stiffer penalty (amount of fines, probation, and length of sentence). This procedure eliminated the confusion in arriving at offender type by multiple charges for any one arrest. It also minimized a distortion sometimes created by the police when they charge arrestees with multiple offenses (hoping that one or more will stick)--charges that ensue from one arrest for one unit of criminal behavior. There are also frequent changes in arrest charges subsequent to the original charge resulting from the criminal justice negotiating process (between defense attorney and the prosecutor). The further removed the initial criminal charge from time of arrest, the further removed is the actual criminal behavior. On the basis of this arrest history analysis we classified the 2,786 Georgia DUI offenders into four subgroups: (1) First-time DUI Offenders who were later found to be social drinkers; (2) DUI Recidivists later found to be alcoholics; (3) DUI and Other Traffic Offenders, found to be problem drinkers and bad drivers; and (4) Mixed Multiple Offenders, found to be problem drinkers, bad drivers, and criminals on the road. For the theoretical base of this classification, see preceding section on Frame of Reference.

Secondly, utilizing the Georgia DUI study data base, these four DUI offender subgroups were analyzed and compared along the following two dimensions: (1) sociodemographic characteristics; (2) social psychological characteristics (drinking type: social drinkers, problem drinkers, or alcoholics; drinking-related perceptions; drinking history).

Thirdly, utilizing our personal interview data, a subsample of 311 white male offenders was analyzed along the following six additional dimensions (that is, in addition to the above two dimensions): (3) self-concept and identities; (4) life history and personal relationship problems; (5) life-style; (6) world view; (7) drinking and driving patterns and attitudes; and (8) reactions to criminal justice processing and the DUI label.

In sum, the present analysis consists of three parts: first, the arrest history analysis leading to the identification of the four DUI offender subgroups; second, an analysis of the 2,786 DUI offenders along the first two study dimensions of sociodemographics and social psychological characteristics utilizing the Georgia DUI study data; and third, an analysis of a subsample of 311 offenders along all eight study dimensions (our personal interview data were utilized in analyzing the latter six dimensions).

Measurement of Variables

1. DUI Offender Subgroups: On the basis of the frequency of arrest by criminal charge, we classified 2,786 DUI offenders into four subtypes: (1) First-time DUI Offenders-- those with no prior arrest history (N=281); (2) DUI Recidivists --those with one or more prior arrests for DUI charges. In some cases these DUI charges were accompanied by less serious alcohol-related charges such as public drunkenness, drinking hard liquor in public establishments other than bars and restaurants, open container in car, etcetera (N=471); (3) DUI and Other Traffic Offenders--those with one or more prior DUI arrests and one or more prior arrests for other traffic violations (N=1,295); and, (4) Mixed Multiple Offenders--those with prior criminal charges other than DUI, prior DUI and other criminal charges, and prior DUI, traffic, and criminal charges (N=739). We realize that some of the traffic and criminal charges other than DUI found in the arrest histories of subgroups (3) and (4) may have been alcohol-related. However, because the traffic charges (exclusive of DUI) were not accompanied by alcohol-related charges, and because the offenders denied any such relationship during the interviews, we accepted official records at face value.

II. Sociodemographics

a. Gender: (1) Male, (2) Female.

b. Age: Constructed by subtracting date of birth from date of survey: (1) 16-20 years; (2) 21-34 years; (3) 35-44 years; (4) 45-64 years; and, (5) 65 years or above.

c. Education: (1) Grade School (1 to 8 years); (2) Some High School (9 to 11 years); (3) High School Completion (12 years); (4) Some College (13 to 15 years); (5) College Completion (16 years); and (6) Post-graduate (17 years or more).

d. Marital Status: (1) Married; (2) Separated; (3) Divorced; (4) Widowed; and, (5) Never Married.

e. Income: (1) Under $10,000; (2) $10,000-$19,999; (3) $20,000-$29,999; (4) $30,000- $39,999; (5) $40,000-$49,999, and, (5) $50,000 and over.

f. Employment Status: (1) Full-time; (2) Part-time; (3) Unemployed; 4) Retired; and (5) Not seeking employment.

g. Race: (1) White; (2) Black; (3) Hispanic; (4)Asian; and (5) Other.

III. Social Psychological Characteristics

a. Drinking Type: All DUI offenders in this study were classified at their attending DUI schools into three categories on the basis of the Mortimer-Filkins (M-F)[5] test: (1) social drinkers (score, less than 60); (2) excessive drinkers (score, 60-85); and, (3) problem drinkers (score, over 85).

b. Drinking-Related Perceptions (of Self and Others): These perceptions were classified into four categories: (1) perceived self drinking problems; (2) perceived ability to control self drinking; (3) perceived hangover effects; and, (4) others' perception toward self drinking. (For specific questions under each of these categories and responses by offender subtypes, see Appendix C, Table C. 1.)

c. Drinking History: This dimension has five components: (1) alcohol treatments; (2) alcohol addiction; (3) job-related consequences; and (4) non-job-related consequences. (For specific questions under each of these categories and responses by offender subtypes, see Appendix C, Table C. 2.)

IV. Self-Concept and Identities: Responses to the following four topical questions during the personal interviews were utilized to measure this dimension: (1) Who are you? (2) How would you describe yourself? (3) In what way are you different from others? (4) How do you think others see you?

V. Life History and Personal Relationship Problems: Responses to the following topical questions during the personal interviews were utilized to measure this dimension: (1) What kind of home did you come from? (2) Did you experience any childhood or adolescent problems at home? If so, explain. (3) Did you have any problems at school? If so, explain. (4) Have you had any community problems? If so, explain. (5) Have you had any legal problems? If so, explain. (6) What kind of personal relationship problems have you had? (7) Have you had any courtship or marital problems? If so, explain. (8) Have you had any health problems? If so, explain.

VI. Life-Style: By life-style we mean the behavioral and orientational adaptations that people make while facing problems in the process of social living; that is, behavioral styles of interacting with others in central life activities (see Henslin, 1977:11-16). Responses to the following discussion topics were utilized for this dimension: (1) language form and content and physical appearance; (2) world of work; (3) organizations, associations, and recreation; and, (4) sex and family life.

VII. World View: We define world view from a nominalist perspective. The world is the universe to which people respond on the basis of their assigned meanings to this entity in everyday life; that is, a social construction of whatever one perceives it to be from one's own social experience, as opposed to the so-called objective world (see Lyman and Scott, 1970; Pfuhl, 1986). Responses to the following topical questions were utilized for this dimension: (1) What does the world mean to you? (2) How do you view the world?

(3) What is your place in this world? (4) What are your life plans? (5) What do you think of the future? (6) What does the past mean to you? (7) What does being a southern male mean to you? (8) What does being a Georgian mean to you?

VIII. Drinking and Driving Patterns and Attitudes: Responses to the following specific questions were utilized for this dimension: 1. What is the length of your usual drinking session? 2. How many drinks did you have within a four-hour period prior to the instant arrest for DUI (Beer, wine, hard liquor)? (1, 2, 3, 4, 5 or more drinks)? 3. How many drinks did you have within an hour preceding the instant arrest for DUI (Beer, wine, hard liquor)? (1, 2, 3, 4, 5 or more drinks)? 4. How many times during the past month have you driven within an hour of having consumed 1, 2, 3, 4, 5 or more alcoholic drinks? 5. Do you consider yourself a binge drinker? 6. Why did you drive after drinking? 7. Were you drinking while driving preceding the instant arrest? 8. Where were you heading at the time of the instant arrest? 9. Did you know you were probably too intoxicated to drive prior to the instant arrest? If so/ did you think you could still drive safely? 10. Do you consider yourself a competent driver after drinking? 11. In the past six months, how frequently did you drive after drinking? 12. When you drove after drinking, were you aware of the risk to yourself and to others? 13. Were you facing any extraordinary pressures or problems prior to the instant arrest? If so, please explain. 14. Under what circumstances, were you likely to drive after drinking? 15. Do you think that driving after drinking is morally wrong? 16. How do you feel about people who drive after they drink? 17. Do you think we need stiffer laws against drunk driving? If so, explain.

IX. Reactions to Criminal Justice System and the DUI Label: Responses to the following topical questions were utilized to determine this dimension: (1) Do you think you should have been arrested in the instant case? (2) Do you think you received a fair trial and sentence? (3) Were you treated fairly by the police? Jailers? Court officials? (4) Do you agree that you violated the law when you were arrested? (5) Do you think the police, jails, and courts safeguard society? Were you benefited by attending DUI school? (6) Do you recommend DUI school attendance for other DUI offenders? (7) What do you think of the DUI laws? (8) What do you recommend to reduce drunk driving? (9) Do you think the current law enforcement practices to keep drivers off the road work? (10) Will they work for you? If not, what will? (11) How do you feel about being labeled and called a DUI offender?

The data analysis of the foregoing dimensions are presented in Chapters 3 and 4.

III. ANALYSIS OF ARREST HISTORY, SOCIODEMOGRAPHICS, AND SOCIAL PSYCHOLOGICAL CHARACTERISTICS

Total Sample

The arrest history analysis of the total sample (N=2,786) discloses a mixed bag of recidivists in that nine out of every ten had been arrested at least once for DUI prior to the instant arrest. Of these, 81 percent had one or more prior arrests on traffic or non-DUI criminal charges. This dispels the stereotypic notion of a "pure" DUI offender type. The sample composes a young (56 percent aged 21-34 years), white (72 percent), mate-less (74 percent), male group (85 percent) of full-time employed (72 percent) offenders who earn less than $20,000 a year. Although most (79 percent) are either excessive or problem drinkers, nearly half did not perceive self-drinking problems, and more than two-thirds claimed they could control their drinking. Further, though only one-half (52 percent) claimed that others perceived them to have drinking problems, a large proportion (61 percent) admitted they had experienced negative, non-job related consequences of alcohol consumption; for example, personal, community, and human relationship adjustment problems, and prior arrests for drunken behavior of one kind or another. Moreover, most of these arrestees had also encountered legal, employment, and life-adjustment problems unrelated to drinking and drunk-driving behavior. Notwithstanding, they unrealistically claimed that they could manage their life situations and control their drinking. Most perceived themselves to be competent drivers when and when not drinking.

Subgroup Analysis

In this section, we identify four arrest history DUI subgroups and examine each on the following two dimensions: (1) sociodemographic characteristics; and, (2) social psychological characteristics.   The exercise here is at the normative and structural level of analysis (see Frame of Reference section).

I. First-time DUI Offenders: These 281 First-time Offenders comprise 10 percent of the total sample. Because their arrest records evince no pattern, we conjectured that they might be non-deviant law-abiding social drinkers. One could argue that, because of age, they had not had time to develop a patterned arrest history, however, they do not vary markedly with respect to chronology from two other subtypes (DUI and Traffic Offenders and Mixed Multiple Offenders). Moreover, crime is a young man's game, and with the exception of alcoholic offenders, criminal arrest charges generally decrease after age 30.

Nearly two-thirds are in the age group of 21-34 years, and over one-half (59 percent) are males. Most are married and living together (60 percent), employed full-time (88 percent), and earning more than $30,000 a year (75 percent). Primarily social drinkers (87 percent), only 1 percent considered themselves to be alcohol addicts. Only 7 percent had experienced hangover effects, and only 1 percent had received any alcohol treatments. Few (15 percent) perceived problems with self-drinking, and only 5 percent thought that others perceived them to have problems with drinking. None reported problems with their ability to control drinking. Thus First-time DUI Offenders as a group are social drinkers, and can probably be reasoned with on a rational basis. Perhaps they can be taught to moderate their drinking consumption within legally acceptable levels, particularly drinking before driving. They probably represent people who inadvertently drink to excess before driving, who are not conscious of being intoxicated when driving after drinking, and, who consume alcoholic beverages with no expectation of having to drive soon thereafter. Before the instant arrest these social drinkers may have had "a little too much to drink" and later realized they made a wrong judgment. In any event the cases in this category underline the point (and caveat) that any consumption of alcohol beverages before and during driving is risky (See Tables 2.1 to 2.4).

II. *The DUI Recidivists:* These 471 DUI Recidivists comprise 17 percent of the sample. Of these, 56 percent had two or three prior arrests, 31 percent had four prior arrests, 9 percent had five prior arrests, 4 percent had six to eight prior arrests. On an average, this group had 3.4 prior DUI arrests. Most of these multiple offenders had at least one of the following specific alcohol-related charges in their arrest histories in conjunction with a more serious DUI charge prior to the instant arrest (public drunkenness, disturbing the peace, purchase of alcohol for a minor, violation of the Georgia Controlled Substance Act, intoxication and disorderly conduct, and driving after declared and before expiration of probation period.) On the basis of their DUI recidivism and specific alcohol-related charges, we surmised them to be problem drinkers.

Most are over 35 years of age (73 percent) and nine out every ten are males. Only 34 percent are married and the others are either separated (8 percent), divorced (36 percent), widowed (3 percent) or have never been married (18 percent). Nearly two-thirds have earnings of more than $30,000 a year from full-time employment. Most (91 percent) are problem drinkers; three-fourths (76 percent) are addicted to alcohol; 84 percent had experienced hangover effects; and, 64 percent had received alcohol treatments. Most (80 percent) are aware of their self-drinking problems. However, more than half claimed they could control their drinking (58 percent). For more details, see Tables 3.1 to 3.4.

Although these DUI Recidivists are obviously alcoholics, their danger and threat to the safety of the public on the road is not clear. While several studies have implicated alcoholics as being significant contributors to serious injury and fatal accidents, several others have viewed them as scapegoats for drunk driving as well as for many other social problems. These studies emphasize disturbing events and mental characteristics or states (such as impulsivity, suicidal proclivity, paranoid ideation, depression, and anxiety) in the causation of traffic accidents and injuries more than drunk driving per se (see Jacobs,

1989:42-54). In any event these multiple offenders appear to be generalized deviants on the basis of arrest history and problem drinking history. As disclosed later on in this work, these offenders claim they do not drive drunk frequently.

III. DUI and Traffic Offenders: This largest subgroup of 1,295 DUI and Traffic Offenders constitutes 46 percent of the sample. Members of this subgroup were more frequently arrested for traffic violations than for DUI with a mean ratio of 4 to 1. The specific traffic arrest citations occur in the following order of frequency: exceeding speed limits; disobedience of any traffic control device or traffic officer; illegal lane change or turns; driving without or with expired/suspended license, fraudulent or fictitious use of license; driving without proper equipment; reckless driving; unlawful passing; causing traffic accidents; possession of an open container of an alcoholic beverage while driving; running from or leaving the scene of an accident; and, other traffic moving violations. The average number of prior arrests for this multiple offender group is 5.2. Because these recidivists had separate DUI and traffic violation charges as well as a combination of the two in some cases in their arrest histories, we consider them to be problem drinkers as well as "bad drivers."

Like First-time DUI Offenders, many of these (63 percent) were in the 21-34 years of age. (There were more females in this subtype [20 percent] than any of the other three subtypes.) They were somewhat evenly distributed between "married/living together" and "never married" categories. Given the combination of their age and marital status, some of these drivers' drinking behaviors are probably centered around dating and recreational patterns; that is, to and from parties, dances, restaurants, and bars. Nearly two-thirds (65 percent) have earnings of less than $20,000, although many (75 percent) have full-time jobs. This indicates that many of this membership may have been engaged in low-paying blue collar jobs (Table 2.1). Unlike DUI Recidivists (none of whom are social drinkers), 16 percent of this subgroup are social drinkers (Table 2.2). However, nearly one-third are excessive drinkers and one-half are problem drinkers. Although one-third (34 percent) are addicted to alcohol and 61 percent had experienced hangover effects, only 20 percent had received any alcohol treatment. Over one-half (59 percent) perceived problems with their drinking but only 26 percent perceived problems with controlling their drinking. Like the DUI Recidivists and the Mixed Multiple Offenders, they claimed that they could control their drinking (Tables 2.3 and 2.4). This irrational denial is characteristic of problem drinkers researched in other studies (see Roebuck and Kessler, 1972; McClelland et al., 1972; Goode, 1994; Jung, 1994).

Thus, one-half of the offenders of this recidivistic subgroup are known problem drinkers and the remainder may be in a progression stage of becoming problem drinkers. Furthermore, a sizable number commit traffic offenses even when not legally intoxicated or, at the least, were not so charged. Some of these traffic offenses probably were liquor related. Should this trend continue these offenders will remain risky and dangerous drivers to themselves and to others. Therefore, they appear to be generalized deviants on the basis of their arrest records and drinking problems.

IV. Mixed Multiple Offenders: The Mixed Multiple Offenders had been arrested on prior DUI charges, on other prior criminal charges, and on prior traffic violations. This second largest subgroup of 739 recidivistic offenders comprise 27 percent of the total sample. Their lengthy and serious non-DUI criminal arrest charges follow in the order of frequency: grand larceny (26%); disorderly conduct (18%); burglary (18%); robbery (16%); vandalism (15%); writing bad checks and forgery (15%); possession and/or use of illegal substances (13%); carrying concealed weapons/possession without permits (13%); aggravated assault (12%); criminal trespassing (12%); fraud (10%); vice and gambling (7%); homicide, including vehicular homicide (4%); and, rape (3%). Other less serious arrest charges scattered throughout these arrest histories include: woman battery, child abuse, domestic non-support, littering, public drunkenness, fighting in a public place, refusal to obey a peace officer, resisting arrest, contempt of court, furnishing alcohol to a minor, giving false name or address to a police officer, hindering apprehension, fishing out of season/taking game without license, hunting from public land, and violation of probation--all in conjunction with more serious DUI, criminal, or traffic offenses. These offenders were more frequently arrested for criminal charges followed by traffic and then DUI charges. The average number of prior arrests for this group is 8.1. These arrest histories and their structural characteristics indicate problem drinkers, criminals, and bad drivers. This subgroup makes up the most dangerous drivers and the most serious offenders in the sample.

These offenders are somewhat older than the First-time DUI Offenders, and the DUI and Traffic Offenders, but are younger than the DUI Recidivists. Clearly everyone is over 20 years of age and most (83 percent) are in the ages from 21 to 44 years. Almost all of them (99 percent) are males and only 23 percent are married or living together. Nearly 70 percent claimed earnings of less than $20,000 and only 56 percent had been engaged in full-time jobs (Table 2.1). Their reports of relatively low incomes and less frequent full employment pursuits probably indicate a sporadic criminal life-style. Like the DUI and Traffic Offenders, 16 percent of this subtype are social drinkers (Table 2.2). But there are more problem drinkers (56 percent) in this category than in the DUI and Traffic Offender subtype (50 percent). Although more than one-half (52 percent) perceived hangover effects from drinking during the night before, only 23 percent considered themselves to be addicts, only 26 percent thought they did not have the ability to control their drinking, and only 11 percent had ever received any alcohol treatment (Tables 2.3 and 2.4).

Thus the Mixed Multiple Offenders are similar to the First-time DUIs and the DUI and Traffic Offenders in gender and age in that they are male young adults. Although drunk driving is generally considered to be a male offense the gender gap is much wider among this subgroup membership than in any of the other subgroups. Despite differences, this category is more similar to the DUI and Traffic Offenders than to the other two subgroups, particularly in drinking perceptions, drinking type and recidivism. Finally and more importantly, unlike the other three types they have long multiple arrest records and have been in and out of correctional institutions on several occasions. Obviously they are generalized deviants and episodic criminals.

Summary

In summary, the foregoing analysis reveals at the first two levels of analysis that all four offender groups comprise young white males. Age wise the DUI Recidivists are older than the other three groups. The First-time DUI Offenders are more frequently married, earn more money, and are more frequently employed than members of the other three subgroups. Obviously they lead a more conventional life-style than members of the other three subgroups. Mixed Multiple Offenders are the least likely to be married, earn less money, and are less frequently employed on a full-time basis than those in the other three subgroups. Furthermore and importantly, the demographics of the Mixed Multiple Offender are more similar to those of prison populations than are the three other subgroups.

When classified by drinking type, a large percentage of the total sample is found to be in the excessive and problem drinker category. As expected, the First-time DUI Offenders are social drinkers and the least problematic of the four subgroups. The DUI Recidivists are alcoholics and risky drivers when on the road, though probably less frequently on the road than the three other subgroups. The DUI and Traffic Offenders are problem drinkers and bad drivers even when they are not legally intoxicated. The Mixed Multiple Offenders are problem drinkers, bad drivers, and criminals--the most problematic subgroup. One of the most important findings of this analysis is that although problem drinkers vary from 50 percent of the DUI and Traffic Offenders to 87 percent of the DUI Recidivists, many deny that they have drinking problems. Though the three subgroups (2), (3), and (4) are similar in some respects, the alcoholism of subgroup (2), the bad driving of subgroup (3), and the criminality of subgroup (4) mark significant differentials.

Table 3.1

Distribution of DUI Offenders by Demographic Characteristics

Demographics	Total (N=2,786) No.	Total (N=2,786) Pct.	1st Time DUI (N=281) No.	1st Time DUI (N=281) Pct.	DUI Recidivist (N=471) No.	DUI Recidivist (N=471) Pct.	DUI+ Traffic (N=1,295) No.	DUI+ Traffic (N=1,295) Pct.	Mixed Multiple (N=739) No.	Mixed Multiple (N=739) Pct.
Age										
16-20 Years	37	1.3	15	5.3	0	0	22	1.7	0	0
21-34 Years	1,549	55.6	179	63.7	128	27.1	813	62.8	429	58.1
35-44 Years	665	23.9	64	22.8	136	28.9	278	21.5	187	25.3
45-64 Years	452	16.2	23	8.2	163	34.6	152	11.7	114	15.4
65+ Years	83	3.0	0	0	44	9.4	30	2.3	9	1.2
Gender										
Male	2,368	85.0	167	59.4	429	91.1	1,041	80.4	731	98.9
Female	418	15.0	114	40.6	42	8.9	254	19.6	8	1.1
Marital Status										
Married	1,002	36.0	169	60.1	161	34.2	504	38.9	168	22.7
Separated	175	6.3	12	4.3	38	8.1	47	3.6	78	10.6
Divorced	585	21.0	9	3.2	169	35.9	175	13.5	232	31.4
Widowed	56	2.0	3	1.1	16	3.4	18	1.5	19	2.6
Never Married	968	34.7	88	31.3	87	18.4	551	42.5	242	32.7

Continued on next page

Table 3.1--Continued

Demographics	Total (N=2,786) No.	Pct.	1st Time DUI (N=281) No.	Pct.	DUI Recidivist (N=471) No.	Pct.	DUI+ Traffic (N=1,295) No.	Pct.	Mixed Multiple (N=739) No.	Pct.
Income										
Less than $10,000	385	13.8	0	0	72	15.3	147	11.4	166	22.5
$10,000 - 19,999	1,115	41.4	21	7.5	87	18.5	689	53.2	358	48.4
$20,000 - 29,999	594	21.3	52	18.5	184	39.1	256	19.8	102	13.8
$30,000 - 39,999	236	8.5	89	31.7	43	9.1	77	5.9	27	3.7
$40,000 - 49,999	76	2.7	46	16.4	22	4.7	6	0.4	2	0.2
$50,000+	79	2.8	54	19.2	21	4.4	4	0.3	0	0
No Response	261	9.4	19	6.7	42	8.9	116	9.0	84	11.4
Education										
High School or Less	1,990	71.4	7	2.5	315	66.9	1,048	80.9	620	83.9
Some College	477	17.2	105	37.4	120	25.5	166	12.8	86	11.7
College Complete	130	4.7	94	33.5	12	2.5	17	1.3	7	0.9
Graduate or Above	79	2.8	69	24.5	3	0.6	5	0.4	2	0.3
No Response	110	3.9	6	2.1	21	4.5	59	4.6	24	3.2

Continued on next page

Table 3.1--Continued

Demographics	Total (N=2,786) No.	Total Pct.	1st Time DUI (N=281) No.	1st Time DUI Pct.	DUI Recidivist (N=471) No.	DUI Recidivist Pct.	DUI+ Traffic (N=1,295) No.	DUI+ Traffic Pct.	Mixed Multiple (N=739) No.	Mixed Multiple Pct.
Employment Status										
Full-Time	2,005	72.0	247	87.9	372	79.0	972	75.1	414	56.0
Part-Time	307	11.0	21	7.4	48	10.2	209	16.1	29	3.9
Unemployed	249	8.9	7	2.5	19	4.0	53	4.1	170	23.0
Retired	94	3.4	3	1.1	11	2.3	21	1.6	59	8.0
Not Seeking Empl.	74	2.7	0	0	3	0.7	9	0.7	62	8.4
No Response	57	2.0	3	1.1	18	3.8	31	2.4	5	0.7
Race										
White	2,014	72.3	253	90.0	393	83.4	920	71.1	448	60.7
Black	666	23.9	17	6.0	53	11.3	327	25.2	269	36.4
Hispanic	33	1.2	3	1.1	8	1.7	13	1.0	9	1.2
Asian	14	0.5	1	0.4	3	0.6	7	0.5	3	0.4
Other	15	0.5	1	0.4	2	0.4	9	0.7	3	0.4
No Response	44	1.6	6	2.1	12	2.6	19	1.5	7	0.9

Table 3.2

Distribution of DUI Offenders by Drinking Type

Drinking Type	Total (N=2,786)		1st Time DUI (N=281)		DUI Recidivist (N=471)		DUI+ Traffic (N=1,295)		Mixed Multiple (N=739)	
	No.	Pct.	No.	Pct.	No.	Pct.	No.	Pct.	No.	Pct.
Drinking Type										
Social Drinkers	575	20.6	244	86.8	0	0	210	16.2	121	16.4
Excessive Drinkers	715	25.7	34	12.1	42	8.9	433	33.4	206	27.9
Problem Drinkers	1,496	53.7	3	1.1	429	91.1	652	50.4	412	55.7

Table 3.3

Distribution of DUI Offenders by Drinking Related Perceptions

Drinking Related Perceptions	Total (N=2,786) No.	Pct.	1st Time DUI (N=281) No.	Pct.	DUI Recidivist (N=471) No.	Pct.	DUI+ Traffic (N=1,295) No.	Pct.	Mixed Multiple (N=739) No.	Pct.
Perceived Self Drinking Problems										
Yes	1,465	52.6	44	15.6	378	80.2	757	58.5	286	38.7
No	1,243	44.3	232	82.6	80	17.0	487	37.6	435	58.9
No Response	87	3.1	5	1.8	13	2.8	51	3.9	18	2.4
Perceived Ability to Control										
Yes	1,936	69.5	269	95.7	274	58.2	882	68.1	511	69.1
No	698	25.0	0	0	178	37.8	331	25.6	189	25.6
No Response	152	5.5	12	4.3	19	4.0	82	6.3	39	5.3
Perceived Hangover Effects										
Yes	1,597	57.3	19	6.7	396	84.1	795	61.4	387	52.4
No	1,093	39.2	259	92.2	58	12.3	450	34.7	326	44.1
No Response	96	3.5	3	1.1	17	3.6	50	3.9	26	3.5
Other's Perception of Self as a Normal Drinker										
Yes	1,457	52.3	14	5.0	381	80.9	796	61.5	266	36.0
No	1,222	43.9	258	91.8	74	15.7	448	34.6	442	59.8
No Response	107	3.8	9	3.2	16	3.4	51	3.9	31	4.2

Table 3.4

Distribution of DUI Offenders by Drinking History

Drinking History	Total (N=2,786)		1st Time DUI (N=281)		DUI Recidivist (N=471)		DUI+ Traffic (N=1,295)		Mixed Multiple (N=739)	
	No.	Pct.	No.	Pct.	No.	Pct.	No.	Pct.	No.	Pct.
Alcohol Treatment										
Received	647	23.2	3	1.1	302	64.1	259	20.0	83	11.2
Not Received	2,089	75.0	275	97.8	160	34.0	1,013	78.2	641	86.8
No Response	50	1.8	3	1.1	9	1.9	23	1.8	15	2.0
Alcohol Addiction										
Addicted	979	35.1	4	1.4	360	76.4	444	34.3	171	23.1
Not Addicted	1,663	59.7	266	94.7	70	14.9	792	61.2	535	72.4
No Response	144	5.2	11	3.9	41	8.7	59	4.5	33	4.5
Job-Related Consequences										
Experienced	377	13.5	4	1.4	246	52.2	80	6.2	47	6.4
Not Experienced	2,368	85.0	275	97.9	219	46.5	1,191	92.0	683	92.4
No Response	41	1.5	2	0.7	6	1.3	24	1.8	9	1.2
Non Job-Related Consequences										
Experienced	1,685	60.5	4	1.4	351	74.5	711	54.9	619	83.8
Not Experienced	1,055	37.9	275	98.2	109	23.2	563	43.5	108	14.6
No Response	46	1.6	2	0.4	11	2.3	21	1.6	12	1.6

IV. THE ANALYSIS OF THE SUBSAMPLE OF 311 WHITE MALE DUI OFFENDERS

This chapter provides an analysis of the subsample of 311 while male offenders on all study dimensions. First, on the basis of the official arrest history data we assign each offender to one of the four arrest history subgroups. Second, we examine each subgroup along the first two dimensions--sociodemographics and social psychological characteristics--utilizing the 1989 Georgia DUI study data set. Finally, from our personal interview data, we investigate and describe each subgroup along the following six dimensions: self-concept and identities, life history and personal relationship problems, life-style, world view, drinking and driving patterns and attitudes, and reaction to criminal justice processing and the DUI label. This subgroup analysis of the subsample along the eight study dimensions resulted in the construction of the four DUI offender subtypes.

Analysis of Official Arrest History Data

Of the 311 white male DUIs interviewed 22 were First-time DUI Offenders; 28 were DUI Recidivists; 172 were DUI and Traffic Offenders; and, 89 were Mixed Multiple Offenders. Among the DUI Recidivists, 52 percent had two or three prior arrests, 34 percent had four prior arrests, seven percent had five prior arrests, and the remaining seven percent had six to eight prior arrests. The average number of prior arrests is 3.5. Scattered throughout their arrest histories were less serious charges for public drunkenness, disturbing the peace, purchase of alcohol for a minor, violation of the Georgia Controlled Substance Act, intoxication and disorderly conduct, and driving after declared and before expiration of probation period.

DUI and Traffic Offenders had been arrested more frequently for traffic violations than for DUI, with a mean ratio of 3 to 1, although, some of these may have been alcohol related. The specific traffic violations occurred in the following order: speeding, running stop sign or light, reckless driving, driving without or with expired/suspended license, improper lane changes or turns, unlawful use of driver's license, driving unsafe or improperly equipped vehicle, driving without insurance or license tag, eluding a police officer (fleeing), and possession of an open container of an alcoholic beverage while driving. The average number of prior arrests for this group is 6.1.

The Mixed Multiple Offenders had prior arrest histories for DUI as well as non-DUI criminal and traffic offenses. Over half of this category (51%) had been arrested on charges of one or more of the following violent crimes: homicide (5%), rape (3%), assault (25%), woman battery (36%), robbery (6%), and child abuse (11%). Seventy-eight percent had been arrested previously on other offense charges: disorderly conduct (53%), illegal trespassing (52%), domestic nonsupport (24%), gambling (42%), writing bad checks (43%), larceny (61%), burglary (51%), vandalism (4%), non-DUI traffic violations (46%), littering (75%), possession of illegal substances (14%). The average number of prior arrests for this group is 8.2, and the average number of charges per arrest for a respondent was 2.9. All had served some time in correctional institutions.

This arrest history analysis suggests that First-time DUI Offenders are social drinkers who are similar to that segment of the drinking/driving population who occasionally drink in moderate amounts before driving; and, who are careful drivers as a rule, particularly after drinking. Perhaps at the time of the instant arrest they were not aware of their intoxicated state, and, perhaps they did not ever become intoxicated intentionally before driving. Thus their drunk-driving culpability may be attenuated. On the other hand, DUI Recidivists appear to be problem drinkers and generalized deviants who drive when knowingly intoxicated. DUI and Traffic Offenders seem to be problem drinkers, risk takers, and "bad drivers" when and when not intoxicated. Mixed Multiple offenders probably drive frequently when knowingly intoxicated and appear to be generalized deviants. Furthermore, their lengthy arrest histories (including some serious and violent criminal charges in addition to DUI's and traffic offenses) indicate a problem-drinking group of bad drivers and generalized deviants, a category representing what T. C. Willett called "criminals on the road." These 311 arrest histories were classifiable into the same offender subgroups as were those offenders in the larger data set analyzed in Chapter III.

Sociodemographics and Social Psychological Characteristics *(Based on 1989 DUI Data Set)*

The majority of the interviewees (N=311) were young (77% aged 21-34), single (70%), employed full-time (74%), blue-collar workers (86%), with less than high school education (63%), and, with a mean income of $13,500. Fifty-two percent lived in metropolitan areas with populations of 100,000 or more, 34 percent lived in towns with populations between 25,000 to 100,000 and the remaining 14 percent resided in areas with populations of less than 25,000. An examination of these subgroups by sociodemographics and social psychological characteristics disclosed no significant differences between this sample of 311 cases and their counterparts in the larger data set (N=2,786) from which these cases were drawn (t-values were insignificant at 95%). Furthermore, as in the larger data set, the findings at the social psychological level support the suppositions at the level of arrest history analysis.

The inter-group comparisons show that the First-time DUI Offender group, when compared with the other three offender subgroups, was more frequently married (N=18), more frequently white-collar workers (N=19), more highly educated (high school to college education, N=19), and earned a higher income (mean earnings of $20,000). These differentials are also similar to their counterparts in the larger sample. No statistical tests were conducted to determine the significance of these appreciable differences between First-time Offenders and the other subgroups because of small sample size.

PERSONAL INTERVIEW DATA ANALYSIS

As indicated previously the data on the dimensions below were collected by the authors during personal interviews with 311 cases, and were not available for the other respondents in the larger data set. A careful content analysis[6] disclosed a similarity (but not identity) among the three recidivistic offender subgroups (DUI Recidivists, DUI and Traffic Offenders, and Mixed Multiple Offenders) for the first four study dimensions: self-concept and identities, life history and personal relationship problems, life-style, and world view, but marked differences (in these dimensions) from First-time DUI Offenders. Therefore, we first discuss the preceding three recidivistic offender subgroups as one general "recidivistic offender" category with reference to these four dimensions; and, then compare it with the First-time DUI Offender category. Next, the last two dimensions, Drinking and Driving Patterns and Attitudes; and, Reactions to the Criminal Justice System and the DUI Label, are discussed separately for each of the four offender subgroups because they differ along these two dimensions.

DUI Recidivists, DUI and Traffic Offenders and Mixed Multiple Offenders

(1) Self-concept and Identities

(a) *Self-Definition*: These men described themselves as white working-class southerners, residents of a particular Georgia county, town, or city, and as members of a specific family group. None defined themselves as criminals; five referred to themselves as outlaws. They voiced a strong sense of place, family name and continuity. Loyalty was frequently professed for the southern region and its customs, as well as for friends and relatives. One DUI and Traffic Offender, a carpenter, speaks to this point:

> You know I went up to Dayton, Ohio, a few years back to work. Got good wages too. But I spent most of my money driving back home. I couldn't stay up there at holiday time. Then, seems like a bunch of my kin folks

passed on. I jess had to come back then. I got sick up there too, and no one to take care of me around. Them people up there are a different breed of cats. They don't believe in nothin but money and bout themselves. Kin folks don't mean nothing to them people, and they ain't got no real friends. They talk funny and "blacks" get treated as good as I did on the job. You know I feared to die up there. Them bastards probably would a put me in that Yankee dirt. Not even called my people. I got the hell outa there one day. Jes packed my bag and took off to home. Hell with all the money and union dues. I'll stay right here in Dixie. Be buried here with my kind of people. If yer heart ain't in Dixie, git yer ass out.

They called themselves honest, hard-working, white men, distinguishable from "trash" (good-for-nothing, lazy men on welfare) and big shots (middle- and upper-class southerners) who really do not (in their terms) work for a living. Their remarks indicated resignation, like their parents before them, to working-class status and marginality. Aspirations and respectability, to them, centered on a regular job and honest living: putting meat and bread on the table and getting by. Status was sought within, rather than beyond, working-class social groups. As one DUI and Traffic Offender reports:

I'm a poor workin man who don't have much education. I know I ain't going nowhere. But the big shots need little people like me to boss around. And I get by. But I know many people think I'm a loser. I take care of my family and put the bread on the table. I stay with my own kind and they don't think I'm a loser.

They expressed a dislike of or ambivalence toward outsiders, and status was sought within work-buddy social groups. Although they reported a self-awareness of economic and social marginality, they voiced strong individualistic feelings and evidenced little working-class consciousness. Paradoxically, they assumed a fatalistic external locus of control. For example, one typical comment by a Mixed Multiple Offender follows:

What will be, will be. Just because you don't understan why something happens means nothin. The cause may be somewhere else. And why worry about it.

(b) Self-Concept in Relationship to Particular Others: Many defined themselves in antagonistic juxtaposition to four other groups within their milieu: 1. outsiders; 2. "big shots" (bosses, businessmen, owners, managers, and professionals); 3. "low class" or "sorry people"; 4. and blacks.

1. Outsiders: These were people from outside the southern region, frequently designated as foreigners and uppity "black lovers," northern skilled workers who had taken their jobs away; union organizers, civil rights leaders, meddling government men, alien company representatives, and unwanted tourists -- all out to change the honest God-fearing, easy-going southern way of life. The outsiders' dress and manners were too fine, their speech too rapid, their demand for expert and quick service too rude; and, they acted like "smart asses." Outsiders were also out-of-state owners, pro-union workers, and foremen who did not accept their human qualities and way of life; and, bosses, particularly outside bosses, who were only interested in "working the hell out of them." Anybody who worked for the federal government in any capacity was considered an outsider, even those who worked in their behalf; for example, Occupational Safety and Health Administration (OSHA) employees. They reported dislike for outside work foremen, whom they "hoodwinked" when possible. Any boss was suspect, but "inside bastards" were preferred to "outside bastards." Tourists and visitors were foreigners to be exploited in any conceivable way; for example, short change; performance of slow and sloppy service; overcharge; discourteous treatment; provoking fights with; etcetera. Except in secondary relationships they shunned contacts with outsiders. In turn, they thought outsiders looked down upon them as inferior southern hicks to stay away from.

2. Big Shots: Those viewed as "superior acting," "educated," "slick," and "airy" manipulators who exploited them. They expressed in different ways ambivalence toward this "higher class of people," whom they envied, felt inferior to, and

distrusted; but, whom they simultaneously admired, envied, and paid deference to. As one verbose Mixed Multiple Offender notes:

> They are educated and a higher class of people. We know they look down on us. Their children go to private schools. Ours go to public schools where the "blacks" go. We go to the public swimming pool. They got their own pools. We go to the Pentecostal and Baptist churches. They go to the Methodist and Presbyterian churches. They go to country clubs and play golf. We go to pool rooms and honky-tonks and hangout. And, you know, fish and hunt. They hunt too but at private clubs. We hunt and fish where we can and when we can get by with it. They live in big houses in fine neighborhoods. We live where we can afford to, in apartments and small houses. We rent. They own. Our folks ride buses sometimes. They always go in private cars. We respect them because they are our people. But we know they are different. We don't mix with them often. We got our own circles.

They were also aware that big shots purposefully avoided social contacts with them--especially the exchange of family visits, dating relationships, and other intimate gatherings including the presence of both men and women. Another Mixed Multiple Offender (a plumber) comments:

> There are enough churches around of different denominations so the big shots can stay away from us. And they do if they can. Even when we go to the same church. Damn rare. We know that fellowship begins and ends at the church door. About the only places we come in contact is at farms, lumber yards, stores and factories. Sometimes hardware stores. And you know, at work. But at work they deal with us through foremen. They're Mister and we are Johns and Jacks. You get the picture?

These two quotes along with other similar accounts indicate that these men consider themselves class bound; that is, they do not work, play, or socialize with their "social superiors." They disparaged "big shots" as being phony and effeminate with "no grit in their trough," and their references to class differences frequently colored their put-downs. As one DUI and Traffic Offender, a short-haul trucker remarks:

> The line ran out when old man Jones died. His son ain't got it. Weak seed.

This quote also illustrates their common belief in biological determinism. Sometimes they mentioned opportunities that permitted them to turn the tables on the elites. A DUI and Traffic Offender (a handyman plumber) relates this story:

> I called my doctor at his home one night. Needed him to come see my wife. She was terrible sick. The Doc he jes asked me 'bout if she had a real high fever, and tole me to git her two aspirins, and call him in the mornin. Week or so later he done call me middle the night to come fix his john what was runnin over. Seems he had a party goin on. I tole him to drop in two aspirins and call me in the mornin.

Whether the foregoing trite tale is literally true or not, it represents a metaphor of social class and class antagonisms. Though these men consider violence an appropriate method to settle personal affronts and put-downs; and, though they frequently resort to the personal (and physical) redress of wrongs, violence was generally intra- rather than inter-group directed.   They reported that even when pressured and derogated by big shots, they had to be polite and show respect--especially to managers, owners, employers, professionals and bureaucrats. One DUI recidivist (a roofer) remarks:

> What you gonna do? The big shots control our lives in more ways than one. They make the laws. They own the cops. So they put you in jail when they want to.

Like when you have a few drinks and drive. They got
the power over the whole system. They are our bosses.
You get violent, it don't pay off. You lose regardless.
There are other ways to skin a cat. You know, smile and
take it. When you find another job tell them to shove it
and walk away. My mamma tole me a long time ago
who to mess wid and who to leave alone.

3. Low-Class or "Sorry" People: These were the unemployed
or recipients of welfare checks, food stamps, and benefits of one
kind or another. Their main grievances were directed toward
able-bodied, unemployed, black and white males and black
unwed mothers. This "ilk," "trash," were blamed because they
were "freeloaders," and too lazy to work. They also considered
public welfare to be a "socialist system" that required them to
take care of bums via taxes. No disdain was expressed for
welfare recipients' deviant behavior, such as drunkenness or
illicit sex, but just the odium "they don't work for a living"--and
lived at their expense. One DUI Recidivist (a warehouse worker)
states:

These people on welfare are no good. They're too
lazy to work. They rather get by on welfare than work
and make a good livin. And the damn government takes
care of them. It's like Russia. Everybody gets taken care
of from the cradle to the grave. From the womb to the
tomb. From the basket to the casket. Why should I take
care of them? I have a hard time takin care of myself.
Them people ought to be forced to work. You know, if
necessary lock them up, or let them starve. And these
black women who make their living on their backs. You
know, having one baby after another is a shame. They
ought to cut their tubes. And, make the fathers pay for
the kids. I have to pay for mine. This country is goin to
hell on welfare. These freeloaders should be cut off.

These men overlooked the fact or did not know that many
on welfare are unemployables, mothers, children, and old
people. They did not count their own occasional unemployment

checks as welfare, nor chastise their friends and relatives who were welfare recipients. The latter groups, to them, were worthy recipients--those who really needed and deserved help. Many others were unworthy drags on the system. As one DUI Recidivist, a factory worker who was drawing unemployment compensation, says:

> Yea, I know a few good people on welfare. One of my uncles and one of my friends gets checks. But you know they are really down and out. They would work if they could find a job. They are different from those freeloaders.

These men claimed to "stay clear off welfare bums"; whom they detested; and, in turn, welfare recipients avoided contacts with them. Another DUI Recidivist, a restaurant waiter, speaks:

> Man, these bums stay clear off me. They know I give them no slack. And that if they get in my way, they are goin to get their asses kicked. If I had a license to get rid of them, they would be long gone. I don't care how much they drink or f--- around, so long as it's not at my expense. They keep their place when I'm around.

Their accounts, however, reveal that these men had more personal contacts with welfare recipients than they let on. Many mentioned relatives and acquaintances on welfare. Significantly, more than one half (60%) admitted that their families of orientation had been on welfare of one kind or another (principally AFDC) at one time or another. However, they were reluctant to discuss any of their particular welfare situations, and expressed shame of prior (and sometimes current) public welfare family status. To them, welfare status designates a condition of immorality because like many southerners, they equate poverty and welfare status with individual responsibility. The following account by one frank DUI and Traffic Offender illustrates the shame and pain of past family welfare status:

You know my family was on and off welfare while I was growing up. My old man was just too lazy to work regular. He would work for a while and everything would be okay. Then he would quit and sit down. Sometimes he would stay at home. Other times he would stay somewhere else. I don't know where. Maybe with another woman, but we didn't get a check. Maybe she was getting it both ways. Anyway, my mamma had to go to the welfare office to feed us, pay the rent and buy the clothes. All of us tried to keep it a secret, but 'twas no use. The neighbors find out quick and that was bad. I felt ashamed at school. But nobody put me down about it. Some of them like some of my neighbors were on welfare too. But that didn't make my mamma or me feel no better. Of course, we first went to some family members, and to some friends. But this was not enough. You see, many of them were on welfare too. Sometimes we didn't know this. They tried to hide it too. You didn't talk about these things. I still blame it on the ole man. Yea, he drank a lot and stepped out on mamma. But that ain't the point. A hell of a lot of men do things like that. Most of the men I know drink, gamble and step out on their wives. A real man can drink, gamble and go out with women. And work and take care of home base. They got balls. You know, men sons can be proud of.

Yet another DUI and Traffic Offender reports on his recent welfare status:

There for a while I couldn't find a job. It hurt like hell because I really tried. My wife could find only part time work. We were in a bad fix. She insisted on going to the welfare office to get some help. I tole her not to do that . . . to hold on and give me a chance to find a job. She wouldn't listen to me and got on me about drinkin. I was drinkin some but not too much. She didn't want me to drink and drive either. But I had to find a job. And you know, everybody drinks and drives, whether they

be working or not. I can drive better drunk than most
people can sober. So can a lot of my friends. The naggin
got so bad I just moved in a while with Louise. She be a
girl I know for a long time. She was working and she
took care of me. Fact is she gave me some money for
home expenses. My wife didn't appreciate nothing. You
know that fool filed for a divorce. She didn't show no
respect or appreciation. I just feel ashamed of her going
to the welfare. She put me down. Louise understands, so
I am still with her. She knows how to make me feel like a
man even when I'm not working, and drinkin.

This and similar quotes suggest that most of these men (60
percent) were not too far removed from family welfare situations
which is understandable in light of their economically insecure
family backgrounds, social class, and precarious work situations.
Also significant in understanding these men are their permissive
attitudes toward heavy drinking; driving and drinking;
gambling, and womanizing; that is, even in the case of
unemployed husbands and fathers. A "real man" could drink
and drive; gamble, drink, and womanize; and still "put the bread
on the table"–even if with the financial aid of a girlfriend.

4. Blacks: The men in these three offender groups voiced a
clear awareness and approval of individual, institutional, and
cultural racism obtaining in their region and immediate milieu.
They were against civil rights laws and such organizations as the
NAACP (National Association for the Advancement of Colored
People), HEW (Health, Education, and Welfare), and HUD
(Housing and Urban Development). Remarks indicated their
desire to live in separate neighborhoods and avoid contacts with
all blacks when possible. All claimed civil rights laws placed an
undue burden on them. Comments by one DUI and Traffic
Offender are illustrative:

The government's civil rights' programs from the
jump were based on force. And too hard on people like
us. Laws don't change people's minds. As time goes by
the laws get worse. We got to go to school with blacks.

We got to live and work with them too. You know everywhere. The government has no right to move them into our neighborhoods. I hate the projects. It's not so hard on the big shots. They move out when blacks move in. I can't because I don't have money to buy another home. They can send their children to private schools. They don't have to go to public parks and swimming pools. They got their own. That's one reason some of them are so liberal. They can hole themselves up from blacks and poor people. People like me can't do this. We got to mingle with them. Like it or not. Even some of the blacks don't like it. But they got no choice either. The white politicians don't help. They know blacks vote. And the liberals are no-good "black" lovers. They really don't like blacks any more than I do. Just an act. The damn hypocrites.

They acknowledged working alongside blacks at all sorts of menial and blue-collar jobs. But, they maintained that conversations and interactions at these work sites were limited to work tasks. Comments concerning these interactions indicate that conversations with blacks were pitched in a phony, "egalitarian" mold--stilted, stylized, and stereotyped exchanges about trivial, impersonal, inane subjects such as the weather, sports, daily events, and the movies. According to them whites and blacks at the work site segregated themselves during rest periods and lunch breaks and went their own separate ways when the work day was over.

Contrary to popular opinion in the south these men expressed a keen awareness of shared cultural elements with blacks; for example, manual labor, diet, language, religion, folk knowledge, humor, recreational pursuits, and customs. They knew that both were working-class wage earners, near the bottom of the economic and social system; enjoyed soul food (pork, collards, turnip greens, fried tomatoes, fried chicken, grits, cornbread, molasses, black-eyed peas, okra, and chitlins); practiced a fundamentalist Protestant religion; shared similar superstitions; and drank, scuffled, hunted, fished, and womanized. Yet they stressed in one way or another what they termed significant differences between themselves and blacks. First and foremost, they claimed to come from "good blood"; and that regardless of whatever economic progress blacks might experience, they could never be white and equal. The first attribute of having good blood is being white. However, simply being white does not mean one has good blood, but it is the first prerequisite. Being white places one in a different order of men, a separate and superior race. They mentioned, to paraphrase, other cultural differences such as: European versus African heritage; country and western music versus soul (jazz and rhythm and blues); respectable dance styles versus "jungle type" dancing; conservative dress versus "loud color" dress; white style talking versus "funky talk"; white straight walking style vs. black strutting; white-gender-double-standard dating patterns vs. black egalitarian dating practices; white modesty vs. black "showing out" behavior; different physical characteristics. To them blacks were ugly people physically; and like animals sexually. Whites were a better-looking and behaving breed of people in every way.

Most of their comments on blacks dealt with what they termed forced integration and the unfair advantages bestowed upon them by the federal government. As one DUI and Traffic Offender reports:

> You know the government forced this integration thing on us. It tried every way to mix up all of us regardless of how we feel. First it was the schools. Then when they found out children go to school where they live, they moved blacks in our neighborhoods. You know with all kinds of laws about real estate and loans helping blacks move in. Then they moved the housing projects to white neighborhoods—our neighborhoods. Next, they tried bussing—moving kids all over town and cross town. What a mess! Next they started the quota thing. They claim not, but they got quotas everywhere. And they got that affirmative action shit, too. The government don't want equality. It wants blacks to have more rights than us everywhere. When they go to school. When they go to college. When they go on to

jobs. When they look for a house, everywhere. Blacks get to be hired over whites. It makes no difference what your qualifications. This goes for government jobs and everywhere else, like factories, police departments, post offices, and fire departments. Blacks get hired first and promoted first. And they get fired last. Man, the whole thing is a mess. And those damned white liberals are behind the whole thing. They are afraid of blacks. Hell, some juries don't even want to convict blacks when they know they are guilty. They are afraid they will riot. The judges are afraid too. What a bunch of flakes. These liberals think its smart to be liberal. Shit, they are educated fools and hypocrites. But, whatever they give them, they're still going to be "losers."

Blacks, to these men, are people of a different and inferior race to be avoided when possible but not hated-- "people that the government gives everything to." They claimed not to know or care about how blacks perceived them but when probed, opined they were probably disliked as "rednecks." Their reports did not indicate racial hatred but the desire for complete segregation. As one Mixed Multiple Offender declares: "we like some blacks as individuals, but it's the group thing we don't like."

Finally, they rationalized away their arrests and difficulties related to heavy drinking and drinking and driving as just normal consequences of a "natural" hell-raising way of life. Most admitted they were occasional law breakers, they said, "like everybody else."

(c) Macho Stance and Ambivalence: As a group they verbalized a macho self-image and stance tied in with heavy drinking, drinking and driving, thrill seeking, virility, physical prowess, and a proclivity to use violence in settling disputes and interactional problems. Furthermore, their responses revealed a dearth of verbal skill and motivation required in peaceful problem solving. Although they externalized an independent bravado, they simultaneously expressed some feelings of social inadequacy and low self-esteem. One Mixed Multiple Offender's comments are illustrative of a weak self-concept and the difficulty in a democracy of designating all work as honorable.

(This is more the case in the south where manual labor and the manual laborer have historically been denigrated.)

> I know I'm a poor working man and don't have much education. I work with my hands but I earn an honest living. But in Georgia, that ain't worth much in the eyes of the upscale people. We say we don't care what the big shots think about us. But we do, and it hurts. It ain't just them. Everybody around here thinks if you ain't a lawyer or a doctor, or an engineer, or a business man with money--or some high-faluting white-collar worker, you ain't shit. It's not fair but that's the way it is. I may not be going nowhere but the community needs people like me. Somebody's got to do the real work. And the big shots need little people like me to boss around. And I guess we need people like them around to run things. I get by. I'm not a free loader on welfare. But I know many people think folks like me are losers. But what the hell would they do without guys like me? And who cares, I got good friends who accept me. And after a few drinks I'm as good as anybody.

(2) *Life History and Personal Relationship Problems*

(a) *Life History Problems*
1. Home conditions: Sixty-eight percent reported growing up in working-class, low-income housing, where their physical needs were barely met, though none went hungry or without basic clothing needs. More than one-third (40%) were products of families that had been on public welfare at one time or another during their formative years. More than half (57%) were from broken homes as a result of divorce, separation, or parental death. Fifteen were reared in orphanages, by foster parents or by relatives. Only 36 percent were reared in intact families where mother and father were ever present. Most parents or surrogate parents (80%) were renters rather than homeowners and were irregularly employed in nonunion, low-paying jobs. Most (73%) were also highly mobile at different job sites and dwelling units. Their low-rental apartments and houses were frequently situated

in mixed residential, commercial areas near liquor stores, pool rooms, bars, beer joints, honky-tonks, and fast-food restaurants. They noted the presence of delinquent gangs, illegal substance use and criminal activities in or around their neighborhoods. The emotional tone of family life for most (64%) was strained, conflictive, and without enough personal attention, love, discipline, and support. Despite this, however, 55 percent claimed close personal ties with their mothers or mother-figures. Mothers frequently worked outside the home, and adult supervision was at a minimum. Mothers and fathers or mothers' boyfriends (in the absence of the father) were continually bickering and fighting over financial problems, the children, sexual jealousies, or conflicts with the neighbors. Heavy drinking by mothers or fathers (or mothers' male companions) usually accompanied these quarrels and altercations. They said the police were called in occasionally to mediate or arbitrate these domestic conflicts. More than one-third recalled their mothers had been beaten up at one time or another by their husbands and/or boyfriends.

Only 20 percent reported close personal ties with fathers or father figures; and, only 13 percent said they were adequately supervised by fathers or father figures. Thirty percent claimed to have been physically abused (whipped too hard) by fathers or father-figures. Nine percent said they were physically abused by their mother (whipped too hard). Only 17 percent said they were adequately supervised by both parents. Most (72%) said that neither parent was around to supervise them adequately. Only 20 percent claimed to have been reared in intact, economically, and emotionally secure homes where supervision was close, adequate, and consistent--and where they enjoyed close personal ties with both parents.

2. Childhood and Adolescent Problems at Home: Most (63%) reported childhood problems centering on fussing and/or fighting with their siblings, parents, and neighborhood playmates. Chief childhood problems centered on rebellion and the lack of parental attention and supervision. Approximately 75 percent reported problems with fathers, father figures, or mothers' boyfriends--most having to do with altercations with these authority figures whom they did not feel were fair, caring,

and consistent in disciplinary measures. None mentioned sexual abuse.

As adolescents three-fourths reported problems with parents concerning three or more of the following: staying out too late at night (60%), lying (55%), running away from home (45%), stealing from family members (30%), fighting with siblings and parents (48%), drinking (70%), using drugs (20%), smoking (90%), being beyond parental control (24%), using abusive and obscene language (40%), refusing to help with household tasks (50%), destruction of home property (3%), bringing home stolen property (30%); possessing illegal firearms (36%). Eighty-one percent reported smoking, and 72 percent reported drinking before age fourteen. Seventy-three percent said they had sex with a girl before age thirteen, 90% by age fifteen. Fifty-three percent reported gambling by age fifteen and 43 percent using marijuana by age sixteen. None mentioned homosexual relations.

3. Childhood and Adolescent Problems at School: Fifty-four percent were frequently absent from school during childhood because of illness, lack of interest, or lack of a parental enforcement policy. Most (62%) did not like school and reported poor grades. As teenagers, 61 percent reported getting in trouble for three or more of the following reasons at school: poor grades and skipping school; fighting with other students and altercations with teachers over classroom discipline; gambling and bringing weapons to school and disrupting the classroom; and, stealing from student lockers. Forty-one percent were suspended from school at one time or another for disciplinary reasons (fighting, stealing, sex with girl on school property, drinking, gambling, weapons carrying, disrupting classrooms). Twenty percent of those suspended were eventually expelled. Eighty-four percent of those expelled fell into the Mixed Multiple Offender group. Only 26 percent mentioned no childhood and adolescent problems at school.

4. Childhood and Adolescent Problems in the Community: Fifty-nine percent noted childhood problems having to do with roaming the neighborhood without parental permission or supervision and consequently getting in the way of neighbors. Fifty percent reported fusses and spats with neighbors and their

children--particularly with male peers and male heads of households. Sixteen percent claimed to have belonged to neighborhood gangs. When teenagers, 61 percent reported getting into trouble for three or more of the following reasons: fighting with male peers (71%), drinking (71%), gambling (31%), stealing (49%), keeping girl friends out too late (47%), vandalism (defacing property) (38%), breaking curfews (28%), unauthorized use of autos (24%), stealing cars or car parts (24%), trespassing (22%), burglary (18%), driving without a license(15%), reckless driving (14%), possession of or selling drugs (11%), breaking bottles on the street (23%), shooting out street lights (18%), shoplifting (23%), sexual relations with underaged girls (12%), disturbing the peace (17%), indecent exposure (8%). Thirty-one percent reported no childhood or adolescent problems in the community.

5. Legal Problems as Minors: Thirty-four percent reported negative contacts with police as minors; that is, warnings and/or police reports for one or more of the following: fighting, gang activity, shoplifting, disturbing the peace, burglary, driving without a license, stealing cars or car parts, possession of illegal substance traffic offenses, drinking, assault, sex offenses. Seventeen percent were placed on probation for one or more of the preceding offenses. Thirteen percent had been committed to either jail or youth development centers of whom 91 percent fell into the Mixed Multiple Offender group. Sixty-six percent claimed no legal problems as minors. From childhood and adolescent accounts it became evident that the more serious delinquent acts (stealing, robbery, burglary, carrying weapons, assault, drunk driving, possession and/or use of illegal substances) were more frequently committed by the Mixed Multiple Offenders than by those of any other subgroups. This group membership also grew up in more problematic homes. Quotes are not recorded for the preceding items (1 through 5) for spatial considerations, and differences among these three recidivistic subgroups are qualitatively noted.

(b) Personal Relationship Problems

These interviewees frequently related personal relationship difficulties with others seemingly generated by one or more of the following: (1) the respondents admitted an impulsive nature and a quick temper; (2) frequent intoxication; (3) presence in risky behavioral situations; and (4) a macho stance (they claimed a necessary position for survival in their milieu). Personal problems generally occurred within the following social contexts: rowdy drinking bouts in honky-tonks, gambling disputes, altercations with other males over females, squabbles with peers over property and goods, quarrels with parents, older siblings, teachers, and authority figures, and conflicts with female companions over sexual control. In reference to the latter, one Mixed Multiple Offender's comments are typical:

> The problem with these women is they got too much freedom. A man has to lay down the law. You know, keep them under control. Now if my woman lets me run the show. Does what I tole her to do. There is no problem. But if she wants to do what she pleases then the shit hits the fan. I tell her what's going down. You know, how things have to be. I tell her it's my way or the highway. You know, a German Shepherd is at your feet or at your throat. Well my woman ain't at my throat. I don't put up with no woman shit specially if I'm drinkin. That's the way things are with my kind of people. I don't make the rules.

About one-third of these men (34%) reported using force at one time or another to, "keep their women in line." As one typical Mixed Multiple Offender explains:

> Now, I don't like to beat up bad on no woman. I wasn't brought up that way. But I got a short fuse. Sometimes they nag you to death about your drinkin. They get a bone and keep chewing on it. If you can't get them off that kick, you got to do something about it. Sometimes they can't think straight anyway. Sometimes I have to put them in their place. Slap them around a little bit or give them the boot. And if they complain about my drinkin, I tell them it's none of their business. I drink before and after them. And I don't let them drive

my car when I been drinkin. I drink and drive and do anything else I want to. I don't want no woman driving me around. Man, everybody drinks and drives. A man don't let no woman drive less he wants to. And if I give her the boot I take my shoe off first. (Obviously this last statement is a play on words, but symbolically significant nonetheless.)

Most blamed their personal relationship problems on others with whom they interacted, their own quick tempers, and drinking. The following comments by a DUI Recidivist illustrate this point:

I get along with good people. You know, stand-up guys and women who know their place. But I don't make it with flakes and smart asses. I try to avoid these kinds of people. But when they get up in my face I have to do something. Most people are okay for a while. Then their bad side shows up. When I tell some jokers they are wrong, they get pissed off and turn on me. You can't tell them nothing. Frankly, most of them are no damn good. You just can't trust nobody. Seems like I just keep running into no-good people. I just got bad luck and when I'm drinkin I don't take no shit from nobody. And where I come from, you got to fight to protect yourself and your name. A dude who won't fight ain't no man.

(3) Life-style

(a) Language Form and Content

1. Physical Appearance and Front: Physical appearance, body movement, mien, and clothing convey social, personal, and self-identity as well as one's stance toward the world--and, in a sense reflect one's biography and place in the social world (See Stone, 1962; Roebuck, Murty, and Smith, 1993).

As observed during the interviews these men were of medium height (5' 7" to about 5' 11" tall) and of stocky build. Most had beer bellies supported by wide belts and large belt buckles. Weight varied from 150 to 225 pounds. All were of a ruddy complexion and most wore long sideburns and/or beards. They wore their fine-textured hair long and unkept. Faces and hands were weatherbeaten, freckled, and sunburned. Many had scars on their faces and arms, and about one-third were tattooed (particularly the Mixed Multiple Offenders). They looked five or ten years older than their chronological age. Usually dressed in t-shirts or flannel shirts and blue jeans, they frequently wore imitation leather jackets or jean jackets. When suited up they wore double-knit polyester leisure suits. T-shirts, often of mixed artificial fibers, were frequently "walking advertisements" for some type of business. Footwear consisted of tennis or jogging shoes, work shoes, or boots, all of an outlet store variety. The most important piece of clothing was the baseball cap, usually advertising some store or fertilizer company. Clothing was light for the weather and ill fitting (overcoats according to them were worn by sissies.) They wore little or no jewelry and, if present, consisted of large gaudy rings and heavy metal or leather bracelets. Watches were rare but pocket knives were ever present. They carried cigarettes (frequently rolled up in t-shirt sleeves), snuff, and chewing tobacco but rarely pipes (an educated sissy's smoke).

They sat in a loose-limbed, slouchy manner and when standing leaned heavily on nearby furniture or walls. Shoulders were drooped, and head, shoulder, and body movements appeared stiff, awkward and exaggerated. Hands and feet moved frequently in a jerky nervous manner. The walking gait was stiff, mechanical, and long-strided. Eyes, lips, and facial features moved frequently and furtively. Facial expressions continually changed (suddenly) and did not appear to be under control. Emotion, irritation, and anger showed in a flushing of the face. Hand, eye, mouth, and body gestures were exaggerated and non-rhythmic as was their language. Greetings exchanged with peers in our presence were marked by vigorous hand shakes, awkward fanfare and flourishes, and loud salutations and back slapping--all interlarded with endearing "smiling" expletives, like "How are you, you old son of a bitch?" Body form and movement did not appear to be symmetrical or well articulated by middle-class standards. Yet, paradoxically enough, they appeared to be self-contained and proud.

2. Language: Language is the most important system of symbols used to construct and communicate meanings. People communicate during interaction through and by gestures, grunts, body movements, facial expression, and verbalizations. Man interprets events and constructs their meanings through language. When people speak they shape and direct their own behavior as well as others' behavior, and the mutually resulting behavior is a product of this interaction. Meaning must arise from experience, and experience is based on and emerges from language, its grammar, and semantics.

These interviewees' language structure was faulty according to standard American English. Typical errors included subject-verb (We is); incorrect tense usage (We drunk a whole gallon of wine); mispronunciation of words (figer for figure); the use of words in an incorrect or awkward context (I' fixin' to go to the store); the substitution of d for a th sound as in dat for that; leaving the g off of "ing" words. (Other substitutions included sez for says; frum for from; en for and; instunce for instance; izn't for isn't; thar for there; sartin for certain and y'all for you all.) When asked about their pronunciation and grammar they indicated to the interviewer reasons to the effect that correct pronunciation and grammar were effeminate and something of little importance. As one DUI and Traffic Offender explains:

> People who talk pretty are sissy. Or they think they're better than the rest of us. Education don't make the man. I get over what I mean, and what I want to say. You understan me, don't you? So what in the hell is the dif. My friends understan me. We all talk southern. And you know its not what you say, but how you say it. We got our own way of saying things like I'm fixing to go. You know what I'm saying.

Most of their expressions, accounts, and stories were experientially based and often exaggerated and dramatized. Regional colloquialisms and ambiguity allowed for flexibility when speaking of size, speed, age, etcetera; for example, "passel" for any number, "99 percent" for most of the time. Content dealt with hunting, fishing, shop talk, stock car racing, ball games, drinking, gambling, fighting, cars, trucks, "dirty jokes," and sex. CB Slang was profuse; for example, accidentally on purpose for drunk driving, alky for liquor, ape for rough trucker, bang up for accident, bear poem for traffic ticket, beaver hunt for cruising women, and camera for radar. They spoke in a rough, ungrammatical, obscene, and profane vernacular. Vocabulary was concrete rather than abstract and parochial with the exception of religious allegorical content. Words and sentences ran together, tenses were mixed, sentences were not completed, syllables were left out, words were slurred, and r's and "ings " were not pronounced. Voice quality was flat, drawly, and characterized by jerky rhythm control, thin resonance and amplitude, slow tempo, and latency of response. Vocal expressions included frequent loud laughing, groaning, coughing, clearing of the throat, sneezing, swallowing and sighing. Vocal segregates (fill-ins) such as "uh," "um," "huh," and "uh-huh" and pauses occurred frequently.

Physical appearance, stance and movement, and verbal and nonverbal communication indicated a southern low socioeconomic status but also an honest effort to express their thoughts and feelings. Beyond mundane instrumental requirements, language to them is essentially a means of entertainment because their primary medium of interaction is oral and locally constructed. There was no pretense about these men and they did not attempt to impress the interviewers. Their accounts were straightforward, internally consistent, and believable.

(b) World of Work

1. Physically Oriented Work: The work accounts of these men with the exception of six white-collar workers, disclosed constricted lives within a particular kind of work milieu. None thought of themselves as pursuing a career, though the work place was central to their identity and way of life. Physical work was the essential component of this milieu, ubiquitous to their life-style and essential to their sense of manliness and stock of knowledge. Pride in physical work, along with roles as southern white males, comprised their raison d'être. Several themes characterized the reality of this work setting: physical

orientation, pride in work accomplishments, occupational roles, living on "the edge of things," male domination, and informal work relations.

2. Physical Orientation: They defined work as physical activity directed toward making a living without the orbit of play. People who do not work with their hands do not really work. Sports and professional recreational activity (hunting, fishing, golfing, etcetera) do not qualify as work. College athletes and professional sports figures, for example, ball players, do not work because they are really playing, nor do professionals such as lawyers, C.P.A.s, bankers, preachers, and professors. Some M.D.s (general practitioners) might work to some extent because they use their hands to make a living. But most practice medicine to make money and enjoy prestige. Not only are non-manual tasks exempt from real work, but those who perform them are neither manly nor trustworthy. Yet, at the same time, they admired and respected professionals. They derogate those above their reach in a fashion that some psychologists would call "reaction formation," or what the man in the street would call "sour grapes." Typical occupations included factory and mill workers, construction workers, short-order cooks and restaurant employees, truckers, fishermen, carpenters, house painters, welders, trappers, plumbers, electricians, warehouse workers, bartenders, farm hands, roofers, cab drivers, and auto mechanics. In brief they were blue-collar workers who worked for wages rather than a salary and did not own the establishments where they worked.

Most took pride in various manual work skills; physical endurance, prowess and strength; seniority within the trade; and a sense of pride at the work site. Many bragged about the ability to fix things, such as clocks, cars, tractors, machinery, plumbing, irons, tools, flat tires, etcetera. They also boasted about how much weight they could lift, how long and hard they could work without rest, and how far they could drive a car or a truck without sleep. Most were proud of being good, all-around handy men. All claimed some specialized knowledge about the performance of one kind of work, task, or line of work and emphasized the length of job experience (but not with one company or employer). As non-union wage earners they had moved around from one job to another seeking to increase meager wages or work benefits. Many said they moved frequently because of the "greedy," "uppity," and "worthless" bosses who exploited them.

Very few acquired work skills in formal school settings, and they expressed disdain for and/or envy of formal schooling, even trades training. One Mixed Multiple Offender explains:

> I don't need no college boy coming here and telling me what to do. And I don't need any joker just out of trade school telling me what to do neither. Every summer they bring in some engineering students who don't know their asses from a hole in the ground. I have to go along behind them and redo the wiring. They don't know how to run a wire. Take those trade-school half asses. They can't do a damn thing either. I have to show them what to do too. I had rather have one worker who learned on the job like me than ten of those trade school bumpkins. You learn it the hard way on the job. Not from books nor trade manuals. They keep talking about apprenticeships and the training periods. It makes no sense to me. I am not getting paid to train a bunch of school-boy apprenticeships. When they come here I want them to know how to do the job from the jump. A good electrician in one place can work in another.

Most compared themselves favorably with white-collar workers in terms of the work place and the pay. As one DUI Recidivist comments:

> Those white collar workers got things soft and easy. They work in offices and around people who are dressed up and carry brief cases. They think they're better than me because they don't have to wear work clothes. Shit, they work for bosses just like I do. And I get more money than they get. I can quit today and find a good job tomorrow because I got a good trade. They can't do that. I don't have to kiss as much ass as they do either. I

got more freedom in my job. If I want to squeeze a beer, I can. They can't.

3. Individualism and Pride in Work: They expressed individualistic attitudes rather than work organizational views, and stressed the quality put in the work task rather than the worth of the work supervision involved. They approached the work sites in an egocentric fashion and emphasized the application of work skills in concrete rather than in abstract organizational modes. They extolled learning by doing on the job. Furthermore, they resented foremen or bosses who supervised them too closely and preferred work schedules permitting them to take frequent rest periods and days off. They said they preferred to work at their own pace and to organize work tasks among fellow workers on an equal and direct informal basis. The following complaint by a DUI Recidivist (a tobacco warehouse floor worker) about his foreman, close supervision, and organization goals illustrates individualism and the desire to personalize the work situation:

I told that pissy-ass foreman I didn't give a shit if the American Tobacco Company didn't sell another frigging cigarette . . . that I didn't smoke the poison shit anyway. I chew. I 'splained to him I didn't care a rat's ass about team work 'twin warehouse workers and the factory and all that marketing bullshit. I tried to git over to him that all what I was interested in was gitting these basket fulls of tobacco off the floor and ready for the drying plants . . . thass all me and the other fellers give a shit about cause thass all we git paid fer. And we do a good job when left alone. If that smart ass foreman who's buckin' for a buyer's job would leave us floor men be, we'd do the job better. We work things out fine mongst us selves. You know one pulls, one sweeps, two of us load and one drives. We all unload at the drying plant. We shift up. If he keeps on a 'messing with me, he can take the whole ball of wax and shove it. I mean the whole shit-a-roo cousin, you know what I mean? You been there, too, right?

Note in the above quote that the warehouse worker personalizes the work situation to his boss and to the interviewer (The interviewer had told him that he too had worked at one time as a floor man in a tobacco warehouse). Their accounts disclosed several reasons (paraphrased here) for attempting to personalize the work place: (1) bosses and employees must know that all people should interact with one another on an egalitarian face-to-face personal basis because such interaction is the only human and correct manner to behave (This is a southern rural or small-town custom inhering in southern folk culture); (2) the boss, other employees and all people connected with the work place must know that they (the employees) count--that they are human beings, worthy of consideration just because they are human; (3) that the more personalized the work situation, the more equal they become to employers and other employees; (4) that personalization gives them leverage over others; that is, from their standpoint when people get to know you (and listen to your personal problems and tales) they become involved with and obligated to you. In brief, they desired a semblance of personal worth and equality.

Another tale follows from a Mixed Multiple Offender (an auto mechanic) who spouts off about his boss (the owner of an automobile dealership and garage); that is, in a way to demonstrate his individualism and independence:

> I worked on that lemon the boss sold that old man every week for two months. I finally told the boss, "It want no use fer me to work on that sucker no more . . . It want no good and can't be fixed even by Jesus Christ." He said to me, "John, you go on out there and fix that car. I know you can do it. Don't give me no more lip. I'm the boss and you do what I say, do you understand?" I tole him, "O.K. Mr. Bossman, you go fix that sucker. Tis your car, shove it and your f---in' job up your ass. I quit. Do you understan?"

Individualism and conservative political stances explain their negative reports about liberal causes, labor unions, government organizations, government help programs, feminism, affirmative action, political correctness, women and blacks at the workplace, etcetera. The following remarks by one Mixed Multiple Offender (a factory worker) expresses these negative views:

> We working class southerners just don't like labor unions. We want to negotiate our own work situation. Our religion tells us a man is responsible for his own fate --and don't say nothing about labor unions or government men to help you. All they do is take your money and they're run from the outside by a bunch of foreigners. All those government programs are for welfare freeloaders and blacks. The government gives them everything but that don't change nothing. They're still "blacks" and bums. I don't like blacks taking our jobs when I know we're better qualified. Now the libbers are in the act. I got to compete with the blacks and the women. Man, the whole country is going to hell.

4. Work Activity and Living on the Edge of Things: Finally, these men were aware of the fact that their vaunted life-style was under siege from a more liberated contemporary way of life; that their common stock of knowledge (derived primarily from the rural and small-town south) conflicts with many ideas they encounter from the media and the ever-changing work place. They were aware of their precarious work status; that the work place is becoming increasingly regulated, impersonal, and competitive; and that at work their definitions of work and respectability, insistence on informal authority, personal negotiations in work relations, and white and male domination are all fading.

Yet, according to them, respectability still means a steady job, a living, and a physical work activity that provides room for their individual contributions (actually all increasingly difficult to find). They said they needed their jobs "to get along" or get by rather than to get ahead or increase social status. Their chief concerns were: status among their peers; taking care of themselves, and the family; loyalty to peers and work buddies; masculinity, and worthiness as a real man; loyalty to the southern region; a repertoire of expletives denoting virility and courage; the ability to hold their liquor like a man; and, freedom to drink and raise hell whenever and wherever they wished.

(c) Organizations, Associations, and Recreation

These offenders manifested a general disinterest and lack of faith in formal organizations such as political parties, labor unions, fraternal lodges, civic clubs, government agencies, schools, colleges, and welfare and rehabilitative programs (including DUI schools and treatment clinics). (Perhaps the history of the south provides some justification for this position.)

1. The Church: Most (92%) had been baptized in Protestant churches and nearly two-thirds (73%) claimed church membership in one of the following denominations: Southern Baptist, Primitive Baptist, Assembly of God, Pentecostal, Church of Christ, Church of God, and Methodist. It is important to note that all of these with the exception of the Methodist church maintain individual church autonomy, and for the most part practice a studied separation from non-fundamentalist mainstream Protestant faiths. These churches stress preaching the gospel, hell fire and damnation, personal salvation, the saving of souls, the literal interpretation of the Bible, divine forgiveness of sin, emotionally expressive church worship, divine audition, and special sanctification, and they downplay the social gospel and modernity as emphasized in mainstream, liberal Protestant faiths. Ministers are called to preach via personal summons from God and are not usually (with the exception of Methodist ministers) seminary educated. They are Bible-believing fundamentalists.

Though mothers, wives, girl friends, and other female relatives attend church regularly, less than 50 percent of these men said they did so; 20 percent went irregularly. As one DUI and Traffic Offender explains:

> Some religion is good for everybody but you don't have to go to church every Sunday. Sunday is my rest day. I really think religion is mostly for women and children. Maybe old men too. But I'm young. The people

who take care of the moral thing . . . the people who hold out hope for us. They are our women. There's so much evil in the world you got to have religion. I'm glad I was raised in the church. It tells me who I am and gives me hope. But I need to get closer to Jesus.

They said they grew up in churches where drinking, gambling, card playing, "screwing around," and dancing were evil, and where they were expected to testify about their sins to the church congregation--and to them, having fun was sinning. Their God was a judgmental, fearsome, jealous, Old Testament punishing deity. On the other hand, salvation depended on a personal relationship with the savior, Jesus, and on faith, baptism, grace, and current religious beliefs (doctrines) rather than on good deeds. Their expressed religious beliefs and concerns focused on hazy, Old Testament stories, orthodoxy, violence, revenge; individual sin, baptism (born again) redemption and salvation; a personal relationship with the Savior; and a literal interpretation of the Bible. Their faith was characterized by fate and supernatural justice (both of which are contradictory by ordinary logical standards). Religion to them comprised a belief system somewhat removed from social problems encountered in everyday life: a belief system based on a murky convoluted mythology, severe justice and piety, sin, punishment, and redemption. Many listened to lay "called" ministers--called to preach rather than to plough corn. Their formative years were suffused with pious exhortations, judgments, and fear of damnation. It should be noted that there is a current social movement in the United States back to religious fundamentalism. (See H. Paul Chalfant, Roger E. Beckley, and C. Eddie Palmer, Third Edition, *Religion in Contemporary Society*, 1994.) In this sense these men are far from being marginals.

The Ten Commandments constituted their law, but a forgiving God was eternal, and it was never too late to repent. One Mixed Multiple Offender points out:

You are supposed to go by the good Book. Those things they tell you in the Catholic Church and those fancy Protestant churches are for the birds. Those educated preachers don't have the ear of God. They tell you about the problems in this world. And they don't know anything about them. Real preachers preach from the Book (Bible). They tell you about the spiritual world. They got a text and they stick to it. They preach about sin and our real personal problems. It's never too late to get right with Jesus. You got to go to him direct. He forgives you for anything you do wrong. You know, if you have the right attitude and beg for forgiveness. I started out right and went wrong. But I can change and get back to Jesus. You really cause your own problems by not getting with Jesus.

Anti-intellectual, individualistic perspectives appeared to explain these offenders' distrust of modernity, science, and professionalism. As one DUI Recidivist states:

A lot of people think you should go to some shrink or social worker about your problems. Or to one of those priests or high-class preachers. Wrong. You got to go right to Jesus. Those phonies just take your money or have you put away. And you don't need no union boss nor welfare agency to take care of you. Take care of yourself with the help of Jesus. Your problems have nothing to do with this crazy system. Right is right, and wrong is wrong. You straighten up and go with God and your problems will melt away. You don't need those fancy doctors either. They can't help you stop drinking. I ought to know. They never did nothing for me. Drinking is a sin that has caused all my problems. I went to Jesus. He helped. But I ain't there yet. Problem is I get out of my misery when I drink. When I'm drinkin I ain't got no problems.

2. Labor Unions: A few (26) said they had belonged to some type of labor union at one time or another (United Auto Workers, CIO, Teamsters, machinist unions, textile unions). But most did not join unions and only four were current union

members. All favored right-to-work laws and open shops. They said they liked labor-union wages, pensions, hospitalization, health insurance plans, unemployment compensation, job protection, recreational facilities, and other benefits. But, they simultaneously complained that unions throughout the country had too much political power, were beyond control, and had too much coercive power over the individual worker. Furthermore, they reported that union dues exceeded union benefits. Additionally, most (85%) reported that the unions in their area were too weak to help them. One DUI Recidivist states:

> We don't have many unions in Georgia. And those we got is low-skill, low-wage labor. You know things like textile and furniture. And you know where blacks and women work. There ain't many unions for workers in the auto, rubber, steel and electrical manufacturing plants--where the real money is. Seasonal labor don't work out well with labor unions. Everybody down here except some working men are against unions. You know, the big shots, the newspapers, and the politicians are all against them. Even the preachers don't like them. Anyway, they don't help you get a job. And they don't help you holding no job. If the boss wants to get rid of you, he will find a way, union or no union. And time you pay your labor dues, you don't make much out of them.

Most (85%) maintained a set of rigid beliefs about unions: for example, the belief that the cost of living differences between the north (where unions are strong and plentiful) and the south compensate for regional wage differences; that the differentials between union and non-union scales and union benefits are offset by union dues. Though they thought that eventually unionization would grow in the south, they neither comprehended the struggle entailed for union success, nor expressed the willingness to pay the price. They blamed union failures in the south on "weak unions" rather than on any organizational weaknesses among workers. They did not seem to understand that unions can be no stronger than the collective will of the union workers and were not willing to pay the price for labor unions. Their only expressed interests in unions were in quick benefits for themselves as individuals rather than in long-term working-class benefits. Furthermore, and more importantly, they said they were afraid of losing their jobs for "talkin unions" and not being able to find another job elsewhere if fired for being pro-union (The authors had heard similar statements within other research contexts).

All opposed the use of compulsion or force of any kind by formal organizations, including labor unions and advocated right to work laws. The "self reliance" and "individualism" of these men was reflected in their work behavior. More than three-fourths (86%) had sketchy work records and had moved frequently from one job to another in efforts to secure slightly higher wages in each move. One DUI and Traffic Offender offers the following typical comments:

> Man, I'm no joiner. Don't waste my time on a bunch of organizations and clubs. They don't do nothing but take your money. Labor unions don't do much for you down here. Maybe some day. But you see I got to think of today. All that sacrifice talk about building unions don't get it for me. I want mine now. I ain't interested in all that shit about others. I have to take care of myself, thank you. If everybody felt the way I do, we wouldn't need no labor unions.

3. Other Formal Groups: None were active in political party activities and appeared about equally split between preference for the Democrat and Republican parties. They disliked the Republican Party because it represents, to them, moneyed interests, and they disliked the Democratic Party because it represents blacks and freeloaders. As one DUI and Traffic Offender says:

> There ain't much difference between Republicans and Democrats. The people at the top of both parties get money and both raise a lot of money. The Republicans raise more because they got more. I don't give nothing to

them. The Republicans want to fix things so rich people can get richer. The Democrats want to give everything to the freeloaders. They say the Republicans are conservative and the Democrats are liberal. One is conservative in holding out for the rich. The other is liberal in spending money for the freeloaders. Take your pick. I don't care for either one. When I vote, I votes for the man.

About 30 percent voted in local elections and less than 10 percent in the last national elections.

Though none admitted membership in the Ku Klux Klan, most (75%) were sympathetic to its white supremacy stand. All were segregationists and bemoaned any form of racial integration. All said they knew people who belonged to the Ku Klux Klan, but adamantly refused to discuss any of them or their activities. Approximately one-third belonged to the National Rifle Association, and all approved of this organization's position on gun control. All owned guns of many different types which they claimed were necessary for self-protection, target shooting, and hunting purposes. Magnums and automatics were preferred along with assault rifles. Most owned pick-up trucks with conspicuous gun racks, and most equated gun ownership with citizenship rights and the masculine role. One DUI Recidivist's comments illustrate this point:

The Constitution gives me the right to bear arms. That means to own and carry guns, and no one can take that right away from me. To own guns is the American way. You know if guns were outlawed, only outlaws would have guns. A man needs protection these days from all these criminals, rapists, and robbers. The head of the household has to protect his women and children. Who knows? The blacks may try to get uppity and take over. They might try to come over to burn my neighborhood. That's when I got to have some fire power. I got different types of guns for different purposes. You know, hand guns, shot guns, rifles, and all kinds. And no one is going to take them away from me. I am going to join the National Rifle Association when I get a little money ahead. Guns don't kill people. Bad people with guns kill people. Hell, if they didn't shoot you, they would find something else. Like cut your throat with a knife. But it ain't wrong to kill in self-defense. And some people should have been dead ten years ago.

More than one-half said they had belonged to one of the following veteran's organizations at one time or another: American Legion, Disabled American Veterans, The Veterans of Foreign Wars or Am Vets. However, only 15 percent reported current active memberships in any of these organizations. Most said they dropped out because of their inability to pay the dues. Many said they dropped out because these organizations had been taken over by big shots. As one DUI and Traffic Offender stated:

> Well, I used to go to the American Legion hall to drink and shoot some pool. And you know you could eat there too if you want. You could take your girl and dance too. But it's been taken over by the big shots and the officers. They run the show. They added many things, where they could bring their women. And the women came in all dressed up and felt they were better than us. And better than our women. I don't feel at ease there any more. It's not like it used to be. My drinking buddies don't like it neither. When we drink, we whoop it up. We can't be ourselves there no more. I never went to the monthly business meetings where I know the big shots run the show. To hell with them. My buddies and I go to the honky-tonks to drink. There we are the big shots. They can't bother us there. The politicians always got some program they want you to join or give money to. I don't waste my time voting for nothing. And I don't have any money for them.

Very few (18) had ever belonged to private lodges or fraternal organizations. Fifteen said they had been initiated into the Masonic Lodge, but only four professed current membership. None volunteered any comments on their activities as Masons.

4. Informal Groups

Fishing and hunting buddies: While formal groups were relatively unimportant to these men, informal groups were essential to their life-style. The most dominant figures here (outside of family group members discussed later on) were male drinking, fishing, hunting, gambling, and honky-tonk companions; all referred to as "drinkin buddies." They said they met these boon companions in childhood neighborhoods, at school, on the job, or through family connections, or at honky-tonks. Most said they "grew up" with members of these groups, and just kept on doing what they had always done together-- "drinking and driving around," smoking marijuana, shooting pool, fighting, working, fishing, and hunting, honky-tonking, double dating, gambling, "hanging out and around," goofing off. Fishing and hunting were not only modes of recreation but crucial patterns of everyday life that had been handed down to them as a "natural," manly, honorable pattern expected of all "real men." One DUI and Traffic Offender states:

> I've been fishin and huntin all my life. My daddy started me off when I was a little boy. I got my first rifle when I was eleven years old. By the time I was fourteen, I had me a shotgun and a hound dog. I never knew no other way. It's natural for man to fish and hunt. That's the way we started out. And I still don't throw no fish back. I eat all of them. I go every time I get the chance. Sometimes I wish I could stay in the woods. I never knew no real man who didn't like to fish and hunt. Course, the city slickers is a different story. But then, they don't know nothing about real life and some of them play at fishin and huntin. And belong to fancy hunting clubs on posted land. Screw them. I hunt where I please, and when I please.

Fishing and hunting usually included a buddy (or buddies), beer, fishing paraphernalia, an assortment of firearms, hunting dogs, pick-up trucks, and boats. Pick-up trucks with gun racks were usually used to transport the boat to the fishing hole or to the hunting designated wooded area. The most important items were the buddy and the beer. Entire afternoons (sometimes longer) might be spent without catching any fish or shooting any game, but a lot of beer was consumed and tall tales were exchanged. Many recounted tragic accidents during these excursions, such as over-turned boats, auto and truck wrecks, accidental gunshot wounds, snake bites, falls, physical injuries, drownings, camp fire burning, and other mishaps. And many of these mishaps appeared to be alcohol related. Remarks by a Mixed Multiple Offender are illustrative:

> You know, if we went fishin or huntin, the beer or some kind of booze went along too--beer for fishin, booze for huntin. Sometimes both, but always one or other. You see the drinkin and talkin together was part of the whole thing. There's no way you can fish and hunt with your buddies without drinkin for companionship. Sure, I know some of the accidents we had wouldn't have happened if we had a been cold sober. But that ain't the point. You take your chances. Beer and fishin go together like bread and butter, or say a horse and a carriage. I don't understan why some people don't seem to see these things. You just don't hunt and fish without beer or booze. To hell with the risks you take. What's that got to do with anything. You can't have no fun at anything less you take some risks. What is the big deal? Of course you got to drink and drive if you want to go huntin or fishin.

They talked about hunting dogs, game fowl, squirrels, rabbits, and deer and all kinds of fish as part of a way of life. In addition to the venison and the drinking stories, deer hunting (the ultra "sport") provided skins for rugs and heads for mounting (as trophies). The mounted head (the larger the antlers the better) served as a machismo symbol along with animal skins and pelts. One DUI Recidivist boasted that a stuffed black bear stood in the center of "my small den." "The bear tells all my visitors what a good hunter I am." In response to the interviewer's question, "Does the bear talk?" He answered, "He don't have to talk. Jes beeze there." He was also very proud of his four coon hounds, deer dogs, and bird dogs.

Drinking Patterns and the Honky-tonk Set: Drinking activities were described within hunting and fishing contexts and regular attendance at honky-tonks, beer joints, truck stops, all-night restaurants, service stations, pool rooms, garages, discount stores, and stock car races. They drank at home, in the car, at work, movies, weddings, parties, and funerals. Much of their drinking took place at honky-tonks and enroute to such places. Work situations usually provided for frequent free periods within and without the work place where (and when) they could drink at certain intervals. Irregular work hours, seasonal employment, and rotating job shifts permitted ample spare time for drinking, an everyday activity for most. Friday and Saturday nights were prime times to get "wiped out" or "shit faced." Beer was the everyday drink of choice, bourbon the preferred weekend beverage. They usually consumed 5-6 beers daily in beer joints and between work and home, and frequently purchased a "roadie" (six pack) to go at the last drinking place. Heavy drinking and driving was a common occurrence and was rationalized even though they were fully aware of the risks involved--risks taken lightly, matter of factly, unrealistically, and fatalistically. Big shots on the other hand could drink and drive without risk of being arrested. As one DUI Recidivist explains:

We, drinkin buddies drink most everyday together. It's the natural thing to do with your friends. The big shots drink in those fancy cocktail lounges and country clubs. I do mine in a honky-tonk. What's the diff? Well if they get drunk, a friend takes them home or maybe the police. If I get caught, it's another story. They might put me in jail. But you know things that happen are meant to be. That's the way things go. No big deal. Hell, people drink and drive every day. I don't want to cause no wreck. But if I crash it's one of those things. So what? Hey, I break the law now and then, but who don't? And I drive careful when I've been drinkin. Most of my drinkin buddies are good drivers like me. You see you have to get use to drinkin and drivin. It takes experience over time. I been at it a long time. I drink most every day, so I got to drink and drive. But you got to compensate when you drink and drive. I can drink and drive all day long without no body knowing it. See those cars outside bars. Those guys know they are intoxicated when they drive home. Cars, bars, roads, and drinkers go together. Who in the hell rides a bus?

Honky-tonks that provide beer, junk food, barbecue sandwiches, pork rinds, pinball machines, pool tables, booths, tables, and juke boxes are preferred social settings[7]. Though beer was usually the only alcoholic beverage sold in these places, patrons were allowed to bring in bottles of bourbon, partially concealed in brown paper sacks during weekends. Activities focus on drinking, socializing and gossiping, sports talk, shop talk, storytelling, cross-sex relationships, and picking up women, playing the pinball machines, and shooting pool, arguing, jousting, and mock fighting--sometimes real fighting inside or outside. A Mixed Multiple Offender describes the sequence of events that generally occur at honky-tonks thusly:

> You walk up to the bar and order a beer in a can or a bottle. It's important to order the kind of beer you want, like "Schlitz," and where you want a can or a bottle. No man asks for a glass. You drink it from the can or bottle. Only some women want a glass. Most of them do like what we do. Then you takes your beer and shoot a game of pool. Or play a pinball machine. After you start everything falls in place. You put your money in the slot and play the game. You put a quarter in the juke box and make a selection. You buy and drink another beer. And you talk to your buddies. Now and then you go to the rest room and take a leak. Real man don't wash their hands. They go in and out as fast as they can. That's all there is to it. But that's what we do. Without the beer and the drinkin buddies, the whole thing would be nothin. Routines the thing man if it's fun things, but not

routine work. That's another story. Drinkin breaks my routine and makes me feel like I'm somebody and you know you have to drive to the joint and drive home later. There's no way out of driving and drinking. Just has to be.

Dancing usually occurs on weekends accompanied by live music. Drinking is considered to be a natural recreational activity there as well as (at times) a relief mechanism for personal problems ("misery drinking"). Most said they drank too much at honky-tonks but claimed to have control over their drinking. As one DUI and Traffic Offender comments:

Sometimes I drink there to get high and have a good time. It helps me to fit in better and dance. I feel like I'm ten feet tall when I'm high. On weekends I drink to get drunk. Sometimes I drink to forget my troubles. Most of the time I drink to be sociable with my buddies. It all depends on the situation. Sometimes I just drink to drink, and to feel good. But I got control. Hell, I can drive better drunk than most people sober. I know when I'm too drunk to drive when I can't find the key hole to open my car door. That ain't often.

Though most preferred one particular beer joint or honky-tonk over others, they drank in several during the week as well as on weekends. This mobility (from joint to joint) required frequent drinking and driving trips over distances from one or two blocks to one to five miles. All preferred driving to and from drinking establishments in their own individual cars, and eschewed designated drivers and seat belts. One DUI and Traffic Offender states:

I want my own wheels so when I want to go I go, and when I want to stay, I stay. My buddies feel the same way. We usually meet at one place but we drive our own cars to wherever we want to go to drink. That designated driver shit won't fly. Those silly people talk about it but it don't work. I'm my designated driver, and

I don't want no woman to drive my car either. A man drives when he has to drive drunk or sober. And I don't fool with seat belts either. Too much trouble. Only big shots wear belts and let their women drive. They can afford fancy cars.

They boasted that their drinking and driving usually posed no problems for them because they were good drivers and controlled drinkers. One DUI Recidivist comments:

Me and my buddies go to a few beer joints nearly everyday. We go to a honky-tonk on weekends. Don't make no difference, we drink and drive nearly everyday. Millions of other people do too. What's that shit about knowing to say when. We're good drivers and we know when to stop drinking. We don't drink too much so we can drive good. Course we try to be more careful if we get a snoot full. We look out for each other. You know, some times we may drive a buddy home. But damn seldom. Usually, it's each man for himself. And that works out. Once in a while we get stopped and arrested. But that's one of those things. You know you got to take chances. When we leave the joint we drive slow and easy, and very careful like. Because we don't want the cops to give us a DUI. You know they are out there looking out for you all the time because their bosses, the big shots want to keep us in line. If they want to get you, they will find a way to get you. They tell you to blow in something, and God knows what happens after that. If you refuse to take a breath test, they put you in jail and take your license away and do everything they can. Like charging you with resisting arrest if you give them any lip. They're real pigs. Problem is I feel real independent when I get high. And then I feel like tellin them to mind their own damn business and to go watch beer commercials. I ran with a few guys in school who later became cops. When that happened we went on our own ways. Man, who can be a cop? I want no part of any cop. You can't trust the bastards. They do what the big shots tell them to do.

(Note that none of these men mentioned the chances of harming others or themselves when driving after drinking. They seem to be primarily concerned with avoiding the police whom they do not respect, because they are enforcers for the upper classes.) The honky-tonks they frequented were not known as pick-up bars but rather as meeting places for working-class men and women. Women unlike men were reportedly "weekenders," but occasionally dropped by during week days to drink and converse with the regulars. They (women) came on Friday and Saturday nights escorted or unescorted. As one DUI and Traffic Offender explains:

You know, there is a crowd of women who come in here to socialize. During the week they come in alone or with girl friends. On weekends, they come alone sometimes, and sometimes with boyfriends. On weekdays we chat with them like we do with our men buddies. You see in a way they are our buddies too. And we date some of them. Sometimes we run into them when they don't have anybody with them. I wouldn't call them pick-ups because we know them. And we drink together like buddies. Course, we take them to bed when we can. No big thing. Friday and Saturday nights are different. They dress up then and come to dance and get picked up. There's a fight once in a while over the women who aren't regulars. You know, the ones that just drop by for a pick up. We usually fight over those wild mares. When I pick up a women, I send her a free drink first. I look her over and make sure she's not with anyone. If I catch her eye and she smiles, then I know I'm in. If she accepts my drink I move in. Sometimes, if I know she's interested I just move in anyway, at the bar or at a table. Sometimes they flirt and then hold back. Then I tell her what she is and walk away. Now these outside mares are the ones we fight over sometimes. Not inside, but outside in the parking lot. I guess me and my

buddies has one or two fights every week or two. Our
friends break us up and we don't usually do no big
damage. Generally, we forget about it by the next day
and carry on like nothin happened. Its fun to drink,
fight, and f---. I feel good, you know, strong, and real
important when I drink. I'm the wrong cat to mess with
then. It's good to drink and feel important. You know,
be somebody.

The above quote and other similar comments indicate
frequent fights over women and personal disputes during
weekend nights, despite close police surveillance. However,
most are not serious and have no consequences. Only on rare
occasions did honky-tonk owners call the police who cruised the
honky-tonk areas on a regular basis. Usually, no arrests were
made even when they did come in to break up fights.
Occasionally, they arrested a few troublemakers for assault and
public disturbance. If weapons were involved and/or serious
bodily harm was inflicted, the police usually arrested all parties
concerned. One Mixed Multiple Offender comments:

The cops drive by the honky-tonk areas during the
weekends. They call our places redneck bars. They
know we're going to drink, f---, fight, on Friday and
Saturday nights. If you don't drink what do you go to
bar for? But, so long as we stay in our places and don't
bother other people . . . don't kill each other, they leave
us alone. But they are always on the look out.

According to these men wide latitudes of behaviors were
permitted in honky-tonks; for example, open sexual flirtation
and sexual joshing; singing, joking, and "showing out" behaviors;
bragging, signifying, exaggerating, strutting, posing, hollering.
However, certain conduct was prohibited: serious fighting,
destructive violence, heavy gambling, soliciting for prostitution,
vandalism, and the overt trafficking in illegal goods and services.
The owners, employees, and patrons feared these behaviors
would bring in the police and/or cause internal operating
disruptions. Profanity and obscenity were commonplace but

usually uttered in a joking or indirect manner; that is, in a non-confrontational fashion. The social actors themselves as well as the owners and the employees were concerned with the control of destructive behavior. Patrons sometimes became intoxicated to the point of losing motor control, and consequently, fell off bar stools, went to sleep, stumbled around, spoke in a slurred fashion, fell on the floor and up against others. Men and women displayed open and marked affection for one another (e.g., fondling and embracing). The close frequent face-to-face contacts among patrons in a crowded, co-mingled, fluid behavior setting made occasional mishaps (jostling, turning over drinks, cigarette burns) and run-ins inevitable. However, most offenses of commission or omission were typically minor social piques that did not cause serious ill effects such as: pushes, bumps, shoves; the usurpation of others' seats at the bar or table; spilling of other's drinks, stepping in other people's territory; mistakenly picking up other's drinks; knowingly or unknowingly flirting with another's girlfriend; neglecting to pay for an obligated round of drinks. Remedial measures such as, "I'm sorry," "pardon me," "forgive me" usually cleared up these gaffes.

When asked about honky-tonky conversation these men reported the following sociability[7] (man-to-man) topics: tall hunting and fishing tales; sports, vehicles (cars, trucks, motorcycles), stock-car racing; heavy equipment, guns and ammunition; trucking, farming, cattle, dogs, drinking, fighting, gambling; enemies list (Yankees, social workers, "blacks," bosses, big government, the United Nations, welfare organizations, foreigners, liberals, city slickers); good eating (greasy food), wild life, road and building construction, funerals, weddings, parties, women and cheap sex; local gossip about who got sick, pregnant, shot, married, or put in jail; and ubiquitous shop talk about how they "put down" bosses. In regard to the latter, for example, one Mixed Multiple Offender reports during the interviews:

> I told my boss at the factory he could shelve that new title that he wanted to give me . . . materials inspector or same shit like that. I told him he could keep the phony title and the phony promotion going with it

. . . all but the money. I told him, "jes give me the extra money and hold the bull shit."

Cross-sex conversation at honky-tonks dealt with sweet talk, courtship ploys, passion, anticipation, tryst logistics, and sexual bantering. As one DUI, and Traffic Offender comments:

> You know we really go after women, but we kid them around too and they kid us back. One morning this waitress ask me: "Hi honey, what can I get you this morning?" I said, "Hi, baby, what will you give me?" She says, "well the special is two eggs, sausage, grits, and coffee." I told her, "is that all I can have?" She told me, "no, but that's all you can get."

Many reported honky-tonk conversations centered on masculine aggression like driving a fist through a wall, loyalty to the boys by staying out late at night regardless of the wife; courage and never backing down from a fight; and, never turning down a good piece of ass. (The authors encouraged these subjects to relate stories on honky-tonk life, because we reasoned that such tales would tell us much about identity, perspective, and everyday life; and provide a window into drinking and driving motivation and patterns.)

Music: These men reported that honky-tonk music, "hard" country music, provided the necessary musical background for their relaxation and entertainment. As Malone (1989) points out, honky-tonk music projects the mood and ambiance of its birth place, the beer joint, and closely reflects southern working-class culture. Honky-tonk has best marked the evolution of southern folk music from rural to urban industrial life. The sad but non-protest lyrics and tonality music evoke emotional pain, isolation, nostalgia, sentimentality, and human weakness. Musical themes focus on drinking and sexual cheating; violence, fighting, and gambling; heartbreak, sinning, suffering, alienation, failure, and unrequited love; good women-bad women-wayward husband triangle, and saints and sinners.

All these men professed a love for country and western music because they said it was "true to life" and their kind of thing. One DUI Recidivist explains his identification with this genre:

> The blacks got their blues and jazz. We got our white soul music. It sounds good and we can dance to most of it. It tells a real story and we can understan the words. Most of these hard rock and roll numbers don't have any words we can understan, crazy stuff. Our music deals with real people in real life. It lays things out where we can see it and feel it. You know like, right and wrong. And it tells you the causes of your problems. And how you alone can solve them. With all the hell raising and pain out there you get a spiritual message. It takes you out of this crazy world that I don't understan. It tells you, you got to solve your own problems with the help of God and good women.

The foregoing quote also illustrates the thematic tie-in of this music with these DUIs, religion and life-style, their individualism, a simplistic definition of right and wrong, and the desire for a constant simple world, enduring and unchanged.

Other Hangouts: These men said they lived a simple life that did not call for much in the way of entertainment beyond hunting and fishing, drinking beer with their buddies, listening to country music, playing pinball machines, shooting pool, visiting with family members, and having sex. Other than beer joints and honky-tonks they haunted all-night restaurants, discount stores, service stations, barber shops, and truck-stops. And sometimes they went to jail. They usually went to restaurants where country-style decor and food prevailed. They went twice during the day: early in the morning for breakfast and late at light after leaving the beer joint or honky-tonk. The early morning breakfast that included only coffee and a doughnut or toast was a place for discussing the notable events in their lives of the preceding day: the weather, gossip, and athletic events such as the Atlanta International Raceway races, and the outcomes of various sporting events. After getting "high" or "drunk" at a local honky-tonk they frequently went to all-night restaurants, such as a pancake house, omelet shop, or a waffle house where coffee, cigarettes, and greasy food made up the menu. That was the time for complaining about the boss, and the work place; a time for complaining about girlfriends and wives, the cops and the big shots; and, monotony of homelife in general. They also said it was a place and time to "sober up" before going home.

They went to discount stores to gossip, look around, and buy cheap clothing, and fishing and hunting equipment, to find out who else was there, and to setup an upcoming weekend for hunting, fishing, or watching sports events on T.V. with companions. All-night service stations were also hangouts for many because "that's where the boys hang out." Frequently these stations offered auto repair services on credit and provided hangout sites for sociability, gossiping, card playing, drinking and camaraderie. The conversations there dealt with how autos work, what was wrong with their cars, and how to fix them. Many claimed to be good "shade tree" mechanics; however, they said they did not have the necessary equipment and car tools to perform a first class mechanic's duties. At this site, they also discussed different makes of cars; the pros and cons of hunting and fishing equipment; weddings, funerals, and obituaries; and, fishing and hunting trips. Secondary and primary group relationships (business, and personal relations) were mixed at these places. One Mixed Multiple Offender's comments reflect the service station scene:

> Sometimes when I get off work or leave the beer joint I drop by John's gas station. He is a good man and I know him for a long time. Most of the time I run into many of my buddies there. It's like being at home. If John is busy and I need something, I go behind the counter to get it and leave the money on the counter. Sometimes I wait on a customer if he's busy. Or one of my buddies might help the customer. We sit around inside and outside and chew the fat. There ain't no women there. It's a man's place. We can say what we want. I might hand John some tools when he's workin on somethin. If I need a beer I get it from the cooler and pay him later. My buddies do the same. If there's no

customers, we play cards and gamble a little. If it's real late we might send out for a bottle, and take a few good drinks. If I have trouble with my car he'll fix it. I pay him what I can and when I can. He understans and goes easy on me. Of course, I'm talking about my self and my crowd. If you go there, you won't get the same treatment. I feel safe there because if someone calls who I don't want to talk to, you know like wife or girlfriend, John tells them I ain't there. Sometimes I answer the phone for him. If somebody wants one of us, I'll check and find out if he wants to talk. If he don't, I'll tell them he ain't there. We look out for each other. When we are drinkin we want no one to bother us.

(d) *Sex and Family Life*

Comments disclosed that these men viewed the male role first as being head of a family and a provider; then as a father, and last as a husband. They claimed to respect women as long as they stayed in their place. According to them females' duties were to take care of the house and children and make the male comfortable in every way. They preferred girlfriends and wives from similar backgrounds to theirs who accepted their macho image of real men. Ideally, women should not work in the labor force, but should she work, she should do so with the express consent of the husband. Interview reports indicated that they did not want their wives or girlfriends to go back to school or to become economically independent or superior to them in any sphere, because they feared the consequential weakening of the provider role. Women at school might learn knowledge alien to them, have elevating experiences, and might find other more interesting men than themselves. They recounted in many ways that most women they knew agreed with them about the male and female roles. For example, they explained in a joking manner that their women did not think a man was good at "diddling," unless he was willing to fight. As one DUI and Traffic Offender reports: "If a man won't fight he's no good in the bed."

They claimed satisfactory relationships with women so long as they did not challenge their masculinity and authority. They became riled when girlfriends or wives acted independently, questioned their authority and knowledge, compared them unfavorably in any way with other men, criticized their success as providers, asked them about their activities away from home, disagreed with the double standard rule, nagged them about their drinking, flirted with other men, or "put them down" in front of other people. They expected female acquaintances of short duration to have sex with them without any emotional commitment on their part. The following remarks by one DUI and Traffic Offender are typical:

> Now you know I never mashed it on no women. I respect them. I never raped nobody. But if I took them out and spent my money I expected them to come across. You know give up the pussy. What the hell does she go out with me for unless she wants to f--- me. I never had time for all that romance and sweet talk, bull shit. A woman is a woman and a man is a man. If she's a real woman she wants to make out. I just put it to them. You like me, fine, then we make out. If you don't please don't waste my time, find yourself another boy. I never took one by force, but sometimes you have to push a little. They don't want to be called pushovers. I don't use no rubbers neither. She has to take care of herself. Some stupes worry about hurting a woman's feelings over a piece of ass. I don't. Man they can turn those tears off and on like a faucet. And sometimes when you think it's on, it's done been off a long time ago. But I can handle them good when I'm drinkin. I get courage then.

All stated they had sex relations with several different women concurrently and as often as they could.

They interacted with members of the opposite sex from grade school through puberty, to marriage within their communities. Few traveled far from home to date. When reaching adolescence, they noted major differences between themselves and big shots' sons: plain clothing vs. preppie clothing; low and average grades vs. high grades; non-membership in clubs and organizations vs. club and organization memberships (for example, Beta Club and Key Club, school newspaper staff, glee club). Furthermore, they took mechanical drawing, shop, physical education, industrial arts and agriculture while big shots' children took courses in chemistry, physics, drama, and foreign languages. One DUI and Traffic Offenders claims:

> By the end of my first year in high school I knew the crowd of girls I couldn't get a date with. I ask out girls from my own neighborhood. You know, girls whose fathers worked with their hands for a living. The girls I took out didn't finish high school. The preppies dated girls who were going to college. You know, like them.

Their first knowledge of sex was crude and unsophisticated and learned from childhood peers and father figures. In high school, as adolescents, they had brief and intermittent sexual encounters with two or three female school mates. None mentioned any homosexual relationships. They married early, usually before twenty-one, and said they really learnt about sex with their wives. As one DUI and Traffic Offender commented:

> I took out three or four girls in high school. You know before I dropped out. I laid three of them, but it was no big deal. It was quick and neither of us really got off right. We didn't know too much about what we were doing. They went on to somebody else soon. I got married to one of them when I was eighteen. We found out about sex together. Now I'm single, and I take a lot of women to bed. And I don't use rubbers either. That's like wading in water with your socks on.

These men considered marriage a legalistic and religious institution centering on living together, the church, the spouse's family, and their own family of orientation. They maintained that, once married, wives should take care of the house, care for the children, maintain family relations with both sides of the family, have meals ready on time, take care of the husband both physically and sexually, not interfere in the husband's work or social relations. On the other hand they had the right to intercede in their wives' work and social relations at will. They did not expect to wash clothes, mop floors, wash dishes, sweep the floor, change diapers, or rock the baby to sleep. The husband could have extramarital affairs should he be discreet, but the wife could not. One DUI and Traffic Offender reports:

> I don't think a man should be a dog when he gets married. He should show his family respect. If he steps out now and then he should keep it away from his family. If he don't, he's a dog and loses respect. What the wife don't know don't hurt her. But only trash throw it in her face. As far as a wife going out with another guy. I'll tell you one thing. If she shacks up with some other guy I will beat her up real bad, and leave her. Fact is I might beat her to death and take my chances with the chair. That's the way I was brought up. And that's the way my buddies think.

They also expected wives or girlfriends not to complain about their buddies and social acquaintances and to accept them in the house as visitors no matter how they might feel about them. On the other hand they had the right to monitor their wives or girlfriends' social acquaintances. However, they said they put up with their wives close relatives when they had to.

As alluded to previously, the sex role of these offenders is defined and supported by what they hear in country music. As one DUI Recidivist states:

> My kind of music, country music, deals with drinkin, gettin laid, going out on your wife. And you know bad women and divorce. The good women always forgives the man. But the man don't forgive the women. He leaves her, or beats the hell outa her. Sometimes both. This may not be right, but it works. Course no man should tell on a woman. Who wants to hear it.

They voiced ambivalent attitudes toward divorces and reported their religion did not permit it. To them divorce was both a sin and a mark of failure. One Mixed Multiple Offender explains:

> It ain't right to get a divorce. My Pa and Ma told me that. Most divorces happen because the men can't control the ol' lady . If you don't handle them right from the jump they become wild mares. But if things get too bad, and you start fighting and hurting one another. And if she runs out on you. If she don't take care of the children. Then she's got to go. But still it's a shame.

The comments of these men show that they continually argued and fought (verbally and sometimes physically) with their girlfriends and wives over their insistence on complete sexual control in all aspects of life; that is, from the way they dressed, acted, used make-up, talked, and related to others. Most disagreements centered on the way girlfriends and wives conducted themselves in the presence of other males. Though a few admitted slapping a girlfriend or wife around "lightly," "when she needed it," none reported beating up any female. However, approximately 40 percent of the Mixed Multiple Offenders and 25 percent of the DUI and Traffic Offenders had been arrested for woman battery. They claimed that they treated women in the same way as other men in their community treated them.

(4) World View

(a) *Machismo:* From these men's responses it is clear that one consistent commonalty coursed through their lives; that is, the concept of "manhood" (machismo). To them manhood was based on the legitimacy of violence, domination, and independence. They also insisted on the privilege of getting completely drunk at certain time intervals and conceived of heavy drinking as a masculine trait tied in with virility, toughness, courage, and violence in settling disputes. Virility included the ability to hold one's liquor (or beer) like a man (so-called controlled drinking). The use of hand guns, fists, or knives was part of this mix. Perhaps their relative economic, social, and political powerlessness along with a southern working-class background explains this proclivity for hard drinking and fighting. If successful, physical force yields temporary power. On this point see Toplin (1975). Their machismo complex appears to be an extension and reflection of regional working-class chauvinism. In any event the interview accounts reveal they did not understand symbolic power, did not possess negotiating skills in lieu of violence, were impulsive and quick tempered, and were not motivated to seek nonviolent solutions to problems. Unlike the First-time Offenders, they said their buddies as well as female companions accepted violence as a male characteristic. One Mixed Multiple Offender speaks to this point:

> If somebody messes with me, I enjoy punching him out. I don't take no shit, and I don't want to shake hands and say I'm sorry. I like to hit him in the face where I can leave my mark. Hey, if I get hit it's O.K., I don't mind taking my licks. They juice me up. I don't talk my way out of a fight. The women love fights. When we go outside the honky-tonk to fight they follow us and squeal and cry about Johnny's gonna hurt somebody or get beat up bad. Or get killed. They pretend they want to stop us. Shit man, they love it. Specially, if we're fighting over them. You know the way they figure it, if a man won't fight he cant f--- good. Fighting, drinking, and getting laid makes a good weekend. If your head ain't bad on Monday morning you didn't have no fun over the weekend.

This macho pose appeared to be somewhat exaggerated but in their minds a necessary trapping for masculinity. Though they were involved in many tiffs, scuffles, and fights, few of these altercations resulted in serious injury and arrests.

Their concept of masculinity was also manifested in the way they avoided such "feminine" words as "sweet," "nice," "pretty," "love," "feelings," "hurt" and "I am sorry." Such terminology to them is effeminate. All insisted they did not like to sit close to another man at any time. They spoke of being sick or being hurt as weaknesses, and said they didn't go to doctors unless they were "really sick" (barely able to get out of bed.) Once in a doctor's office or a hospital, the primary aim was to get out as soon as possible. Health problems such as arthritis and back pains were usually channeled to chiropractors rather than to licensed physicians. Though they rarely engaged in recreational physical activities other than hunting, fishing, and fighting, they said they were in good shape. This despite the fact that they didn't give off the impression of being as fit as they claimed; most had beer bellies and were a little on the flabby side for their chronological age.

They avoided asking others for help when possible and did not like to stop and seek directions when driving, even when lost. When unable to decipher a road map, read a blueprint, or understand a driver's manual, they refrained from asking knowledgeable people for assistance. They went to "loan sharks" when in a financial bind rather than to family members or welfare agencies. To them, asking for help signified weakness. When facing emotional problems, they refused to go to doctors, psychologists, or social workers, but instead insisted on riding them out with drinking buddies. Such expressions as "I'm not crazy. I never been crazy. So why go to a shrink," were common. Dieting was something females do. Real men do not restrict their consumption of food or alcohol. In fact, abstaining from alcohol was considered feminine. As one Mixed Multiple Offender comments:

> Man, I don't diet. I eats and drinks what I want to. Only women and big shots diet. You know you are going to die of something sooner or later. So why get all het up about it. Enjoy yourself. It's later than you think.

Self-care was also feminine, and they were not too concerned about their physical appearance. They spent little time and money on toilet articles, dentists, and clothing. One DUI and Traffic Offender explains:

> I don't worry about how I look. So long as I don't look like an old man. Only women and big shots got to worry about how they look and clothes. People can take

me or leave me. Spending time and money in head
shops and cologne and clothes is crazy. What you sees
is what you get. If you keep clean you smell O.K.

Finally, they attempted to avoid any kind of dependency,
particularly welfare. As one reports: "welfare is for the lame, the
blind, the weak, and the free loaders. I'm a man."

(b) Marginality, Risk-taking, and Fatalism: The remarks of these
men clearly demonstrate that they comprise a socially,
economically, and politically weak working-class group
articulated to a semi-traditional society. They love the outdoors
for both work and recreational activities and hold a whimsical
life ambition to live on their own farm and work it. Though
placing great emphasis on working for an honest living, work is
not central to their life scheme as it is for many middle-class
Americans. Work is primarily a necessary means to survival, a
means of avoiding the shackles of welfare and the federal
government and a necessity to support "good times." In fact they
play down middle-class values encompassing such things as
getting an education, planning a career, avoiding violence,
saving money, correct speech and dressing properly, "nice" home
ownership, social status, and respectability.

Present oriented, these men live in the here and now and are
too busy "just making it" for any prolonged serious concern
about the future. Meat and bread must be put on the table today,
and all sorts of bills have to be paid at the end of the month.
What is going to happen a year or more from now is distant,
problematic, and unworthy of their serious consideration. They
live in a concrete world of work, home, and leisure where
thought, emotion, and action center on physical, mundane
activities. The objects and utensils surrounding them are of the
practical work-a-day variety. They interact in this milieu with
their own kind and think and talk about things in a restricted
social world: going to work, wages, and bosses; time off,
hunting, fishing, boating; strength, endurance, alcohol, beer
joints, and "making it"; war, sex, fighting, sports talk; kinfolk,
wives and children; good eating, and outside and inside
enemies.

They live in a provincial world and present an anti-intellectual and anti-aesthetic persona. They fear and dislike modernity and those things they know little about, which they perceive as foreign objects beyond their reach; for example, any kind of theory or symbolism, sophisticated art, classical music, haute couture, ballet, the legitimate stage, and literature. They do not like jazz or rhythm and blues because "it's black music." Nothing is accepted from popular culture unless, like country music, it fits into their life-style. Education, art, and book learning are for other kinds of people unless they help them make quick money in some way. To hear them tell it, they are always too busy "making it" for all that education stuff. As one DUI Recidivist notes:

> Now what in the hell is all that Shakespeare shit and crazy music doing for anybody. I sure can't use none of it. I guess it is for high-class women and big shots.

Their fundamentalist religion is a given without having to think or talk about it in any analytical way. Certainly their faith fits in with and reflects a fatalistic, individualistic, and physically oriented working-class life-style. Along with drinking, blind faith gives them solace, a purpose for living, and ties them in with their immediate and extended family, and with friends and peers. Essentially they are preoccupied with their mundane world: work, leisure time to spend as they choose in drinking, socializing, and just "takin' it easy." They live in a small close-knit world increasingly besieged by inside and outside enemies. In brief, they are hard-drinking, hell-raising, violent, risk-taking fatalists. Remarks by one DUI and Traffic Offender are illustrative.

> Man, I work hard. When I get off I want some excitement. Let the good times roll. I go to the honky-tonk and live it up. I drink when I want to and how much I want to. If I get in a fight who cares. If I get drunk so what. That's life. If I meet a woman and get something, fine. I don't care who she belongs to if she wants to go with me. Course I don't pick on my buddies'

women, less they come on strong. If I get picked up by the police—-too bad. I don't want a DUI, but you have to take your chances. I don't want to crash either. Who does? If you want to have a good time and live like a free man, you have to cut loose and raise some hell. I have to let it all hang out now and then. God takes care of drunks, fools, and little children. But those damned cops are always out there looking for me. If I break no law they should leave me alone. Most people drink and drive. I got to admit though, I get a kick out of driving fast. It's a power trip. I like those fast chases on T.V. And if you've few drinks it's a bigger thrill.

They did not conceive of themselves as living a deviant lifestyle or as being deviant in any way. Life was hard and they enjoyed what there was of it to grab. When probed in the area of heavy drinking and drunk driving, fighting, and being arrested, they glossed over such behaviors as a "natural" part of their lives that they had to live with. As one explains:

Life is just that way. I play the hand I was dealt. You know, being what I am. And you know coming from where I'm coming from. I couldn't be no different.

Summary
The substance of the foregoing study dimensions on ethnographic analysis renders support for the suppositions and findings at the first two study levels of analysis. That is, DUI Recidivists, DUI and Other Traffic Offenders, and Mixed Multiple Offenders (in particular) have engaged in various deviant and/or criminal activities from early adolescence. The offenses of the DUI Recidivists are alcohol related, those of the DUI and Traffic Offender are liquor and traffic related and petty in nature, and those of the Mixed Multiple Offender include a variety of serious but episodic offenses pitched at a low modus operandi level. None appeared to be or claimed to be professional criminals. Their arrest histories and dispositions indicated a category of petty habitual criminals. More than

three-fourths of these men were problem drinkers, however, the overwhelming majority denied driving or alcohol-related problems. Such denial indicates faulty thinking, poor judgment, risk-taking, and shortsightedness.

They defined themselves as white working-class southerners in contrast to southern trash who did not work for a living and to big shots. Their self-identity and sense of direction was developed through self-reflection and participation in social relations, that is, self-directed joint actions in the form of social encounters, transactions, interactional routines, and team performances. From an early age they were enmeshed in a subculture of violence. Their self-identity and role-taking behaviors evolved through membership in peer groups within a particular region and social class in a world of work, associations, organizations, and institutions, and regional social space. Their associations with violent peers and participation in deviancy and law-breaking were related reciprocally; that is, their associations with deviant peers lead to increasing deviancy through the reinforcing environment offered by their peer groups. Engaging in deviancy, in turn, leads to increases in associations with deviant peers.

Their behavior was found to be both instrumental (designed to accomplish goals) and expressive (had symbolic value). One must look behind the acts themselves to find the "reality" of these social actors. That is, what did these acts mean to them? Their life history and lifestyle demonstrated impulsivity, hedonism, thrill-seeking, risk-taking habits, proclivity to violence, and a pattern of deviant behavior from an early age. In brief they possessed low self-control and possible negative emotionality (for a definition of negative emotionality, see Caspi et al., 1994). They grew up and lived as adults in permissive, exciting, and problematic environments. Products of economically marginal homes, they had received limited parental affection, guidance, or discipline. By early adolescence they had developed anti-authoritarian attitudes (particularly toward older males in power-wielding positions) and rebellious non-conforming behavioral patterns indicating a generality of deviance. They were keenly aware of their inferior working-class status and felt that their social betters disapproved of their life-style, monitored their activities, kept them down, and controlled their lives.

First-time DUI Offenders

Of the 22 men in the subsample, 20 are profiled below. The remaining two (blue-collar workers) had similar profiles to men in the three other offender groups discussed above.

(1) *Self-Concept and Identities*

They characterized themselves as "white-collar" or "middle-class" southerners and sought social status and companionship among middle-class family, friendship, and associational groups (churches, civic clubs, and occupational organizations). Relatively articulate and self-assured, they were less macho and expressed more conventional self-concepts than did the men in the three other arrest-history categories. They took pride in home ownership, white-collar jobs, education, and respectability and exemplified a sense of place, family, and continuity. They distinguished themselves from the rich, a few of whom they claimed to know and to socialize with, and working-class southerners, some times referred to as rednecks. To them, the rich were elites and role models with whom they sought social intercourse. They divided the working class, those beneath them, into two groups: (1) freeloaders, trash, or "welfare cases," all disrespectable, and (2) poor but decent working-class people, although still beneath them. One recounts:

> I went to college and I'm a professional. Therefore, I don't have any business being in this DUI mess like most of these working-class men I went to DUI school with. It isn't that I feel superior to them, but we just don't have anything in common. We didn't go to school together, live in the same neighborhood, or work together. We don't socialize or go to the same church. We are just two different classes of people.

Blacks, to them, are people of a different race to be avoided. Though their remarks reflect racial and class prejudice, they were less anti-black than the men in the other three arrest-history categories. Regarding race and class questions, they invoked a rhetoric of ethnic pluralism as a means to enjoy "democratically" what they had always had in the south: differential life-styles within a segregated society; white neighborhoods, churches, and social clubs; and white occupational and professional organizations, and so on. They avoided city parks and swimming pools or the use of public transportation and other public facilities where working-class whites and blacks were likely to be. One explains:

> We never use public facilities much anyway. We have our own clubs. My children go to a private religious school. Not too expensive either. To tell you the truth I don't want to associate with many kinds of whites and no blacks. Unless of course I have to deal with them at work. And my DUI school experience convinces me even more that I am right about both of them. I associate with people of my own class and race and avoid social contacts with rednecks and blacks who don't like my kind of people.

They surmised that working-class southerners and blacks looked upon them as respectable citizens. However, they were not concerned with how these different groups perceived them one way or the other. As one comments:

> I really don't know how those working-class men feel about me and my kind. I guess they think we are respectable people who treat them right at work. But then it makes little difference to me what they think. If they don't like me, they don't have to work for me or for people like me. But who are they going to work for? As for blacks I never think about them one way or the other. I treat them right, and they treat me with respect. Of course I can talk only about those I come in contact with, which is damn few.

They tolerate white outsiders (outside the south) of the same social class as themselves who do not by expressed thought or action disrupt the southern way of life. However, they frown upon outside working-class whites, because of class differences in and of themselves and because of their assumed pro-union and pro-black views. One explains:

> I don't see much difference between myself and white people like me from outside the south if they come down here and act right. You know, stay away from the pro-union and pro-black positions, okay. If not they can get the hell out, or stay away from me. I really don't care how they feel about me one way or the other. They are really outsiders and will stay that way as far as I know.

(2) Life History and Personal Relationship Problems

They reported a white-collar, lower-middle or middle-middle class family background and said they grew up in intact families where they claimed to have enjoyed economic and emotional security. For the most part they reported strong ties of affection with parents, siblings, and other close kin, for example, grandparents, uncles, aunts and cousins. They noted few if any serious childhood or adolescent problems, school problems, community problems, or legal problems. Personal relationship problems were infrequent. Though mildly patriarchal in point of view, they expressed less problematic and more egalitarian relationships with women than offenders in the other three arrest history categories. Most (17) said their mothers exerted more influence on them than their fathers. One of these speaks:

> I got along fine with both parents. But I was with my mother for longer periods of time. My father was a workaholic. He was too busy with other people and their children. This macho thing makes no sense. Real men don't have to prove their masculinity. They treat women as equals in most ways. Of course the man has to be the

head of the family, but he has no right to dump on his girlfriend or his wife. The say-so between men and women should not vary too much in degree. Frankly I never had personal relationship problems with women, girlfriends, or wives. Treat them right and they will love you to death. If you are a real man you don't have to prove it.

(3) Life-Style

(a) Language Form and Content

1. Physical Appearance and Front: These men were similar in gross body type to men in the other three arrest history categories, though slimmer and firmer in muscular tone. Clean shaven, they wore their well-trimmed hair at medium length. Skin color was ruddy but smooth and not weatherbeaten, and physical features and body conformation appeared solid, regular, and symmetrical. They looked well kept and of their chronological age. They were dressed in short-sleeved, cotton sports shirts, blue jeans and slacks, and moccasin-type dress shoes. Most wore light blue jeans jackets or windbreakers. Belts were of medium width without large buckles. Clothing ensembles were of natural fabrics (cotton, wool, and silk), and colors were fashionably matched.

They presented a quiet self-contained mien and sat in a semi-erect, relaxed fashion with their legs close together and arms and hands folded slightly inward and resting lightly in their laps or on desk or table tops. They positioned their bodies in a facing stance to the interviewer, and made direct eye contact without staring. Facial expressions were controlled, and they made no exaggerated gestures or body movements of any type. Obviously they had learnt how to qualify, moderate, stimulate, and neutralize facial and body as well as verbal expressions. Hands were kept away from the mouth and out of the pockets. Obviously they had been taught "good manners."

2. Language Form and Content: Verbal reports and accounts centered on work careers, family and sociability (including drinking behavior), and respectability. Vocabulary

was mixed with both concrete and abstract content and suffused with regional metaphors and allegories. (Southerners of all classes tend to be good story tellers and speak rhetorically and allegorically.) Voice quality was low, softly pitched, drawly, and characterized by relaxed articulation, smooth rhythm control, full and rich resonance, and moderate tempo. Their whole demeanor expressed self-assurance, body balance, and a relaxed tentativeness. Speech and gestures were synchronized and complementary. They did not indulge in loud talking or laughing and spoke out in a clear, correct (for the most part), precise manner. In brief, they were middle class all the way.

(b) World of Work

Seven of these men were small business owners, five were store or plant managers, four were sales representatives for private companies, three were accountants, and one was a paralegal. They exerted their work energies in a white-collar world of business and professional activities as owners, bosses, and managers, and they shared the class rewards and perquisites of a semitraditional society. As one business owner comments:

> I come from a good family, went to college, and after joined my father's business. I worked hard and led a respectable life. Sure I got a good house and live in a nice neighborhood, and I don't associate with riff-raff. I deserve what I got, and I don't want to give it away or share it with a bunch of lazy people and blacks. I use my head, not my hands, to make a living. Of course this DUI arrest has cost me time and money. I didn't hurt anybody, just drove with a few drinks, and ran a red light. Those cops should go out after the real criminals and leave people like me alone. But I have to admit, I was high when I got arrested.

(c) Organizations, Associations, and Recreation

These men lived in a highly protected, relatively affluent, and segregated social world removed from the everyday lives of working-class whites and blacks. They belonged to and participated in many formal and informal organizations.

Church: Recreation activities centered on the church, the country club, the golf course, the hunting lodge, fraternal organizations, and the home. Six were mainstream Baptists, seven were Methodists, five Presbyterians and two Episcopalians. To them, religious form appeared to be more meaningful than religious content and the Bible was viewed as literature. (See Robin Fox Lane, "The Bible as Story, Chapter 20," *The Unauthorized Version: Truth and Fiction in the Bible*, pp. 355-374, New York, NY: Alfred A. Knopf, 1992.) As one Methodist comments:

> I go to church as a habit. It's expected of me and people like me. You learn good principles, but I don't go for all that hell fire and damnation and life after death jazz. Some people see others as saints or sinners. I 'm neither one. I drink when I feel like it. There is nothing wrong with drinking and having a good time. A man has to relax. I need relaxation because I work too hard. To most of my friends, going to church is a habit and no big thing. Going to church helps most people, but I'm not a fanatic. I avoid religious topics. Live and let live. Actually I don't give a damn one way or the other about peoples' religious beliefs.

All belonged to two or more of the following organizations: country club, hunting lodge, civic organization, fraternal or veterans' organization. Sixteen played golf and 18 spent leisure time hunting and fishing. All said entertaining friends at home was very important to them and their way of life. They reported social drinking (and at times heavy social drinking, more than four drinks at one sitting) as a part of their recreational activities, but all claimed in different ways that alcohol, to them, was a social lubricant. However, their remarks suggest that they occasionally drank to get high. In brief all were heavy social drinkers. Typical remarks about drinking and driving by one of these offenders follow:

I have a drink or two nearly every day but consider myself a social drinker. I have a few drinks at the country club every weekend with my friends, and a few drinks with my friends after playing 18 holes of golf. And I might have a few drinks on a fishing or hunting trip but usually beer. The hard stuff and hunting and fishing don't go together. When you are in the woods or in a boat you don't have any business drinking the hard stuff. Of course I have a wet bar at home where I entertain my friends. And then we serve wine at dinner sometimes--especially if we have company. I serve more liquor to my friends than I drink myself. In all I drink about a pint of booze a week, plus one or two beers. If we have a party at home, I'll drink more. I don't mind driving when I have had only one or two drinks, but I try to avoid driving when I have had more than that. I might drive after drinking more than three drinks now and then, but I don't like to do it. Usually I let my wife drive when I have more than three. It's those crazy drunken rednecks society has to worry about. They drink too much and don't know how to drive.

Another offender's drinking comments follow:

I do most of my drinking at home or at the country club. Or you know at parties at friends homes. I belong to a circle of friends who drink when hunting, fishing and visiting one another. We usually visit each other along with our wives. I don't drink with just anybody-- just my equals. Drinking to me is a sociable thing. I never drink alone. If I go to a party or go out to dance, I always have a few drinks. Drinking goes along with my social activities. I always offer my friends a drink when they come to my house or office. When some of us get together to play poker I have a beer or two. I also drink beer when hunting and fishing. I occasionally drive when I have had a few drinks. You know two to three, and sometimes four, but not more. I get high on special occasions, like my birthday, somebody else's birthday, or a party. Occasionally I will have a drink or two at home before dinner. This usually happens when I have had a hard day at the office. I always control my drinking and never get stumbling-down drunk. People who do this show no respect for others. No man should be drunk in front of his family. I may get tipsy now and then. But I don't get drunk. Of course if you drink, sooner or later you will get high in spite of yourself. You know, slip up. That has happened to me but not often. Then I don't guzzle the stuff. I'm a sipper. And even if I go to a party late, I don't try to catch up. I mean I don't drink three or four drinks in a hurry to catch up. I try to pace myself. I'm very careful about when, where and with whom I drink--usually after five, at home and with friends. Now if other people with me want to drink more, that's their business, but I don't hang out with drunks and rednecks who go out of control.

(d) Sex and Family Life

Sixteen of these men were married, three were divorced, and one was single. Eleven graduated from college and ten had some college education. Their courtship and marital patterns followed those usually found in the middle class. Generally they dated several different girls in high school and college, dated one girl toward the end of their college career, and married within a year following college life. In their late teens before they had sexual intercourse with a girl, none reported promiscuity at any life stage. They preferred and wound up with girlfriends and wives with similar backgrounds to themselves. They envisioned the masculine role in the family as first husband followed by provider, then father and then head of the household. As one recounts:

I don't think my courtship and marriage was very different from the people I grew up with. I dated several girls in college and high school but settled down to the one I married when I graduated from college. I always used condoms because I didn't want to get any girl in trouble, and I was selective about going to bed. I treated girls like I expected men to treat my sister. I never wanted to hurt anybody. You know I never promised them marriage just to make out. We had sex together like friends. I didn't pick up women in bars. That's risky and who wants to go to bed with a loser and catch something. Like my crowd, I started drinking some when I was a late teenager. But we never got drunk often. I always tried to control my drinking.

These men reported a typical middle class, suburban life-style, and claimed near-egalitarian relationships with women. As one relates:

Well, I live an ordinary way of life. I finished high school, went to college, and then went to work and got married. My wife and her family are pretty much like my mother and father. We live in the suburbs with a two-car garage, and I have a mortgage like everybody else. We do okay but I wish I had more. This DUI arrest has cost me. I don't like the stigma that goes along with it. I thought I was a careful driver and I don't usually drink and drive--that is, drive when I have more than two or three drinks. I just got unlucky this time. But I don't blame the police. I was too high to drive. I left a party and I was on my way home. If my wife had been with me, she would have been driving. But I have to face the music and be more careful in the future. I guess I had six drinks within two hours when they picked me up.

(4) World View

They viewed the world from a southern middle-class perspective, and their lives were enmeshed in pursuit of white-collar careers, family respectability, religious and political correctness, and sociability among peers. Political moderates, they accepted the economic and political system as is and were satisfied with their position in the system and their life-style. They lived in a much more abstract realm than did working-class southerners. Proud of their status they said they deserved to be where they were. Though church goers, they were concerned primarily with this world and material possessions. Life revolved around work, family, and friends. Though relatively well educated, they expressed little analytical criticism of the status quo. As one states:

> Those pundits and some politicians are always talking about social change. I see no reason for great social change. Water seeks its level and birds of a feather flock together. Anyway, the more things seem to change, the more they remain the same. I like my world. I got a job, a family, and good friends. I'm not looking for anything else. Of course I don't like all that government spending on bums and welfare cases. Why should I have to pay for someone else's fun? Those welfare women should get off their backs and go to work. I support my children.

(The preceding quote shows not only conservatism but some similar views to those of the working class.)

Summary

First-time DUI Offenders defined themselves as white middle-class southerners. Most (91 percent) grew up in middle-class families where affection, supervision, and discipline were present. None of these were adjudicated juvenile delinquents, and all appeared to have made adequate adjustments as adolescents and as adults. With an exception of 9 percent who resembled the members of the other three subgroups, the First-time DUI Offenders possess self-control and appear to have well-integrated personalities.

DRINKING AND DRIVING PATTERNS AND ATTITUDES AND REACTIONS TO CRIMINAL JUSTICE PROCESSING AND THE DUI LABEL

Drinking and Driving Patterns and Attitudes

All 311 white males were asked during the interviews to respond to specific questions directed to their drinking and driving patterns and attitudes within the context of Georgia DUI laws.

1. First-time DUI Offenders: The reported median length of drinking sessions for these offenders was two hours and, for most, beer was their drink of choice. They consumed alcoholic beverages at the rate of two beers or one mixed drink per hour. Five reported having had one drink, six reported two drinks, seven reported having had three drinks, and four reported having had four drinks within an hour preceding the instant arrest for DUI. Eleven reported driving one or two times within an hour after having two drinks or less during the past month; five did so three times after consuming three drinks or less; one did so four or more times after having five or more drinks, and the remaining five reported none. Nineteen of these offenders agreed with and respected the current Georgia DUI laws at the time of the instant offense. Three reported that legal BAC limits for arrest were too low. As one of these three reports:

> I only had three beers when I got arrested. I know we have to have DUI laws and people should respect them. Without those laws, the roads would be much more dangerous. Just because they don't stop every drunk driver, doesn't mean they don't stop many of them. But I don't think I was high enough to get arrested. You know even the beer commercials that advise you to know when to say when allow you to drink three or four beers or drinks and still drive. I'm a social drinker. The cops should go after those reckless drunk drivers and leave people like me alone.

None considered themselves to be binge drinkers. Sixteen said they thought they were sober enough to drive without mishap, and the remaining six said there was no one else to drive them home. As one explains:

> My friend was supposed to drive me home after the party. But he was higher than I was. So I had to drive. But I thought I was sober enough to drive safely. The cops say I was speeding. I wonder if they don't want people to drive fast, why do they make fast cars?

Only one reported drinking while driving--sipping beer preceding the instant arrest and he admitted that this was legally and morally wrong. Ten said they stopped by a bar to drink with friends enroute home after work. As one of these reports:

> I meet my friends at the bar two or three times a week to have one or two drinks before going home. But I don't overdo it. This time I did but I thought I was more sober than I actually was. The thing is people in my crowd drink. How can one drink and not drive? You got to go places and then go home.

Nine stated they were heading home following a party. Three said they were enroute to a ball game. Only four reported they thought they were probably too intoxicated to drive before the instant arrest but still thought they could drive safely enough to avoid an accident and arrest. All considered themselves to be competent drivers after drinking. As one explains:

> I and many of my friends have a drink or two before driving but we are good drivers. We keep things under control, and drive very carefully after a few drinks. That's the way it goes with people in my crowd. They are not the problem.

Four said they had never driven after drinking in the past six months, ten drove rarely in this time period, and the remaining eight did so occasionally. Twenty recognized the risk (to themselves and to others) they took when driving after drinking. Only two said they were unaware of such risks. Twenty did not report any extraordinary pressures or problems prior to the instant arrest. One said he was having difficulty with his wife at the time, and the other reported pressure from his employer. Neither thought these problems caused their drinking or instant arrest. All said they were likely to drive after drinking following a social engagement or a party. Sixteen, however, said they thought that driving after drinking more than three drinks was morally wrong. As one of these states:

> One should never drive after drinking more than two or three drinks because it's morally wrong. Driving after drinking increases the chances of hurting someone else. I do it now and then, but it's wrong. You really should not drink very much if you know you have to drive soon after.

Four said the morality of driving after drinking depended on circumstances. As one of these points out:

> If you can help it you should not drive after drinking more than three drinks. But sometimes when there is no one else to drive, you have to do it. But never drive when intoxicated.

The remaining two said it was morally justifiable to drive after drinking, if one were not intoxicated. One of these says:

> It's O.K. to drive after drinking if you have had only a couple of drinks. I mean if you are not high. But you are still taking a chance. They stopped me for speeding. Some people blame the cops, but they have to do their job. We have to have DUI laws, and I respect them. I'll respect them more from now on. But you know even the beer ads tell you it's okay to drink and drive if you are

not high. The whole damn culture says it's okay to drink. And everybody drinks and drives sometimes. We have drinking laws and speeding laws but both are legal. But it's okay to drink and the car companies sell fast and powerful cars. They know people are going to drink and drive.

In summary these offenders do not frequently drive when intoxicated and generally respect DUI laws. They do not intentionally drive when they are aware of being intoxicated; and they do not intentionally get intoxicated before driving. Furthermore, when driving after drinking, they try to drive safely and obey the traffic laws. Nonetheless these DUIs illustrate the point that any drinking within an hour prior to driving is dangerous, risk-taking behavior--though they would not agree. They understand the ambivalence involved in the permissive attitudes toward drinking and driving and the DUI laws. Further, they perceive the cultural contradictions inherent in the advertisement of fast cars and booze and the ready availability and approval of both. Finally, they define themselves as social drinkers and differentiate themselves from run-of-the-mill drunk drivers (the others) whom they think should be under control.

2. DUI Recidivists: The median length of drinking session for this group was five hours, and the drink of choice was beer during the week and hard liquor on weekends. They consumed alcoholic beverages in the amount of five beers or five mixed drinks within an hour prior to the instant arrest. Fourteen reported driving three times within an hour after having three drinks or more during the past month; nine did so four times after consuming five drinks or less, and the remaining five did so five or more times after having five or more drinks. Five considered themselves to be binge drinkers occasionally. Eighteen said they drove after drinking because they drank every day. All reported the need for DUI laws but thought they were too rigid (legal BAC levels were too low) and claimed that special consideration should be extended to drinkers who did not cause serious accidents. Most (20) stated they drove very

carefully after drinking and thought this should be considered
when the police stop them. As one explains:

> Just because I drink regularly, don't mean I cause
> accidents on the road. I drive carefully when I drink.
> The public and police blame alcohol for every problem.
> Traffic accidents is one of them. That's why the DUI
> schools don't work. They tell you to stay away from
> alcohol. They don't know most accidents are caused by
> people who don't know how to drive--drunk or sober.
> We're just the scapegoats. Millions of people drive when
> they drink too much. And they drive fast too. Cars are
> made to run fast. The car companies advertise speed.
> No wonder we have so many accidents.

Most (23) said they tried to avoid driving when they were
too intoxicated. As one notes:

> I drink some every day. So you see, driving there
> and getting home gets me the DUI. I don't drive long
> ways, because I don't want more trouble with cops.
> Whenever I can, I get a buddy to drive me to the bar if I
> been drinkin. Then I get another one to drive me home.
> If I am too high, I just stay home. But if high at the bar, I
> have to drive home. The cops know I'm a drinker but
> that I don't make no trouble. I don't cause no crashes.
> Cut me some slack. Leave me alone. Go after those
> drivin recklessly. Leave me alone less I break some
> traffic law. Maybe give me a some kind of special
> license.

Eight said they had to drive home after drinking. One of
these explains:

> I go to a bar four or five times a week. I have to
> drive myself home sometimes if I can't find somebody to
> take me. I drink when I go fishing and hunting. You
> know, sip a few beers on the road. But I don't get in no
> wrecks. The cops know this. But they lock up who they

want to. Man, if they locked up everybody who knows they're too high to drive there wouldn't be enough jails to hold them.

The remaining two said they drink and drive like everybody else. Sixteen reported drinking while driving preceding the instant arrest. As one of these said:

> You know I sip a beer on the way home. You know a roadie. But I don't hurt nobody. I drive real slow and careful too.

Fifteen said they were heading home from a bar or honky-tonk at the time of the instant arrest; seven were heading from one bar to another, and the remaining six were enroute to a nearby place to purchase more booze. As one reports:

> When you give outa booze, you got to go and get some more. So you have to drive. I try to get somebody to drive me. If not, I do what I have to do. Many people drive when they know they drank too much. Some have to.

Twenty-two said they did not know they were intoxicated before the instant arrest; the remaining six said they knew they were intoxicated but still thought they could drive safely. All considered themselves to be competent drivers after drinking. As one claims:

> I drink and drive only if I have to. I don't want those cops after me. It's not drinking but bad driving that causes accidents. I'm a good driver. I don't want to hurt nobody. And I don't.

Twenty-four reported they drove occasionally after drinking in the past six months; the remaining four said they drove rarely after drinking. Twenty-five recognized the risk to themselves and to others they took when driving after drinking. One of these explains:

> I know I risk myself and other people when I drink
> and drive. That's why I don't drive when I can help it.
> But I drink some every day.

Twenty-three reported facing no extraordinary pressures or problems prior to the instant arrest. Three reported domestic pressures and two reported job-related pressures, but only one of these five reported such pressures caused the instant arrest. Twenty-two said they were likely to drive after drinking when they had to. Six said they were likely to drive after drinking when they did not think they were too intoxicated to drive. Twenty-three admitted it was wrong to drive after drinking but they could not help it. As one states:

> Man, I know I shouldn't drive after I been drinkin
> heavy. But I can't help it. I'm an alcoholic.   The cops
> should consider my condition.

The remaining five expressed no feeling of moral or legal wrong doing by driving after drinking. As one of these reports:

> Who gives a damn about the morality or the legality.
> I just don't want to risk getting a DUI, if I can help it.
> But I do drink and drive when I've got to.

These problem drinkers appear to be alcoholics, drink every day, and are likely to be dangerous and high-risk drivers whenever driving. Though, they do not intentionally drive when intoxicated, or intentionally get intoxicated before driving, or drive recklessly after drinking, they are potentially at risk to themselves and others whenever behind the wheel. They exemplify some respect for DUI laws but think they are too strict and that they should receive special consideration because of their drinking problem. They note the prevalence of drinking and driving and the advertisement of fast cars and booze as cultural incongruities.

3. DUI and Traffic Offenders: The average duration of these offenders' drinking session was 3.5 hours. Beer was the drink of choice during weekdays and hard liquor during weekends. They

consumed alcohol at a general rate of three beers or three mixed drinks per hour. Sixty-three reported having had two or three drinks within an hour preceding the instant arrest, 67 had three drinks, 42 had four or more drinks. Seventy-three reported driving four times or less within an hour after having three or less drinks during the past month; 88 did so five times or less after consuming four drinks or less; and the remaining 11 did so six or more times after having four or more drinks. Fourteen considered themselves to be occasional binge drinkers. Ninety-two said they drove after drinking because it was the "normal thing to do." Fifty-five said they were control drinkers and therefore thought they could take care of the driving situation after drinking. Twenty-five said it was necessary to drive after drinking because they drank frequently. Most of these (151) disagreed with DUI laws whereas the remaining 21 generally agreed with them. One of the majority maintains:

> Drinkin and drivin are necessary to take care of business. Most Americans do it everyday. You can get more done when you socialize at a bar. But, after you drink you got to drive. And you know, it's easier to pick up a woman too, if you drink with her. The cops should not pick up anybody who ain't broken no traffic law. If he's drunk when arrested then charge him. But not before. Anyway all my friends drink and drive.

Thirty reported drinking beer while driving preceding the instant arrest. Eighty-five said they were heading home from a bar or honky-tonk at the time of the instant arrest; 35 were heading from one bar or honky-tonk to another, or to a friend's home; 36 were going to or from a fishing or hunting trip; 11 were going to a party or ball game; and, the remaining five were enroute to purchase more booze. Eighty said they knew they were probably too intoxicated to drive before the instant arrest, of whom 77 thought they could still drive safely. One hundred and twenty respondents considered themselves to be competent drivers after drinking, and did not think that any driver should be arrested for DUI unless he or she had committed another violation. None of these thought the DUI laws were enforced objectively. As one of these argues:

> I know I'm a competent driver after I been drinkin, but I have jes been unlucky gettin into accidents. I'm a pretty good driver. I have been drivin for 10 years. Of course I like to drive fast, but those slow drivers cause more accidents than I do. Why have laws about speeding when cars are built for speed? Those cops out there don't understan this. All they want to do is bust people for DUI or speeding. That's how they make their living. There should be no law against drivin and drinkin. Drinkin is legal. So is driving. Drinking makes you intoxicated. Tell me how you can know the driver is intoxicated. Cops have no right to arrest you unless you violate a traffic law or cause a crash. They pick out those they want to bust. They don't bust country club people in big cars but poor people like me.

The remaining 52 thought they were adequate drivers after drinking. They too were opposed to any per se DUI laws. As one of these comments:

> If you drive as much as I do, you are bound to have an accident now and then. People have accidents whether they been drinkin or not. The DUI laws are unreal. No one should be stopped unless he violates some other law besides DUI. The cops can get you if they want you. So why worry about it? They keep saying a bunch of people get killed every year in traffic accidents and they blame it on DUIs. So why sell liquor and fast cars? Why make freeways and roads that are built for speed. I haven't killed anybody and I'm still alive. And there are too many laws about drinkin and driving. I got to get something out of life. Let the good times roll. If the good Lord calls you, you got to go. The old people who can't drive should stay off the road. Maybe we should have special slow cars and slow roads for them.

Twenty reported they drove regularly after drinking within the past six months; 71 drove so occasionally; and 83 did so rarely. One hundred and sixty-five said they were aware of the risk to themselves and to others when driving after drinking. As one of the latter explains:

> I know I'm taking a chance when I drive and been drinkin too much. And I know I could get in an accident. And that I may be busted by the police for DUI. But you see, life is one risk after another. You take a chance when you walk out the front door. I don't want to get in no accident. Who does? You just got to take your chances. And drinkin and drivin ain't so bad if you are lucky. Many people drink and drive every day. That's what cars, booze, and good roads are made for. They pick on poor people they know been busted before. Let us have some fun. You know, whoop it up, get high, and feel like somebody. Anyway, that's how I grew up. And that's how I live. And it's fun to drive fast. Everybody knows this. The car commercials tell us about the power of their cars. The booze commercials show you how things go with booze.

Seven stated they were not aware of such risks. One hundred and sixty-seven reported facing no extraordinary pressures or problems prior to the instant arrest. Eighty-six reported they were likely to drive after drinking under normal circumstances; 50 were likely to do so when driving from one bar to another, or enroute home; and 36 when traveling to and from hunting and fishing trips or parties. Few (21) said that driving after drinking was morally wrong. The following remarks illustrate the attitudes of most of these offenders toward drinking and driving and DUI laws:

> If you want to live like a man and have some fun, you got to drinkin and drivin. That's what cars and the roads are made for. No matter how much you worry, you can't stop these hard-surfaced roads and speedy cars. As long as you got all those drivers on booze,

someone's going to crash. There's nothing wrong with drivin after drinkin, if you know how to handle it. When I get behind the wheel, I am goin where I have to go. I don't worry about no traffic, the weather, being high, or seat belts. You know the cops or nothing else. And cops have no business busting people for DUI unless they cause an accident. DUI and speeding laws don't make no sense. Cops can bust anybody they want too. They don't bust many drivin a cadillac. All my friends drink and drive. They don't strap themselves down with those silly seat belts neither. You can't move around with those things on.

Most offenders in this category are high-risk, deviant drivers when and when not intoxicated. Moreover, they disparage the DUI laws and uphold driving after drinking as an acceptable way of life. Some become intoxicated intentionally before driving, drink when driving, drive frequently when they know they are intoxicated, and are aware of the consequential risks they take with their lives and those of others. These drive like they live, defiantly, recklessly, and dangerously. As young, hedonistic drivers they view the "law and order" approach to drinking and driving (and speedy driving) as unfair punishment and inconvenient. On the other hand, they claim our society approves of drinking, advertises booze and makes it readily available, permits drinking and driving, passes ambiguous DUI laws that are difficult to enforce evenly and fairly, and manufactures and advertises powerful, speedy cars for our highways. They also note inadequate public transportation system that "forces" some people to drive--drunk or sober.

4. Mixed Multiple Offenders: The average length of drinking session for this group was one and one-half hours, and beer was the choice of drink for most. As one reports:

I don't hang out in any place too long. I have to keep moving. I can squeeze a beer or two in the car while I'm takin care of business.

All reported having had at least three drinks preceding the instant arrest. Forty-four reported driving three times or less within an hour after having two drinks or less during the past month; 32 did so four times or less after consuming three or less drinks; and, the remaining thirteen did so four or more times after having three or more drinks. Only four considered themselves to be occasional binge drinkers. Eighty-one said they drove after drinking because they "had to" regardless of the law and risk involved; because it was the normal thing to do; or because they did not agree with the DUI laws. As one explains:

> I got to take care of business whether I'm drinkin or not. You can't worry about the law every day because they keep changing. Drivin after drinkin is the American thing to do. I got so many things going, I can't worry about the law. The DUI laws are unfair anyway. Everybody drinks and drives. The cops lock up only those they want to. We don't need no DUI laws. Nobody should be arrested unless they cause an accident. Then if they're drunk give a DUI. The law don't worry about the people who steal millions of dollars with a pencil. The law is made by rich people and enforced by cops to keep people like me down. To hell with the law. I've always been an outlaw anyway.

Eight had no specific answer to the question as to why they drove after drinking and appeared to think this question silly and undeserving of an answer. Eighty-two reported drinking while driving preceding the instant arrest. As one points out:

> No one should waste time sitting around drinkin in a bar. You can do a lot of things while drinkin. Nobody goes huntin and fishin without booze. The bottom line is, I drink when I want to like everybody else--in my car, on the way to work, and on the way home from work. Drinkin don't bother me. I can handle it if the cops would jes leave me alone. Now, if I have a wreck then come after me.

They said they were heading to one of the following places at the time of the instant arrest: bar, home, friend's house, relative's house, work place, night club, hunting or fishing places, pool room, honky-tonk. Only two reported they were too intoxicated to drive prior to the instant arrest. Many admitted driving fast after drinking but claimed the police were after them anyway because they had a record. One recounts:

> I drive fast, 'specially if I've had a few drinks. You know a little reckless. I got speeding tickets before. The cops are after me cause of that. You know it's fun to drive fast and feel the power. The car companies sell cars by showing their speed on T.V. Who wants to buy a slow, four-door car?

Sixty-five reported they drove regularly after drinking in the past six months, 20 did so occasionally, and the remaining four rarely. Most said they were aware of the risk to themselves and others when they drove after drinking. Several paraphrased reasons for such behavior as follows: (1) indifference and insensitivity for their or others' safety; (2) the thrill and excitement of fast driving and drinking; (3) taking chances as a way of life; (4) fatalism; (5) disrespect for DUI laws; and (6) the presence and approval of booze and fast cars in our society. The following comments by four different men in this category are illustrative:

> (1) I don't think I drive too fast. But the police do because I got some tickets before. He knows he can say anything he want because nobody listen to me but they listen to him. I know the risk in drivin and drinkin. But that's life. If you crash, that's the way it is. Who gives a damn? And the DUI laws are for the birds. Nobody pays any attention to them 'til they get busted. Everybody drinks and drives. Why you got booze and cars.

> (2) I live in the fast lane. I ain't no 8:00 to 5:00 man. I got to have a nice sports car that can really run. And foxy chicks. Sure, I like to drink and gamble, and drag

race too. But, who lives forever? I just want to have a good time while I'm here. Yesterday or tomorrow don't mean nothin to me. It's what happens today. You need bread to live good. So when I need it, I go out and get it.

(3) I been a hell-raiser all my life and I got a record too. But that don't change my life. Drivin and drinkin is no big deal. When you go out you got to drive. When you drink you got to drive home. I don't plan it. I just do it when I have to. Stupid DUI laws stop nobody. They are nonsense if you get caught. Most don't. I'm tired of hearing drunk drivers kill people. If I wanted to kill somebody, I'd do it. I don't need to make no accident.

(4) Everybody knows that drivin and drinkin heavy is risky. Sometimes you win, sometimes you lose. No one lives forever. When it's your time, you got to go. So who gives a damn about DUI laws. There should be none. As long as they make cars and booze, people are going to drive and drink. The two go together like a horse and buggy. Some times the police lies about how fast people are drivin. Highways are made to speed on. It don't make no sense to bust people for speeding and DUI, less they cause some kind of accident.

None reported facing any extraordinary pressures or problems prior to the instant arrest. They said they were likely to drive after drinking under any circumstances, and none thought that it was morally wrong to do so.

Obviously, these problem drinkers from time to time intentionally became intoxicated before driving; drive frequently when aware of being intoxicated; drink while they are driving; and intentionally drive recklessly (too fast) without concern for their and others' safety. Though recidivists, they continue to violate the law despite prior convictions and penal sanctions. Moreover, they have no respect for or faith in DUI laws. Criminals on the road, they are dangerous drivers. They too, like members of the other three subgroups, note the cultural contradictions concerned with drinking and driving--and offered them as an excuse for their illegal behaviors.

Reactions to Criminal Justice Processing and the DUI Label

1. First-time DUIs: For the most part, most of these offenders (20) reacted to the instant arrest in a quiet, complying manner and cooperated fully with the arresting officers, jailers, and magistrates. During brief stays in jail (from one to two days) they adjusted to routine with little difficulty. All were released on bail but experienced the hearings and sentencing procedures (which involved license revocation, suspended sentence with an agreement to attend a state endorsed drunk-driving school within 120 days, required for license reinstatement). Eighteen found the DUI school experience worthwhile, interesting, beneficial, and sobering. Two thought it was a waste of time. These eighteen thought they should have received probation without going to jail.

Eighteen said all criminal justice procedures pertaining to them were equitable. Two thought they had been treated unfairly and thought all procedures were worthless and/or inconvenient. The stay in jail was shameful, degrading, and painful to all but perhaps helpful by way of deterrence. A typical statement by one offender follows:

> Man, it was bad enough getting arrested, but when they processed me at the jail. You know the scene. . . they took away my dignity. When that drunk tank cell door clanged shut, I swore I would never be in jail again. And I knew my family and friends would know soon that I was a jail bird. I knew then I had to cut down on my social drinking and stop drinking anything before driving.

The two dissatisfied and bitter offenders protested their arrest to all officials and were verbally abusive toward the arresting officer who charged them with resisting arrest (these charges were dropped later).

Fifteen suggested that a pre-sentence investigation should have been conducted and that some form of extra counseling be added to the drunk driving school curriculum. Five offered no treatment recommendations and thought that license suspension was enough for offenders like themselves.

All disavowed the label DUI which they viewed as a temporary, unfortunate designation and insisted they would not be arrested again for DUI, that they would be more careful about drinking and driving in the future. Twenty of these men experienced considerable shame and guilt about the instant arrest. Most thought the DUI laws and the criminal justice processing of DUIs were necessary but inadequate, but none offered any fundamental overhaul measures. All suggested stiffer DUI penalties for whom they termed "the real drunk drivers."

2. DUI Recidivists: All of these men had been in jail before for public drunkenness and did not find it particularly degrading. Most proclaimed that arrest, court procedures, sentencing, license revocation, and drunk-driving school were a fruitless inconvenience. Most (24) expressed negative feelings toward the arresting officer, though they said they were treated routinely or fairly at arrest. Four were initially charged with resisting arrest, however, these charges were dropped before sentencing. Most (21) were indifferent and/or mildly antagonistic toward jailers, the sentencing magistrate, and the DUI school personnel. Twenty labeled themselves alcoholics, and complained they had not received any "real" treatment for their illness and insisted that DUIs like themselves be treated on an outpatient basis by "real therapists" over a long period of time. They also suggested that they and their counterparts be given provisional drivers' licenses following improvement under treatment at a well-established local treatment center. As one of these reports:

People like me don't belong in jail. We should be classified at some diagnostic center as alcoholic and sent to an outpatient treatment program. I know I should not drink and drive, but I can't help it. And I have to drive. The rest of these DUIs who aren't alcoholic should be locked up for a long time. They are the killers. I'm no criminal, just an addict.

Eleven praised the DUI schools they attended but said they should have received further treatment. Most (22) rejected the DUI label for themselves but thought it applicable to non-alcoholics. They expressed ambivalent attitude toward the current DUI laws and criminal justice proceedings which they considered necessary but inadequate, that is, unfair to poor people and alcoholics. Most appeared to believe in a magical power of "therapy" but were unaware of what kind of "therapy" they needed or wanted.

3. DUI and Traffic Offenders: Most of these men (151) expressed mildly negative attitudes toward all the actors in the criminal justice system from the arresting officer, police in general, magistrates, judges, and jailers---and all DUI procedures implemented by these officials. The DUI schools, to most of them, were a nuisance and an inconvenience in that they did no good or harm. Nineteen were charged with resisting arrest in the instant case. To them, most of the criminal justice players were phonies. Most reported that the DUI laws and the criminal justice processing of DUIs were part of a class system devised for big shots (middle- and upper-class people) to monitor and control working-class people like themselves. Driving after drinking, to them, was a way of life and an affirmation of freedom. Most insisted they were hounded by the police, while millions of other drunk-driving "big shots" and "fat cats" were left alone and quickly dismissed if arrested. The legal processing procedures of DUIs were a charade, a show for ignorant, "demanding for justice chumps" who insisted that something be done about the inevitability of drunk drivers and drunk driving.

According to this majority, the police should not arrest anybody for drunk driving unless they caused a traffic accident. Their reasoning was that everybody drinks and drives, so why single them out. Those DUIs responsible for traffic accidents should be punished, not for deterrence which they didn't believe in but because they deserved to be hurt for what they did, wittingly or unwittingly. The comments of one of these men are illustrative.

I should not have been arrested. Hell, I didn't hurt nobody. The whole thing's a scam, man. Everybody drinks and drives. I know some cops drink and drive too. They don't mess with the big boys. All that drunk driving school bullshit sucks. I know all that shit they teach, and I'm not an alcoholic. As long as you get cars and booze you're gonna have drunk drivers. Drinkin and drivin is an American pastime. What about those who don't drink and drive but still cause accidents and kill people? The cops got to get a quota, because the public is screaming about drunk drivers. Next year they'll scream about something else, but it won't do no good to nobody. Get rid of cars and booze. Get rid of bars and highways. Get rid of cops. Then you'll get rid of DUIs. Now if I hurt somebody drivin, hurt me back, but don't give me that deterrence bull shit. All that court shit, taking my license, and putting me in jail did nothing but inconvenience me---and other people like me. But I don't want to hurt nobody.

A minority of 21 expressed indifference to their arrests, official personnel, and legal procedures; however, they claimed that DUI schools were worthwhile. Though still mildly antisocial, these 22 men expressed vague notions of improving themselves and abiding by the law in the future and appeared to be considering a change in life-style. One of these comments:

I know I've been a hell raiser all my life. But it's got me nothing but trouble. I ain't got much religion but I know I've got to change my life or wind up in prison or dead. And I really don't want to hurt people. The DUI school taught me this time a lot more than before. I've never listened to anybody in my life before. Maybe I need to change. I'm going to seek some counseling from somebody. I don't plan to drink and drive anymore. Fact is I plan to quit drinkin and get my shit together. You know, like a steady job, find a good woman and settle down--and stay off the street.

The majority (151) were familiar with the DUI label that the police and the criminal justice system had tagged them with, but they rejected this designation as meaningless and unfair. As one explains:

> They convicted me of a DUI, but it doesn't make sense. Many people drink and drive, but they don't get arrested. They got to arrest someone to keep the public calm. So they arrest people like me. I know about this game all my life. I don't care what they call me.

A minority of 21 expressed the view that they understood and accepted the DUI label and that it had been fairly applied but that such a tag no longer applied to them, because they had changed. They did not expect to be arrested again on a DUI charge and planned not to drink and drive again.

However, as made clear most of these offenders noted (in their words) what they termed to be incongruities and hypocrisy involved with the DUI problem; however, beyond making the DUI laws more permissive and "equitable" they offered no positive measures for the control of drunk driving. As one stated:

> I'm not in the treatment business, but I know what we got now won't get the job done.

4. Mixed Multiple Offenders: These offenders expressed similar views to those voiced by the majority of DUI and Traffic Offenders; however, theirs were more negative. All but two (87) disapproved of DUI laws. However, unlike the offenders in the other three groups, none offered any remedies for drunk driving or drunk drivers. Present oriented, hedonistic, and apparently without care for their or others' safety, they were only concerned with avoiding arrest and jail. To them there are two classes of people: (1) the caught, and (2) the uncaught. As one reports:

> Everybody drinks and drives. Some get caught. Most don't. Big shots go free. You go around but once. Why not have a ball, and live like a free man. I like to

drink and I like to drive. So does everybody else. Its a matter of who gets caught. You know I got a record and the cops are after me. So I'm here. All that bullshit about changing the laws and dishing out more punishment for drunk drivers is a crock. Why not stand up and dance? The more people you got and the more cars, the more drunk drivers. Put the heat on the cops and you get more DUIs. Who cares? Next year the public will have another pet crime to rave about. If you go through what I gone through, you will do exactly what I did. The laws you talk about are made to hold guys like me down.

The label DUI meant nothing to these offenders one way or the other. They already knew they were known as DUI repeaters, but from their perspective they did what they had to do. All claimed in many different ways they did not understand the rationale of the DUI laws or their implementation and that the police should not arrest drinking drivers unless they committed a crime other than DUI. Though many admitted doing time occasionally for what they called "slip ups," they did not discuss their criminal activities in detail. As they put it, "Everybody breaks the law now and then, and if you get caught you just do the time." None appeared to have specialized criminal skills, connections, or career aspirations.

V. DUI DETERRENCE, TREATMENT, AND MECHANICAL CONTROL MEASURES

The underlying rationale of deterrence measures and the drunk driver appears to inhere in the notion that drunk driving is not a "real crime"; that is, "but for the grace of God go I" syndrome and perhaps even a realization that the criminal law can never solve what is in origin a broad social problem. Deterrence theory assumes that a rational drinker knows that consuming more than three or four drinks within an hour prior to driving would place him at risk of driving impairment and arrest for drunk driving. To the contrary, the reality is that following the consumption of two or three drinks, the prospective driver's rationality diminishes and a euphoric false sense of self-confidence (i.e., the perception that additional consumption of alcohol would not impair his driving abilities) develops. Private motor vehicular transportation and pervasive position of alcohol as society's "favorite and acceptable drug" lead many to accept the risks inherent in drinking and driving in return for automotive "freedom" (Light, 1994). As the ethnographic data disclosed in the preceding chapter, most study subjects rationalize away driving after drinking on a number of non-legal motivations: personal convenience, social freedom, thrill-seeking excitement, omnipotence, perceived support from media advertisements for drinking and driving, and rebellion against the system. Therefore, drinking and driving is questionably an entirely rational behavior, yet that is what deterrence requires (personal communication from Frank P. Williams, III; February 15, 1995).

General and Specific Deterrence Measures

The evaluation studies of general deterrence efforts directed at the general driving public to reduce drunk driving (via legal sanctions) produce marginal, long-term deterrent results (Snortum, 1988; Homel, 1988; Nichols and Ross, 1990; Kingsnorth, Alvis, and Gavia, 1993). Some who endorse a theory of general prevention (Berger and Snortum, 1986; Snortum, 1984; Votey, 1984; Grasmick, Bursik, and Arneklev, 1993) suggest that the moralizing and educative effect of legal change involving deterrence and shame is likely to manifest itself in the long rather than the short run. In any event, at best, the deterrent effect of legal sanctions appears to be minimal and of short duration because of the uncertainty and inconsistency of enforcement policy. Berger and Snortum (1986) found in one cross-sectional survey that personal moral commitment against drunk driving was a strong deterrent. Grasmick, Bursik, and Arneklev (1993) support and extend Snortum and Berger's emphasis on the moral factor deterrent through and by two cross-sectional surveys. They argue that a reduction in self-reported drunk driving in a community between two identical surveys conducted in 1982 and 1990 can be attributed to intense legislative activity and moral crusading at the national and local levels during that period. They conclude that the reduction in self-reported drunk driving in the community was due to an increase in the threat of shame for this offense. Green (1991) observes a significant relationship between motivation to drive while under the influence of alcohol and the threat of social disapproval by significant others in a study of 550 randomly sampled adults from the Minneapolis/St. Paul metropolitan area during fall 1983 and fall 1984.

Moskowitz (1989) observes from a review of literature the efficacy of three alcohol-specific policies in the area of primary prevention of alcohol problems (including drunk driving): (1) raising the minimum legal age to 21 years; (2) increasing alcohol taxes; and, (3) increasing the enforcement of drinking-driving laws. He suggests, based on a systems perspective of prevention, that prevention policies may lead to shifts in social norms regarding use of beverage alcohol and thereby reduce alcohol-related problems including drunk driving. Ross (1992) argues that drunk driving is the logical outcome or culmination of the condition that both drinking and driving are interwoven in the institutional life of the contemporary United States. He maintains that drunk driving decreases to the extent to which drinking itself decreases. Policies that increase the costs of alcohol, for example, taxation on alcohol, are likely to reduce the incidence of drunk driving. He also argues that drunk driving decreases to the extent to which driving itself decreases. Therefore programs that delay and restrict the driving of the young may prove to be a deterrent factor. He further suggests a surcharge on alcohol beverages served in on premises outlets; proceeds of which might be used to subsidize evening taxi service for patrons of drinking establishments (Ross, 1990).

Fell (1990) suggests bartender and alcohol server training, free rides for alcohol-impaired drivers, designation of non-drinking drivers, and responsible party hosting as strategies for reducing alcohol-related traffic collisions.   Nichols (1990) proposes that treatment and deterrent approaches should be combined and supplemented with other important efforts such as public information, reduced incentives to drink excessively, raising drinking age, and alcohol education programs for youth. Hingson and Howland (1990) claim that some of the laws to deter drinking and driving passed in the 1980s have achieved declines in alcohol-involved driving and fatal crashes, both through establishing general deterrence and through heightening informal social pressure not to drink and drive. Additional efforts are needed to institutionalize community awareness and concern about drinking and driving and to target unaddressed components of alcohol-related traffic fatality problem, such as passengers who ride with impaired drivers and persons who illegally provide alcohol to minors.

A few statistical models evaluating the individual or social costs of drunk driving and the relative effectiveness of DUI deterrent policies have been offered.   Kenkel (1993) discussed the need to examine the phenomenon of drunk driving from the perspective of two choice margins: the demand for alcohol and the demand for driving when under the influence of alcohol. Following this framework, Mullahy and Sindelar (1994) measured the effect of the tax cost of alcohol, specific DUI penalty costs, per capita alcohol consumption, and socioeconomic and demographic characteristics on driving after "having had too much to drink." They found that an individual's decision to drive while drunk is negatively affected by the expected full price of driving drunk. Wilkinson (1987), in his policy simulation model, examined the relative effects of six specific DUI deterrent policies on fatalities: (1) increasing minimum legal drinking age to 21; (2) strictly enforce the 55-mph speed limit; (3) require outlets to stop serving alcoholic beverages by 2:00 a.m.; (4) increase the price of a gallon of ethanol by $10.00 (14.8% on the average); (5) mandate a minimum fine of $100.00 for the first DUI conviction; and, (6) allow the percentage of young drivers and drinkers to fall by 10%. Results indicated that the first three of the six policies are effective in reducing fatalities. Scribner, MacKinnon, and Dwyer (1994) demonstrated an ecological association between alcohol-outlet density and alcohol-related motor venicle crashes in a cross-sectional study of Los Angeles County cities. They implied that a reduction in the density of alcohol outlets would decrease alcohol-related motor vehicle crashes.

Evaluation studies of "specific deterrence" measures (fines, jail terms, license suspensions or revocations, court-ordered treatment or educational programs, and legal "get tough" policies) directed at the individual DUI offender to deter subsequent DUI violations yield mixed and minimal results (Homel, 1988; Ross, McCleary, and LaFree, 1990; Morse and Elliott, 1992; Kingsnorth, Alvis, and Gavia, 1993). However, there is some evidence that license revocation may be an effective sanction for reducing DUI recidivism (Nichols and Ross, 1990; Homel, 1988; Preusser, Blomberg, and Ulmer, 1988; Lund, 1992). Ross (1991) has called for the decriminalizing of routine drunk-driving cases and the replacement of routine drunk-driving court proceedings with punishment based on administrative procedures. License suspension and revocation (on the arrest spot by the police) and the removal of all driving privileges would be formally withdrawn after a short period, at which time the police action could be appealed to an administrative hearing. Typically licenses would be taken away for a period of 90 days for the administrative offense of driving with a BAC level exceeding a tolerant limit (generally 0.10%). License revocation could exceed this time period should a person refuse to take the breath test. Routine cases are defined as those in which BAC levels are not exceedingly high, and are not associated with endangerment in the sense of dangerous, reckless behavior, or any realized harm, such as injury or property damage. Criminal penalties for driving in defiance of a revocation order would result in incarceration, lengthened license revocation, and vehicle impoundment. Such administrative action would unburden the criminal justice system of routine minor DUI cases, thereby allowing more time for serious cases.

Specific Treatment Measures

The federally sponsored Alcohol Safety Action Projects (ASAPs), beginning in the 1970s and phased out in 1983, and similar currently operating DUI diversionary programs in local communities under local, state, or federal auspices generally place more emphasis on modifying drinking behavior, *per se*, than on drinking and driving behavior. Their secondary coercive prevention measures include a variety of regimens to reduce DUI recidivism ranging from education to outpatient counseling or therapy; for example, group counseling, individual counseling, DUI schools, threat of legal measures (for example, loss of license), and alcohol counseling and treatment. These programs combine treatment and deterrence measures and vary in structure ranging from education courses of two to six weeks to "therapy" for more than a year. Though evaluation studies are difficult to come by and hard to assess, they suggest that such programs may lead to a decrease in arrests and repeat offenses among social drinkers, but no such reduction has been found for heavy drinkers (Nichols, 1990; Jung, 1994:312-313). Nichols (1990) points out that such treatment programs may not be effective among DUI repeat offenders because they do not have to prove they have gained control of their drinking problem pursuant to license reinstatement. It has been suggested that DUIs in these programs be required to prove evidence of sobriety before they may be relicensed. Evaluation studies further suggest that education and treatment programs should be viewed as adjuncts, not as alternatives, to deterrent efforts.

Alcohol treatment programs and the courts at times refer DUIs to Alcoholics Anonymous (based on a self-help orientation and a quasi-religious philosophy) and to therapeutic programs based on medical and/or psychological models stressing, for example, aversive conditioning, contingency contracting (operand conditioning), social learning (reinforcement), family treatment, and shock therapy. Evaluation studies on these referrals yield mixed results. Some programs seem to deter some types of offenders but not others, particularly the heavy binge drinkers. A few studies (Sobell and Sobell, 1973; Sobell, Sobell and Toneatto, 1991) claim success with controlled drinking programs for alcoholics under treatment; that is, as determined by the improvement evaluations of two experimental groups, one given a criterion of abstinence, while the other given a goal of controlled drinking. Their findings have been questioned by those favoring abstinence (Gruenewald, 1991; Vingilis, 1994). Donovan and Marlatt (1982) recommended a controlled drinking program for one DUI personality subtype found in their studies (the non alcoholic). The program recommended for this type included reduction in drinking, help in the reduction of drinking, aid in identifying situations with high risk for DUI, and how to cope with them. However, Fillmore and Vogel-Sprott (1995) found that individual differences in expectations about the behavioral effect of alcohol could differentially affect performance, even though the group of individuals all expect and receive the same beverage.

Rosenberg and Davis (1994), in a national survey of 196 alcohol treatment services, discovered that only 23 percent of the respondents found moderate drinking acceptable for their patients. Of these acceptors, 80 percent worked in outpatient programs and 70 percent reported moderate drinking as appropriate for only 1-25 percent of their clientele. While 58 percent of acceptors gave their "own professional experience" as a basis for their acceptance, 80 percent of non-acceptors based their decision on disease model. Even Norman Denzin, a sociologist, would reject a moderate drinking treatment program based on the thesis that alcoholism is a disease of self, time, emotion, and social relationships. He points out that as drinking careers advance, alcoholic drinkers lose the ability to abstain from drinking or to control the amount consumed. During this process the alcoholic drinker develops an alcoholically-divided self in which there is a profound sense of separation of the drinking-self and the world of everyday social affairs. Alcohol continues to be used in an attempt to exert control over the social world, but this results in a false sense of control, false pride, bad faith and denial (Denzin, 1987a, 1987b, 1987c). Under these assumptions, moderate drinking programs would not be acceptable as successful treatment alternatives--especially in lieu of the fact that an overwhelming number of DUIs are problem drinkers.

DUI CONTROL MEASURES

Electronic Monitoring

Since the middle of the 1980s, the home confinement option or "home incarceration," as an alternative to jail sentences, has attracted considerably more support with the introduction of electronic monitoring (EM). EM monitorees are sentenced to probation which may include participation in alcohol and/or drug counseling or other programs as part of a total treatment package. Home confinement is designed to provide close control in the early probationary period. As of 1992, 45,000 EM monitors were handled in the U. S. by 1,200 different agencies. Though first proposed and utilized for DUI offenders, EM now includes, in addition to DUIs, DULS (driving under license suspension), parolees, and a variety of additional offender populations that are supervised by a wide range of state and local criminal justice agencies from departments of correction, probation, and parole to court systems. Probation departments usually supervise EM programs, which generally entail (for the probationers) fees ranging from $1 to $15 per day across the United States--less than one-third of the cost of jailing (Petersilia 1986, 1987; Lilly et al., 1993).

The EM device is usually in the form of a tamper-proof bracelet worn on ankle or wrist. The offender must have a private, residential telephone line without answering machines or cordless telephones. The "passive" or programmed contact device monitors the offender through a central computer that dials the home telephone at random intervals with a recorded message instructing the probationer to state name and time of day and then insert the coded wristlet into a special base unit attached to the telephone to verify presence. The "active" or continuous monitoring device includes a bracelet transmitter and a small receiver in the home telephone. If the probationer moves more than some 150 to 300 feet from the telephone, the signal transmission is broken and a departure code is sent to the central computer to alert the probation department and print out the offender's name and time of violation (Friel, Vaughn, and del Carmen, 1987). Various types of EMs may be set to restrict the probationer to home and job, and to a few hours each week for shopping and errands. There is some evidence that the restricted regimen forces clients to plan their time very carefully and thereby imposes some order on a once-disordered life (Maxfield and Baumer, 1990).

Lilly et al. (1993) from an evaluation of an EM program (the "front end" of a probation term for drunk driving during three different phases lasting over seven years) found that EM was implemented with few equipment or client complaints, was very cost effective, and was successful in that nearly all clients completed their EM period successfully.

Probation success declined, however, during the post-probation period. Though EM is intrusive it appears to be more effective than jail sentencing. More than one half of the DUI offenders in local jails at the time of the last national survey in 1989 had prior jail time for DUI. More attention should be given to the post-EM portion of probation. EM of course may be used in conjunction with other deterrence measures.

Breath Alcohol Monitoring

Breath Alcohol Monitoring is a dual technology approach that is effective in monitoring offenders with a history of alcohol abuse and/or alcohol-related offenses such as DUI. The system employs a visual telephone that installs in the offender's home and an individual breath alcohol tester. Offender can be monitored for house incarceration and alcohol consumption through randomly generated telephone calls by the central receiver station. The offender is required to take a breath alcohol test at each call. In the event the offender attempts to abort the test by not blowing sufficiently or passing the tester to another individual, an error message will appear. Each random call produces a photographic record, date and time stamped, and the presence of the offender and his breath alcohol reading.   The individual alcohol testers are maintained on calibration schedule to ensure accurate results. Violation reports are generated whenever an offender fails to respond to a phone call, fails to send a picture, has a positive alcohol reading, or the phone is busy for 15 minutes or longer (For specifications of the Alcohol Monitoring System, see Keith, 1992).

Ignition Interlock Devices

As demands for more effective legal deterrents for drunk driving increase a number of states within the past five years have authorized judges or state agencies to use breath analyzer ignition interlock devices as an optional sanction in drunk-driving cases. In most cases, interlocks when ordered are utilized in addition to the fines, license suspension, jail sentences, probation and treatment programs that have been used in the past. To date, approximately 16 states have passed similar legislation; 30 states have introduced legislation that supports--or would make mandatory--the use of interlocks with convicted drunk drivers (Kent, 1990). As of 1991 more than 16,000 interlock systems had been installed throughout the United States (Linnell and Mook, 1991). An ignition interlock devices is a system that connects a breath analyzer to an automobile's ignition. To start the engine of an interlock-equipped vehicle, the driver must blow into the analyzer that measures blood alcohol levels. Should the test show the would-be driver's blood alcohol meets or exceeds the calibrated setting on the device, the car will not start. This is usually referred to as a "Blow-and-Go" Unit which costs about $70 to install. Since 1993 most jurisdictions utilizing interlock systems require a "Rolling Retest" unit that requires a breath retest between two and ten minutes after initial start and at 40 minutes after first retest. If the user does not blow a prompted retest or if he or she fails the retest three consecutive times, the horn will sound repeatedly until the car is turned off. The "Memo Minder" will automatically reset itself for five days.

Therefore, the driver must return to the service center for early monitoring within the five-day period or else the vehicle will be rendered inoperative. Retest times and return time can be specified by the court. "Memo Minder" reminds the interlock user of a monitoring appointment. If the interlock user still does not return to the service center by the due date, the vehicle is rendered inoperative. If the unit detects a system by-pass, it will sound the horn repeatedly until the car is turned off and the Memo Minder is reset, allowing the user five days to return to the service center for early monitoring. A Data Logger keeps a record of the user's activity, recording date and time of each test, and whether or not it was passed or failed. It also records a system bypass; that is, jump start. The internal data logger can record up to 12,000 events. Optional features include a CBPA (Coordinated Breath Pulse Access), a learned breath code that must be passed in addition to the breath alcohol test before the vehicle can be started. It is an added deterrence to an unauthorized party blowing a breath test for the designated driver. VDP (Variable Drive Program) allows the interlock device to tender the vehicle inoperative during specified time periods set by the court. Finally, if specified by the court the BAC level can be set higher or lower to accommodate medical problems, medication, etcetera(Guardian Interlock Responsible Driver Program, 1993).

Morse and Elliott (1992) utilizing data from the Hamilton County Drinking and Driving Study (HCDDS) in Ohio (an ongoing research project that involves a quasi-experimental study design with matched probationary license suspension with "letter to drive" (N=273) and interlock comparison (N=273) groups) conducted a study designed to evaluate the effectiveness of interlock devices; that is, as a deterrent to a repeated drunk driving arrest in a sample of persons convicted of DUI. Survival rates (based on rearrest for DUI in Hamilton County) across a 30-month risk period during which interlock installation, license suspension, and probation sanctions were in effect, revealed that interlock devices significantly reduced the likelihood of a repeated DUI arrest as compared to license suspension. The DUI rearrest rate for the license suspension group (exclusively) was approximately three times as great as that of the interlock group across all time-at-risk periods though the interlock group had a greater number of prior DUI arrests than did the license suspension group. Similar findings have been reported by Baker from a Calvert County, Maryland, study (1990). This skewed difference in rearrest clearly supports a continuing use of the interlock device along with a "letter to drive" as a court-ordered alternative to license suspension alone, or as an option utilizable in conjunction with (most likely following) license suspension.

Ignition interlock devices appear to have a multilevel deterrent effect. First the interlock design physically prevents an intoxicated driver from starting the car by shutting down the electrical system. Second, over time it could possibly become an important behavior modification tool that discourages the driver from drinking at all. That is, faced with the daily need to interface with an interlock, many offenders might find the motivation to control their alcohol problems. Those offenders sentenced to interlocks can remain productive members of society and be able to work and support themselves and family without posing a risk to roadway safety. Interlocks may provide a safety net for pretrial release of felony DUI offenders, reduce jail populations, and also be used in conjunction with other control (for example EMs) and treatment measures (for example intensive probation). Finally, given the findings that a majority of those with suspended licenses continue to drive anyway, interlock devices would appear to provide a viable option for deterring persons convicted of DUI from repeated drinking and driving (Baker, 1990; Nichols and Ross, 1990; Morse and Elliott, 1990).

Smart Cars

Engineers are currently improving on a technology that would thwart the drunk driver already behind the wheel of a moving car. Installed computer sensors on experimental designs can now identify erratic driving and bring the car to a slow shut down while alerting other drivers, including the police, by sounding the car's horn and blinking the lights. Auto makers and government researchers have successfully tested this technology for years, but the car companies have shown scant interest in inserting these sensors in cars. This reluctance is similar to that in the past for seat belts and air bags. Alcohol-detection devices could become standard equipment, but the auto makers claim that this protection costs too much. What else is new? The public does not begrudge the cost of fire detectors in buildings. Perhaps consumers will eventually be willing to pay for anti-drinking systems in cars or DUI offenders could be forced to pay for this installation in their vehicles (Kelley, 1994.)

In conclusion, should the technological deterrence measures prove to be effective, they provide a quick fix at least in short run without undue concern about altering individuals' attitudes, values and/or drinking habits (Jacobs, 1989:170-171). However, in the long run planned social change can only be attained by establishing effective programs for behavioral modification in changing driving population's norms, attitudes, and values toward drinking and driving. This calls for an experimentation of an array of programs requiring partnerships between law enforcement agencies and community organizations.

VI. SUMMARY AND CONCLUSIONS

This study delineates four subtypes of white male DUI offenders: (1) First-time DUI Offenders, (2) DUI Recidivists, (3) DUI and Traffic Offenders, and (4) Mixed Multiple Offenders from a pool of 2,786 Georgia DUI offenders who had attended 65 state-certified DUI schools throughout the state during a three-year period (1986-1989). Nine out of every ten are recidivistic offenders whose deviant and/or criminal behavior appears to be generated from two interrelated sources: (1) the generality of deviance; and, (2) subcultural interaction. While a deviant and violent subculture encompassing heavy drinking and driving provides a prescription for the multiple DUIs' behavior, the script is negotiated, modified, and implemented through and by symbolic interaction among social actors possessing low self- and external controls.

1. Generality of Deviance: This study shows that the generality of deviance theory (incorporating low impulse control) underlines the behavior of all four subtypes. First-time DUI Offenders are less deviant in all respects than the other subtypes. The personal interview data demonstrate them to possess more self-control and to have lived in respectable middle-class environments affording more effective external controls than members of the other three subtypes. Though deviant and/or criminal behaviors were found to be similar among DUI and Traffic Offenders and Mixed Multiple Offenders, the latter's deviant acts were more persistant and grievous. The arrest histories of the Mixed Multiple Offenders are lengthier than any other subtype and indicate a more threatening, violent, and pervasive deviant and/or criminal life-style than those of other subtypes. However, contrary to the premise of the generality of deviance theory pertaining to patterned deviant behavior, DUI Recidivists, as adults, were alcoholics and exemplified over time a DUI pattern. Most citizens, including male alcoholics, drive regularly in our society. Finally, members of all three recidivistic subtypes (2, 3, and 4) possess low self-control and are the products of particular working-class environments that have provided weak external controls. Our extended DUI classification modal goes beyond the traditional dichotomous categories of DUI first-timers vs. DUI recidivists and identifies the most deviant and dangerous type of offender, subtype 4, the Mixed Multiple Offender.

2. *Subcultural Interaction:*   The subcultural behavioral prescriptions for the three recidivistic subtypes (2, 3, and 4) are similar in many respects to those found in Walter B. Miller's lower-class subculture and, Marvin E. Wolfgang and Franco Ferracuti's subculture of violence. The roots of this regional subcultural script are portrayed in Wilbur J. Cash's, *The Mind of the South* and Bertram Whyatt-Brown's book *Southern Honor: Ethics and Behavior in the Old South.*   These subcultural elements, though anchored in the past, are present and ever developing in peer groups among the DUIs under study. That is, the symbols (language, physical appearance, front, body language, manner), and social meanings generating these DUIs' instrumental and expressive behaviors are found to inhere in a deviant southern, working-class subculture characterized by (1) lower-class social, political, and economic marginality and alienation; (2) a mythical embroidered historical past; (3) awareness and consciousness of kind; (4) a specialized regional argot; (5) a "savage ideal" including romanticism, militarism, violence, cruelty, revenge, and chauvinism; (6) religious fundamentalism, hedonism, and sensuality linked to risk taking and a pattern of anti-social behavior including: thrill seeking, womanizing, gambling, brawling, law breaking, problem drinking, and drinking and driving; (7) a regional macho cognitive perspective interpreting and justifying deviant and law-breaking behaviors as normal male recreational pursuits; (8) a vaunted individualism (stemming from a regional and defensive self-concept); (9) racial prejudice, and a militant Protestantism; and (10) anti-modernity, anti-liberalism, anti-intellectualism, and anti-

aestheticism. The following comments by three different Mixed Multiple Offenders serve as a metaphor for this group's ideology: (1) "Oh God, it's so much fun to sin!"; (2) "I'm a southern rebel born to raise hell," and (3) "The big shots should get off our back."

The DUI's identities are developed from a regional, subcultural, and class socialization process, and their interactions follow the principles of symbolic interaction. That is, the DUIs act toward things on the basis of the meanings that the things have for them in their everyday life, and the meaning of such things is derived from or arises out of social interaction with others. These meanings do not derive from the law or abstract principles of what is right or wrong--but rather, are developed through an interaction process with peers. The situated moral meanings of subtypes 2, 3, and 4 as expressed to us during the interviews, rationalize away many aspects of the conventional middle-class moral code and the law-- particularly the moral and legal codes specific to violence, law-breaking, and drinking and driving. They exemplify negative reactions toward the criminal justice system's enforcement of DUI laws and reject for the most part the DUI label. DUI laws, policy, and procedures are necessary though inadequate for a few but unfair and fruitless for most. The DUIs in these three subtypes justify their illegal behaviors on the basis of having a good time, following natural masculine pursuits, meeting peers' expectations, and acting like everbody else. Like other social actors, they create and maintain rationalizations for their conduct in order to make such behavior acceptable to themselves as well as to others. Though perhaps more deviant, their life-style is similar to that of other working-class southerners.

Rationalism and Realism: These offenders (in all four subtypes) appear to act on what they deem to be a rational basis rather than from any unconscious motivation. Though skeptical of DUI laws and their enforcement, the recidivistic offenders like the First-time Offenders appear to be straightforward, honest, and realistic within their own frame of reference. Loyal to their own kind, they have a strong sense of place, family, and continuity. The DUIs in subtypes 2, 3, and

4 though lacking, in a full sense, of a working-class consciousness, are keenly aware of social class biases and injuries in their everyday lives. All sections of this country, and particularly the south, have had little success in selling the idea that all work, including manual labor, is honorable in a democracy, or in glossing over the not-so-hidden injuries of class.

Despite sensing flaws in the political and economic system, subtypes 2, 3, and 4 are willing to work for a living but think the welfare system should be "fixed" to prevent free loading. They are aware of the pseudo (white) liberals' hypocrisy in pressing for Civil Rights programs so long as the results of such measures do not affect their own segregated life style--but at the same time affect theirs. They resent middle- and upper-class morality and control and view "the big shots" as hypocrites. From their position they see through the ambivalence of the American Public's position on drinking and driving; that is, it's O.K. to drink before driving if you don't drink too much, and if you don't get caught. (How much is too much?)

Furthermore, they understand that factors other than drinking account for auto traffic accidents and that passing stringent laws against drinking and driving will continue to be of marginal effectiveness unless and until strong anti-drinking and driving values and norms support such legal provisions. Most importantly of all, they perceive that working-class people who drive inexpensive cars and dress inexpensively are discriminated against in drunk-driving arrest procedures and subsequent sentencing practices. That is, the big shots (middle- and upper-class southerners) are less likely to be stopped for drunk driving and, when stopped, are less likely to be arrested or convicted than are working-class people. To them, their drunk-driving arrests are but one example of upper-class efforts to monitor, censure, control, and criminalize them and their life-styles. In their view, middle- and upper-class people claim falsely to lead conventional life-styles and to refrain from reckless drinking and driving. Therefore, they complain that their drinking and driving behavior as well as their other recreational pursuits are unjustifiably monitored and controlled.

Treatment and Control Suggestions by DUI Offender Subtypes

The correctional (treatment) literature notes a potpourri of potentially or actually conflicting elements and techniques as applied to a generalized offender type. However, some recognized scholars argue against the generalized treatment approach and recommend a search for those principles, processes and factors that produce relevant and effective mixes for specific offender types--usually based on risk level (high, medium, low) as well as personality-based classifications, typologies, development levels, and cognitive levels (Hunt, 1971; Quay and Parsons, 1971; Palmer, 1974; Megargee, Bohn, and Sink, 1979; Jesness and Wedge, 1983; Palmer, 1984; Van Voorhis, 1987; Palmer 1992, 1994). Multiple targets and methods are more likely to be needed with serious or multiple offenders than with others (Palmer, 1994:151-153). Our suggestions for treatment and control measures with DUI Offender subtypes follow.

1. First-time DUI Offenders: This subtype comprises a middle-class group of well-adjusted social drinkers, who possess relatively strong self- and external controls. Generally they control the amount of alcohol they consume and where, when, and with whom they drink. Usually law-abiding citizens, they respect and agree with the DUI laws, do not drive when consciously intoxicated, and customarily hold their drinking before driving to a maximum of three drinks. Identifying with the criminal justice system, they are ashamed and remorseful about the instant arrest. They disavow the DUI label as an unsuitable designation for themselves but as an appropriate tag for working-class DUI recidivists. They say that: people like them are not really DUIs; their behavior in the instant arrest is an aberration; they are not really "like that."

The literature on deterrence and treatment demonstrates that DUI school education and early intervention programs work effectively with such first-time offender social drinkers.

As H. Laurence Ross suggests, routine cases among this subtype should be decriminalized and handled administratively with temporary license revocation and given a "letter to drive." Additionally, DUI school attendance and community service requirements could be imposed wherein they might serve as effective teachers' and counselors' aids in working with DUIs who have drinking problems. Perhaps moderate control drinking programs might prove worthy of experimenting with some members of this subtype. For a definition, benefits, and risks of moderate drinking, see National Institute on Alcohol Abuse and Alcoholism, *Alcohol Alert, No. 16, Ph 315*, April 1992.

2. DUI Recidivists: The arrest histories, social psychological characteristics, and ethnographic data of this subtype clearly indicate alcoholics. They compose the oldest and most serious drinking subtype and are more immersed in the deviant heavy drinking subculture than any other category. Identifying themselves as white, working-class southerners with drinking problems, they possess low self-control and weak self-concepts. As subtypes 3 and 4, they are relatively less educated than the First-time Offenders, politically conservative, rustic, and poor. Furthermore, unlike First-time Offenders, they are also religious fundamentalists, individualists, anti-intellectuals, hedonists and militant southerners. Envious of white-collar and professional workers they feel inferior to those who do not work with their hands and verbalize a macho self-image mirrored in heavy drinking, driving after drinking, drinking while driving, thrill seeking, fighting, gambling, and womanizing.

These alcoholics drink and drive every day to and from work and beer joints, from bar to bar, and from honky-tonks to home; that is, when they are unable to find rides with others. They do not intentionally drive when intoxicated, intentionally get intoxicated before or during driving, or drive recklessly after drinking.   Moreover, they refrain, when possible, from long distance driving, driving on highways, and driving in heavy traffic. They maintain that because of their careful and limited driving, they do not cause crashes or serious accidents. We did not probe into respondents' traffic accidents and were therefore unable to verify these claims. However, we are inclined to accept such statements as within the range of probability as based on their perceptions.

These impulsive low self-controlled, present-oriented, hedonistic, and nonconformist offenders' reasons for drinking may be translated into the following explanations: (1) they possess a highly favorable attitude toward heavy drinking ("drinking is the normal thing to do;" "alcohol is good," "useful" and "important" in their lives); (2) they receive strong environmental support for heavy drinking among significant others in a drinking working-class milieu; (3) drinking serves as a euphoric rewarding agent in reinforcing social interaction; (4) drinking serves as a euphoric rewarding agent in reinforcing self-esteem; and, (5) alcohol effects give them pleasure. These self-explanations for drinking were frequently proffered within the context of story telling about womanizing, drinking, shop talk, bravado, hunting and fishing, fighting, and partying. Heavy drinking among these men appears to build self-esteem and a sense of personal power that in turn leads to more drinking, drunkenness, DUIs, conflicts with women and other adjustment problems. Their personal, economic, social, and political powerlessness anchored in a deviant southern working-class subculture and weak self-control explain their thrill seeking, risky, alcohol-dependent life-style. Norman Denzin (1987a,b,c), a sociologist, observes on the basis of lengthy interviews with alcoholics the existence of an "alcoholically-divided self" wherein alcohol is consumed in an attempt to exert control over one's social world, which results in a false sense of control, false pride, and denial. These men appeared to have such an alcoholically divided self. On the other hand, they realistically perceive the ambivalence in American social structure concerned with drinking and driving.

These men did not find incarceration following the instant arrest degrading, however, they consider arrest, jail time, and court procedures inconvenient, unfair, and fruitless. Indifferent or mildly antagonistic toward the criminal justice system and DUI schools, they reject the DUI label and DUI laws as applied to them because they claim to be a specialized group of alcoholics or problem drinkers. They deny responsibility for the instant arrest and state that the police should "leave them alone." Demanding public and official understanding, they insist on receiving specialized long-term outpatient treatment for alcoholism instead of criminal sanctions. They feel they should receive a special kind of license enabling them to drive while they are undergoing alcohol treatment.

Because members of this subtype are alcoholics and drink and drive regularly, they pose a potential threat for highway and street safety despite claims of limited and careful driving. We recommend that these offenders' licenses be revoked and that they be placed on a long-term treatment plan for alcoholism such as Alcoholics Anonymous wherein they could learn how to be at ease without drinking and establish an identity as a recovering alcoholic. By socializing with others who are struggling to overcome similar problems they could develop a new view of themselves and social recognition as people attempting to overcome alcohol dependency. *They should also be taught there is no magical alcohol treatment to cure them.* Besides eliminating alcohol dependency, the treatment programs should incorporate methods to improve self-esteem, occupational work skills, educational levels, and to provide them with alternate avenues for gaining personal power other than alcohol. In effect, they must first be diverted from the drinking subculture in bars and honky-tonks. The use of electronic monitoring or breath alcohol monitoring, at least in the early treatment stages, would keep them at home and serve this purpose. Their licenses would not be reinstated until they submit evidence of sobriety. Such license should designate the car they are permitted to drive and the limited hours they can drive. In the meantime they should be required to pay a surcharge to subsidize transportation to and from work, treatment facilities, and other legitimate locales. Upon reinstatement of their license, ignition interlock devices should be installed in the specific automobile they are permitted to drive under the close supervision of a probation department (see Chapter V for a description of technological control devices).

Should they receive a DUI during or following treatment, consideration should be given to permanent license revocation. In the case of indigents, the agency of jurisdiction would undergo the initial cost of surcharges and technological device installations on a collectable revocation loan basis. Some of these costs could be retrieved from the liquor and beer producing, distributing, and retailing industries. Consistent incremental behavioral improvement on the part of the offenders would be rewarded by reducing the required loan premium by a certain percentage.

3. DUI and Traffic Offenders: The analysis of this largest subtype discloses problem drinkers, risk-takers, and bad drivers. They commit traffic offenses even when not legally intoxicated. Similar to DUI Recidivists in identity, life history, and personal relationship problems, lifestyle, and world view, yet they do not define themselves as alcoholics, do not engage in "misery drinking," and tend to be more hostile and violent. Their self-concepts are somewhat stronger than those of DUI Recidivists.

Further, unlike the DUI Recidivists, they do not claim problem drinking is responsible for their DUIs. To them, drinking and driving is the normal thing to do, and they claim they are competent drivers even when drinking. These drivers on occasion intentionally drink before driving to the point of intoxication, drink to the point of intoxication while driving, and drive recklessly and dangerously when drinking or not drinking. They do not appear to be overly concerned about their deviant drinking and driving behavior which places themselves and others at risk. Additionally, they view the DUI laws as "silly," "unfair," and "ineffective" statutes and claim that there should be no DUI laws *per se* because everybody drinks and drives--but only the caught get penalized. According to them, the police should not stop any driver unless he or she causes a traffic accident. Most express negative attitudes toward the social actors in and the procedures of the criminal justice system. DUI laws and practices are "unfair," "nuisances," and "inconveniences." They reject the DUI label because, "Everybody drinks and drives and only those who get caught are tagged." They recognize the ambivalence and cultural contradictions in American society dealing with drinking and driving and rationalize away their behavior on the basis of the ready availability of alcohol and fast cars and misleading advertisements in this regard.

Control and preventive measures with this fatalistic subtype must center on long-term treatment for problem drinking, defensive driving education, and effective counseling (correctional and spiritual) programs to alter deviant life-style and negative attitudes toward the law, including DUI laws. These offenders should be required to attend seminars organized and paid for by auto manufacturers, dealers and advertisers, and the liquor industry to dispel the false images that their advertisements have created (for example, the association of having a good time, glamour, power, status, and false pride with drinking and drinking and driving activities. For additional information on this point, see Cox et al., 1992). Some beer companies claim they sponsor the "know when to say when" and advocate moderate drinking. However, "when to say when" in some cases is interpreted by drinkers to mean three or four drinks (Atkin, DeJong and Wallack, 1992). Instead, the proposed seminars should promote slogans such as "say no drinking before driving," "drive only in legal limits," and "drinking is neither glamorous nor sophisticated." Correctional sanctions should include stiffer penalties such as license revocation for an extended period of time, increased fines, and prolonged jail sentences. License reinstatement should be based on sobriety, stringent driving license tests, and basic changes in attitudes about drinking and driving, and drunk-driving behavior. As in the case of DUI Recidivists, they should be required to pay a surcharge for subsidizing their legitimate transportation needs while they are undergoing treatment.

Following an interim case review they should be subjected to electronic monitoring, breath alcohol monitoring, and/or interlock devices in conjunction with their individual treatment program. The speedometers on their individual cars should be calibrated at a reduced speed. Their cars should carry color-coded marked license plates designating them to be bad drivers and DUIs, which would be eventually replaced with normal license plates following cessation of bad driving and drinking and driving. Partial support for the latter measure is found in the literature on "shame," "embarrassment," and "remorse" theories. Finally, those who receive DUIs during or following correctional sanctions or treatment measures would have their licenses revoked for a lengthier period of time.

4. Mixed Multiple Offenders: This second largest subtype includes the most dangerous offenders in the sample. Episodic, non-professional criminals, they are also reckless and drunk drivers. Their profiles, when compared with other subtypes, resemble more closely those of prison populations. The ethnographic data show them to be similar in some respects to the two other recidivistic subtypes, particularly to the DUI and Traffic Offenders, in terms of identities, life history and personal relationship problems, lifestyle, and world view. However, they do not consider themselves to be alcoholics, nor do they engage in "misery drinking." Behaviorally, they are more problematic than any other subtype in that they demonstrate in childhood, adolescence, and adulthood the most violent, delinquent, and criminalistic life-style. Antisocial behaviors include: truancy, smoking, drinking, vandalism, sex offenses, stealing, fighting, brawling, use of drugs, weapon carrying, burglary, robbery, aggravated assault, rape, woman battery, and DUI--a generalized escalating pattern of deviancy beginning at an early age.

Their drinking and driving patterns frequently focus on deviant activities as well as on recreational pursuits, and therefore, they find it usually necessary to drive after drinking frequently. As in the case of DUI and Traffic Offenders, they view the DUI laws as ludicrous, unfair, ineffective, unnecessary, and not applicable to themselves. They react negatively toward the criminal justice system that according to them entails only nuisances and inconveniences. Like subtypes 2 and 3, they are products of subcultures of violence and of weak externally controlled environments. They have displayed low self-control throughout life.

Careful screening procedures should be applied with this group based on their prior arrest history and the circumstances involved in the instant arrest to determine the eligibility for their enrollment in community-based crime prevention and treatment programs, including jail time, house arrests, and various kinds of half-way house confinements. Along with alcohol treatment they should also receive correctional and spiritual counseling, helping them to avoid further criminal behavior. These screening procedures would also indicate those permitted to drive even with technological control devices (EM, breath alcohol monitoring, and interlock). Correctional sanctions should include driver license revocation for a prolonged period. As with the other recidivistic types they should be required to pay a surcharge for subsidizing their legitimate transportation needs. As in the case of DUI and Traffic Offenders, the speedometers on their individual cars should be calibrated at a reduced speed limit. Additionally, their cars should carry color-coded marked license plates designating them as bad drivers and DUIs which could be eventually replaced with normal license plates following cessation of bad driving, and drinking and driving. The foregoing control and treatment measures would occur within a long-term intense probationary supervision regimen following initial incarceration. Finally, those who receive DUIs during or following correctional sanction or treatment measures would be considered for permanent license revocation and prison sentences. Those determined ineligible for the above treatment and control measures should have their drivers' licenses permanently revoked and serve jail or prison sentences.

As a general deterrent measure, the car companies may be mandated to manufacture smart cars for future public consumption. Until such mandate is complied with, those who own smart cars would receive auto insurance premium discounts. Hingson and Howland (1986, 1990) maintain that the passage of legislation, when accompanied by public debate and media attention, helps to create a moral climate that results in strong though informal social pressure not to drink and drive. Perhaps this is true for the general driving population and some First-time Offenders. However, members of subtypes 2, 3, and 4 require specific effective deterrent and control measures.

Finally, many scholars suggest that early interventions are more likely to be effective over the life-course of deviants, delinquents, and criminals than are later interventions because there seems to be considerable stability of individual differences in deviant acts over time. Specific early intervention methods that have been found to be relatively effective include: behavioral interventions (token economy, modeling, behavioral contracting), family interventions, social-cognitive interventions (social skills training and social problem solving, cognitive self-control), academic and vocational education, work programs, individual counseling, and external controls (Palmer, 1994:10-21). Although these measures are not directed toward young DUI Offenders *per se*, they may prove of experimental value with them.

Implications and Recommendations for Future Research

The generalizability of any data set and research findings on amorphous population groups of this kind are somewhat tenuous. However, the DUI offender typology delineated in this study, based on generality of deviance and a subcultural-interaction perspective, demonstrates an empirically derived meaningful differentiation within the DUI category. Moreover, our ethnographic analysis discloses the social world of the southern working-class white male drunk driver and his social reality of drinking and driving. This body of knowledge provides researchers and policy makers with a better understanding of this offender population. Additionally this study proposes feasible treatment and control measures for each subtype. We suggest that our findings may be generalizable to other DUI populations--certainly from populations similar to that of Georgia. Evidently, we need drunk driving studies on a variety of population groups representing different geographical areas and social class levels in order to obtain a wider spectrum of DUI offenders (Jacobs, 1989; Perrine, 1990). Drunk drivers and the social problem of drunk driving of which they are a part may vary from place to place. We hope we have made a start in the right direction.

Future empirical research on drunk drivers should be guided by explicit theoretical frames of reference. Researchers must be aware that they are dealing with a problematic group of offenders whose drinking behavior is only one facet of a thrill-seeking, deviant life-style. Heavy drinking, as a significant part of this life-style, provides self-esteem, a feeling of personal power, and pleasure within a particular subcultural milieu. Because there is no one pure type of DUI offender and no adequate DUI typology, there is further need to develop, and refine, a more useful classification of drunk drivers beyond extant subtypes. One unresearched aspect of such a classification is a definition and an analysis of the drunk driver's specific legal infractions involved in his or her arrest history; for example, DUI BAC levels and traces of other illegal drug use, kind of DUI traffic infractions, accidents, crashes, wrecks, loss of human life, etcetera. In brief, what do the police reports record about each of the drunk drivers' infractions and inferred motivations involved in each arrest? Finally, the arrest history and ethnographic analysis demonstrated in this study could be extended to other DUI offender population segments; for example, to female DUIs, black DUIs, and DUIs in other geographical areas.

Endnotes

[1] Dr. Alfred J. Farina, Research Psychologist, Research Division, National Highway Traffic Safety Administration provided the following formula for calculating BAC based upon self-reported pre-arrest drinking behavior of the jail inmates (See for details, Greenfeld, "Drunk Driving," p. 8, 1988).

$$BAC(h) = [(A/(r \times p))/10] - (h \times K)$$

where,

$BAC(h)$ = Blood alcohol concentration at time h

A = grams of ethanol consumed = [(liquid ounces ethanol) x (.82)]/.035

r = reduced body mass (.68 for males and .55 for females)

p = weight in kilograms = weight in pounds/2.2046

h = hours drinking

K = estimated rate at which the body metabolizes ethanol (.015 ounces per hour)

[2] The construct of social type was first developed by George Simmel. According to Lewis A. Coser, "The type becomes what he is through his relations with others who assign him a particular position and expect him to behave in specific ways. His characteristics are seen as attributes of social structure." (See Coser, L.A., *Masters of Sociological Thought: Ideas in Historical and Social Context*, New York: Harcourt, 1977.)

[3] For a discussion of this point, See P.L. Berger and T. Luckman, *The Social Construction Reality: A Treatise in the Sociology of Knowledge*, New York: Doubleday, 1966; and W. Bankston, Q. Jenkins, C. Thayer-Doyle, and C. Thompson, "Fear of the Drunk Driver: Analysis of an Emergent Social Problem." Paper presented at the annual meetings of the Southwestern Sociological Association, Austin, TX: March 1986.

[4] We modify Goffman's typology and schema in three respects. First, we divide personal identity into two parts: (a)

biographical identity, and (b) presented self and activity to others.   Second, "ego identity" is extended to include self-identification to self and to others and renamed self-identity.

5 The Mortimer-Filkins (M-F) test, also known as HSRI Protocol (Highway Safety Research Institute, University of Michigan), includes: (1) a self-administered questionnaire; (2) an interview schedule, administered by probation officers, providing information about the subject's drinking patterns, health, activities and other background data; (3) a questionnaire and interview summary sheet; (4) a tally sheet of blood alcohol concentration (BAC), and driver and criminal record; and, (5) a treatment evaluation sheet. (For additional details of this instrument, See R. G. Mortimer, L. D. Filkins, J. S. Lower, M. W. Kerlan, D.V. Post, B. Mudge, and C. Rosenblatt, *Court Procedures for Identifying Problem Drinkers: Report on Phase 1.* Los Angeles: University of Southern California, Highway Safety Research Institute, 1974.)

6 We utilized content analysis in this study to compare the specific content, form, volume and substance of the interviewees' responses regarding their self-concepts and identities, life-history and personal relationship problems, life-style, world view, drinking and driving patterns and attitudes, and reactions to criminal justice process and the DUI label. For further discussion of content analysis, see Murty, Ugenyi, and Roebuck (1989) and Krippendorf (1980).

7 Social settings are characterized by the following elements: (a) Freedom of actors both in initiating and terminating interaction and in terms of the latitudes of behavior permissible; (b) Equality, in that all actors are supposed   to act as if all are equal in status and thus open for encounters; (c) Novelty, the anticipation that something unusual or out of the ordinary will probably occur; (d) Stepping out of the real world into a play world where behavior is autonomous and consequential only for the here and now; (e) Space and time circumscriptions, i.e., behavior is limited in both location and duration; (f) Order that, though more

problematic here than in more conventional settings, is generated by actors in their behavioral routines; (g) Permanency, which refers to the sometime anticipation of actors that their play group will endure over time; and, (h) Secrecy, i.e., an air of secrecy may obtain among members within such a setting demarcating their setting and their membership.

Appendix A

National Trends in DUI Arrests

In 1992 there was about one arrest for driving under the influence of an intoxicant for every 106 licensed drivers. Between 1975 and 1992 arrests for DWI increased nearly 72 percent while the number of licensed drivers increased by 33 percent. Arrest rates for DWI were highest among 21-year-olds and reached their peak in 1983 with a rate of one arrest for every 39 licensed drivers of that age (Table A.1). Compared to 1975, data for 1992 reflected declines in arrest rates for drivers of 16-17 years old and every group over the age of 40 (Table A.2). Between 1983 and 1992 the number of DWI arrests per 100,000 licensed drivers dropped 32.8 percent for 21-year-olds, 36.2 percent for 22-year-olds, 35.6 percent for 23-year-olds and 32.3 percent for 24-year-olds. Since 1983, all 50 states and the District of Columbia have gradually passed new laws raising the minimum age for the purchase and public possession of alcoholic beverages to 21 years. Per capita arrest rates for DWI for those aged 18-20 years have decreased by 47 percent since then--almost one-and-one-half times the rate of decrease for those aged 21-24 (34 percent). Lower arrest rates may be a reflection of changing drinking behavior among young adults as a result of raising the minimum drinking age to 21. National surveys of high school seniors indicate that seniors in 1992 (that is, after all 50 states and the District of Columbia had raised their drinking eligibility age to 21 years) reported less prevalent daily drinking and driving in the month preceding the survey than did seniors in 1980 (before the drinking ages were raised). Additionally, a smaller percentage of seniors in 1992 reported engaging in binge drinking (5 or more drinks in a row at least once in the two weeks prior to the interview) than did seniors in 1980.

Table A.1

Arrest Rates for DUI, 18- to 24-Year-olds, 1976-92

Age	Number of DUI Arrests per 100,000 Licensed Drivers in:								
	1976	1977	1978	1979	1980	1981	1982	1983	1984
18 Years	1,068	1,288	1,344	1,486	1,586	1,596	1,787	1,623	1,526
19 Years	1,133	1,453	1,478	1,623	1,802	1,869	2,141	2,086	1,973
20 Years	1,148	1,481	1,551	1,779	1,867	2,031	2,334	2,359	2,209
21 Years	1,212	1,554	1,615	1,778	1,947	2,124	2,503	2,536	2,479
22 Years	1,118	1,462	1,514	1,593	1,839	1,969	2,352	2,505	2,383
23 Years	1,063	1,368	1,415	1,535	1,738	1,892	2,192	2,400	2,300
24 Years	1,023	1,316	1,347	1,459	1,622	1,780	2,126	2,265	2,210
All Drivers	768	914	901	925	982	1,041	1,184	1,244	1,145

Continued on next page

Table A.1 --*Continued*

Number of DUI Arrests per 100,000 Licensed Drivers in:

Age	1985	1986	1987	1988	1989	1990	1991	1992
18 Years	1,428	1,480	1,094	1,036	1,034	1,085	958	857
19 Years	1,848	1,780	1,327	1,244	1,253	1,307	1,185	1,086
20 Years	2,117	1,961	1,536	1,390	1,395	1,418	1,342	1,302
21 Years	2,408	2,292	1,850	1,740	1,755	1,825	1,696	1,705
22 Years	2,538	2,310	1,842	1,694	1,687	1,770	1,609	1,598
23 Years	2,296	2,257	1,798	1,658	1,624	1,698	1,562	1,546
24 Years	2,285	2,213	1,792	1,627	1,648	1,583	1,536	1,533
All Drivers	1,140	1,131	1,067	1,101	1,049	1,084	1,048	938

Note: Percents may not add to 100 due to rounding. Table excludes licensed drivers and arrests for those less than 16 years old. For those 16 and older there were 129,671,000 licensed drivers in 1975 and 173,125,396 in 1992. There were 945,757 DUI arrests in 1975 and 1,624,500 in 1992. The age distribution of known arrests for DUI was applied to the total number of estimated DUI arrests.

Sources: (1) Laurence A. Greenfeld (1988); (2) FBI, *Uniform Crime Reports, 1987 through 1992*; and, (3) U. S. Department of Transportation, *Highway Statistics, 1987 through 1992*.

Table A.2

Comparison of Licensed Drivers and Estimated Arrests for Driving under the Influence by age—1975 and 1992

Age	1975			1992			Percent Change in Rate 1975-92
	Percent of Drivers	Percent of Arrests	Arrests per 100,000 Drivers	Percent of Drivers	Percent of Arrests	Arrests per 100,000 Drivers	
Total	100.0	100.0	729	100.0	100.0	938	+ 28.7
16-17 Years	3.7	1.8	352	2.0	0.8	316	- 10.2
18-24 Years	18.9	25.3	979	12.6	23.3	1,408	+ 43.8
25-29 Years	12.9	15.0	847	10.9	19.9	1,389	+ 64.0
30-34 Years	10.3	12.2	867	12.0	18.9	1,193	+ 37.6
35-39 Years	8.5	10.6	909	11.6	13.9	913	+ 0.4
40-44 Years	7.9	9.8	904	10.4	9.3	678	- 0.3
45-49 Years	8.0	8.9	812	8.6	5.8	510	- 37.2
50-54 Years	7.9	7.3	675	6.7	3.4	391	- 42.1
55-59 Years	6.8	4.6	490	5.7	2.1	282	- 42.4
60-64 Years	5.7	2.7	347	5.4	1.3	187	- 46.1
65 + Years	9.5	1.8	141	13.9	1.3	69	- 51.1

Appendix B

Sources of Data and the Sample

A. The 1989 Georgia DUI Study

The Criminal Justice Institute of Clark Atlanta University conducted a three-year study (October 1, 1986 through September 30, 1989) to evaluate the effects of driver improvement courses on DUI offenders. This project, by adopting a standard "consecutive admissions" strategy, included a representative sample of 2,786 DUI offenders, who attended 67 out of 146 driver improvement course clinics between August 1986 and January 1987. The 67 clinics were selected on the basis of cluster sampling to accomplish a geographic representation of the state.

During the year 1986, there were approximately 1.8 million arrests for driving under the influence. Even though this arrest data may not exactly represent the number of persons arrested (for the reason that some persons may have been arrested more than once for the same offense) a crude comparison of the sample distribution with the distribution of arrests by age, gender, and race provides a general notion regarding the sample representativeness.

Table B.1 clearly indicated no significant differences between the distributions of the study sample and the national arrest data by age or gender. However a significant difference was observed for distribution by race, indicating the possibility of some underrepresentation of whites and overrepresentation of blacks in the sample. Perhaps this difference may disappear if the sample distribution is compared to that of Southern region, for which data are not readily available.

Table B.1

Comparison of Sample Distribution and National DUI Arrests as of 1986 by Selected Variables

Variable	Study Sample	Total DUI Arrests in the U.S., 1986
Age		
16-20 Years	1.3	10.6
21-34 Years	55.6	57.5
35-44 Years	23.9	18.4
45-64 Years	16.2	12.2
65 + Years	3.0	1.3

X_2 (excluding the first and last age groups) = 1.0018; DF=2; Significance= .6059

Gender		
Male	85.0	88.5
Female	15.0	11.5

X^2 = .38536; DF=1; Significance = .5347

Race		
White	72.3	88.7
Black	23.9	9.7
Other	3.8	1.6

X^2 (for white and black categories) = 7.5153; DF = 1; Significance = .0061

The sampled cases were divided into two mutually exclusive categories: (1) First-time DUI Offenders; and, (2) second-time (or more) DUI Offenders. First-time DUI Offenders are those with no previous DUI arrests. Second-time (or more) offenders are those with at least one former DUI conviction; that is, one DUI charge prior to the instant conviction. Of the 2,786 cases 1,842 were found to be First-time DUI Offenders and 944 were second-time (or more) DUI Offenders. These two types were compared along the following dimensions: drinking type (social, excessive, and problem drinkers); demographics (age, gender, education, marital status, income, employment status, ethnicity); social-psychological characteristics (perceived self-drinking problems, perceived ability to control, perceived hangover effects, others' perceptions toward self-drinking); and behavioral characteristics (alcohol treatments, alcohol addiction, job-related drinking consequences, non-job-related drinking consequences, drinking history of family). These data were collected at the time of DUI school enrollment through two-hour personal interviews (conducted with each program participant at the respective DUI schools by six Clark Atlanta University interviewers: one black male aged 27 years; one white male aged 36 years; three black females aged 30 to 45 years; one white female aged 28 years. Two had undergraduate degrees, and the remaining four had Masters or above, all in behavioral sciences). Four interview questionnaire instruments were utilized: (a) sociodemographic background inventory, (b) Mortimer-Filkins (M-F) test, (c) Michigan Alcohol Screening Test (MAST), and (d) DUI Screening Questionnaire. The analysis found significant differences between the two groups on all dimensions except for income and ethnic background. Demographically, second-time (or more) DUI Offenders were older, more frequently white, male, mateless, poorer, and less educated than the first-time offenders. Along all dimensions they exemplified more negative characteristics than did the First-time DUI Offenders; e.g., problem drinkers constituted 58 percent of the First-time DUI Offenders and 73 percent among the second-time (or more) DUI Offenders. This study would have been more discriminative with reference to serious dangerous DUIs had the classification criteria included non-DUI arrest history analysis as well.

The present study reclassifies all of these 2,786 cases into four types based on an analysis of their complete arrest histories: (a) First-time DUI Offender, (b) DUI Recidivist, (c) DUI and Other Traffic Offender, and (d) Mixed Multiple Offender.

B. The Official Arrest Histories

These data were obtained from the Department of Public Safety and the Georgia Crime Information Center in the following manner.

The Department of Public Safety: Following the instructions of the Department of Public Safety, the Clark Atlanta University project staff provided it with the sampled offenders' names, license or social security numbers, dates of birth, race, and sex on a preformatted magnetic tape. Driver history reports were downloaded to magnetic tape and were merged into Clark Atlanta University's computerized data file. These reports included all DUI and other traffic arrest charges.

Georgia Crime Information Center: As in the case of the Department of Public Safety, the Clark Atlanta University project staff provided the Georgia Crime Information Center with the sampled offenders' names, license or social security numbers, dates of birth, sex, and race on a preformatted magnetic tape. However, in lieu of magnetic tape, criminal records were returned to the project staff in the form of "rap sheets" (as originating from each offender's local police department) and a hard copy printout. These arrest histories include all arrests (DUI charges, other traffic charges, and other criminal charges) by date, place, time and charge. Although these arrest histories may not be completely exhaustive because some out-of-state rap sheet entries may not have been available, we consider them adequate for the task at hand. In fact, all cases are Georgia residents.

From the above two sources we constructed a complete arrest history by date of arrest and criminal charge(s) for all sample cases.

C. Personal Interview Data

At the close of the 1989 Georgia DUI study interviews with all white male respondents (N=2,017) were asked, "Will you be available for another interview at a later date if further personal information is needed? If yes, provide your address and telephone number." A total of 1,822 agreed to an additional interview. From February 1989 through July 1990, the authors were able to contact 730 of the 1,822 prospective interviewees. Address changes, disconnected or changed telephone numbers, and unanswered calls limited the numerical contacts. Between February 1989 and July 1990, 311 of the 730 were interviewed. Scheduling problems precluded interviews with the remaining 419 cases because of residential mobility, job schedule interferences, domestic situations, legal problems, and failure to "show up" for an interview. Each of 311 white men was interviewed for one and one-half to two hours at prearranged locales (respondents' homes and researchers' offices). All interview schedules were structured in a five-part topical format: (1) Self-concept and identities; (2) Life history and personal relationship problems; (3) Life-style; (4) World view; (5) Drinking and driving patterns and attitudes; and (6) Reactions to criminal justice system and the DUI label. Following the conclusion of all interviews, the two interviewers compared the responses they had collected individually. The response patterns were found to be internally consistent, plausible, and similar.

Appendix C

Table C.1

Distribution of DUI Offenders by Drinking-Related Perceptions

Drinking-Related Perceptions	Total (N=2,786)		1st Time DUI (N=281)		DUI Recidivist (N=471)		DUI+ Traffic (N=1,295)		Mixed Multiple (N=739)	
	No.	Pct.	No.	Pct.	No.	Pct.	No.	Pct.	No.	Pct.
1. Perceived Self-Drinking Problems										
Yes	1,465	52.6	44	15.6	378	80.2	757	58.5	286	38.7
No	1,243	44.3	232	82.6	80	17.0	487	37.6	435	58.9
No Response	87	3.1	5	1.8	13	2.8	51	3.9	18	2.4
(a) Feel Bad About Self-Drinking										
Yes	1,373	49.3	27	9.6	373	79.2	735	56.8	238	32.2
No	1,374	49.3	251	89.3	90	19.1	538	41.5	495	67.0
No Response	40	1.4	3	1.1	8	1.7	22	1.7	6	0.8
(b) Concerned About Self-Drinking										
Yes	1,320	47.4	63	22.4	359	76.2	610	47.1	288	39.0
No	1,384	49.7	211	75.1	93	19.7	651	50.3	429	58.0
No Response	82	2.9	7	2.5	19	4.1	34	2.6	22	3.0

Continued on next page

Table C.1--Continued

Drinking-Related Perceptions	Total (N=2,786)		1st Time DUI (N=281)		DUI Recidivist (N=471)		DUI+ Traffic (N=1,295)		Mixed Multiple (N=739)	
	No.	Pct.	No.	Pct.	No.	Pct.	No.	Pct.	No.	Pct.
(c) Feel Guilty About Self-Drinking										
Yes	1,110	39.8	47	16.7	233	49.5	601	46.4	229	31.0
No	1,593	57.2	229	81.5	227	48.2	646	49.9	491	66.4
No Response	83	3.0	5	1.8	11	2.3	48	3.7	19	2.6
(d) Feel Annoyed by Criticism of Self-Drinking										
Yes	1,045	37.5	8	2.8	286	60.7	534	41.2	217	29.4
No	1,654	59.3	271	96.5	176	37.4	703	54.3	504	68.2
No Response	87	3.2	2	0.7	9	1.9	58	4.5	18	2.4
2. Perceived Ability to Control										
Yes	1,936	69.5	269	95.7	274	58.2	882	68.1	511	69.1
No	698	25.0	0	0	178	37.8	331	25.6	189	25.6
No Response	152	5.5	12	4.3	19	4.0	82	6.3	39	5.3
(a) Feel as a Normal Drinker										
Yes	1,974	70.8	273	97.2	263	55.8	912	70.4	526	71.2
No	756	27.1	1	0.3	199	42.3	356	27.5	200	27.1
No Response	56	2.1	7	2.5	9	1.9	27	2.1	13	1.7

Continued on next page

Table C.1--Continued

Drinking-Related Perceptions	Total (N=2,786) No.	Pct.	1st Time DUI (N=281) No.	Pct.	DUI Recidivist (N=471) No.	Pct.	DUI+ Traffic (N=1,295) No.	Pct.	Mixed Multiple (N=739) No.	Pct.
(b) Can Stop Without Struggle at One or Two Drinks										
Yes	2,149	77.1	278	98.9	315	66.9	980	75.5	576	77.9
No	602	21.6	0	0	152	32.3	296	22.8	154	20.9
No Response	35	1.3	3	1.1	4	0.8	19	1.5	9	1.2
(c) Can Hold Liquor Better Than Others										
Yes	1,225	44.0	8	2.8	313	66.5	605	46.7	299	40.5
No	1,403	50.3	261	92.9	135	28.6	606	46.8	401	54.2
No Response	158	5.7	12	4.3	23	4.9	84	6.5	39	5.3
(d) Always Able to Stop Drinking When Desired										
Yes	2,075	74.5	274	97.5	230	48.8	906	70.0	665	90.2
No	668	24.0	0	0	223	47.3	368	28.4	68	9.2
No Response	43	1.5	7	2.5	9	1.9	21	1.6	6	0.8
3. Perceived Hangover Effects										
Yes	1,597	57.3	19	6.7	396	84.1	795	61.4	387	52.4
No	1,093	39.2	259	92.2	58	12.3	450	34.7	326	44.1
No Response	96	3.5	3	1.1	17	3.6	50	3.9	26	3.5

Continued on next page

Table C.1—Continued

Drinking-Related Perceptions	Total (N=2,786) No.	Pct.	1st Time DUI (N=281) No.	Pct.	DUI Recidivist (N=471) No.	Pct.	DUI+ Traffic (N=1,295) No.	Pct.	Mixed Multiple (N=739) No.	Pct.
(a) Cannot Remember Part of the Conversation From Evening Before										
Yes	1,599	57.4	2	0.7	410	87.0	865	66.8	322	43.6
No	1,145	41.1	278	98.9	53	11.3	401	31.0	413	55.9
No Response	42	1.5	1	0.4	8	1.7	29	2.2	4	0.5
(b) Drinking Created Problems with Intimates										
Yes	1,654	59.3	31	11.0	394	83.7	827	63.9	402	54.4
No	1,012	36.3	246	87.6	58	12.3	398	30.7	310	41.9
No Response	120	4.4	4	1.4	19	4.0	70	5.4	27	3.7
(c) Had Blank Spots When Tried to Remember Prior Conversation										
Yes	1,371	49.2	2	0.7	397	84.3	686	53.0	286	38.7
No	1,342	48.2	276	98.2	59	12.5	577	44.5	430	58.2
No Response	73	2.6	3	1.1	15	3.2	32	2.5	23	3.1
4. Others' Perception of Self as a Normal Drinker										
Yes	1,457	52.3	14	5.0	381	80.9	796	61.5	266	36.0
No	1,222	43.9	258	91.8	74	15.7	448	34.6	442	59.8
No Response	107	3.8	9	3.2	16	3.4	51	3.9	31	4.2

Continued on next page

Table C.1--Continued

Drinking-Related Perceptions	Total (N=2,786) No.	Pct.	1st Time DUI (N=281) No.	Pct.	DUI Recidivist (N=471) No.	Pct.	DUI+ Traffic (N=1,295) No.	Pct.	Mixed Multiple (N=739) No.	Pct.
(a) Friends or Relatives Perceive as a Normal Drinker										
Yes	1,906	68.4	270	96.1	159	33.8	908	70.1	569	77.0
No	809	29.0	3	1.1	301	63.9	348	26.9	157	21.2
No Response	71	2.6	8	2.8	11	2.3	39	3.0	13	1.8
(b) Others Complain About Subject's Drinking										
Yes	1,344	48.2	12	4.3	377	80.0	681	52.6	274	37.1
No	1,391	49.9	262	93.2	85	18.1	595	45.9	449	60.7
No Response	51	1.9	7	2.5	9	1.9	19	1.5	16	2.2
(c) Family Members Feel Concerned About Subject's Drinking										
Yes	1,502	53.9	16	5.7	406	86.2	823	63.6	257	34.8
No	1,177	42.2	256	91.1	49	10.4	421	32.5	451	61.0
No Response	107	3.9	9	3.2	16	3.4	51	3.9	31	4.2

Table C.2

Distribution of DUI Offenders by Drinking History of Self

Drinking History	Total (N=2,786) No.	Total (N=2,786) Pct.	1st Time DUI (N=281) No.	1st Time DUI (N=281) Pct.	DUI Recidivist (N=471) No.	DUI Recidivist (N=471) Pct.	DUI+ Traffic (N=1,295) No.	DUI+ Traffic (N=1,295) Pct.	Mixed Multiple (N=739) No.	Mixed Multiple (N=739) Pct.
1. Alcohol Treatment										
Received	647	23.2	3	1.1	302	64.1	259	20.0	83	11.2
Not Received	2,089	75.0	275	97.8	160	34.0	1,013	78.2	641	86.8
No Response	50	1.8	3	1.1	9	1.9	23	1.8	15	2.0
(a) Attended A. A.										
Yes	663	23.8	3	1.1	304	64.5	272	21	84	11.4
No	2,088	74.9	276	98.2	160	34.0	1,004	77.5	648	87.7
No Response	35	1.3	2	0.7	7	1.5	19	1.5	7	0.9
(b) Had an Alcohol or Other Drug Treatment Problem										
Yes	615	22.1	2	0.7	301	63.9	246	19.0	66	8.9
No	2,115	75.9	276	98.2	159	33.8	1,024	79.1	656	88.8
No Response	56	2.0	3	1.1	11	2.3	25	1.9	17	2.3

Continued on next page

Table C.2--Continued

Drinking History	Total (N=2,786) No.	Pct.	1st Time DUI (N=281) No.	Pct.	DUI Recidivist (N=471) No.	Pct.	DUI+ Traffic (N=1,295) No.	Pct.	Mixed Multiple (N=739) No.	Pct.
2. Alcohol Addiction										
Addicted	979	35.1	4	1.4	360	76.4	444	34.3	171	23.1
Not Addicted	1,663	59.7	266	94.7	70	14.9	792	61.2	535	72.4
No Response	144	5.2	11	3.9	41	8.7	59	4.5	33	4.5
(a) Had Alcohol Beverage Before Noon										
Yes	1,130	40.5	3	1.1	356	75.6	590	45.5	181	24.5
No	1,616	58.0	276	98.2	108	22.9	685	53.0	547	74.0
No Response	40	1.5	2	0.7	7	1.5	20	1.5	11	1.5
(b) Had DTs, Severe Shaking, etc., After Heavy Drinking										
Yes	247	8.9	0	0	178	37.8	52	4.0	17	2.3
No	2,488	89.3	279	99.3	285	60.5	1,213	93.7	711	96.2
No Response	51	1.8	2	0.7	8	1.7	30	2.3	11	1.5
(c) Number of Days in a Week Usually Had at Least One Drink										
Daily	512	18.4	0	0	348	73.9	124	9.6	40	5.4
3-5 days	798	28.6	49	17.4	105	22.3	484	37.3	160	21.6
0-2 days	1,340	48.1	230	81.9	16	3.4	650	50.2	444	60.1
No Response	136	4.9	2	0.7	2	0.4	37	2.9	95	12.9

Continued on next page

Table C.2--Continued

Drinking History	Total (N=2,786) No.	Pct.	1st Time DUI (N=281) No.	Pct.	DUI Recidivist (N=471) No.	Pct.	DUI+ Traffic (N=1,295) No.	Pct.	Mixed Multiple (N=739) No.	Pct.
(d) Number of Drinks Had in a Usual Occasion										
1-3	1,416	50.8	245	87.2	41	8.7	688	53.1	442	59.8
4 or more	1,217	43.7	34	12.1	376	79.8	531	41.0	276	37.3
No Response	153	5.5	2	0.7	54	11.5	76	5.9	21	2.9
(e) Had Hangover in the Morning for Drinking the Night Before										
Seldom	2,194	78.7	268	95.4	82	17.4	1,161	89.7	683	92.4
Mostly	450	16.1	0	0	360	76.4	76	5.9	14	1.9
No Response	142	5.2	13	4.6	29	6.2	58	4.4	42	5.7
(f) Had a Drink to Cure a Hangover										
Yes	985	35.3	2	0.7	370	78.5	395	30.5	218	29.5
No	1,730	62.1	276	98.2	84	17.8	868	67.0	502	67.9
No Response	71	2.6	3	1.1	17	3.7	32	2.5	19	2.6
(g) Experienced Hands Shaking or Trembling in the Morning										
Yes	500	17.9	0	0	360	76.4	105	8.1	35	4.7
No	2,214	79.4	279	99.3	93	19.7	1,157	89.3	685	92.7
No Response	72	2.7	2	0.7	18	3.8	33	2.6	19	2.6

Continued on next page

Table C.2--Continued

Drinking History	Total (N=2,786) No.	Pct.	1st Time DUI (N=281) No.	Pct.	DUI Recidivist (N=471) No.	Pct.	DUI+ Traffic (N=1,295) No.	Pct.	Mixed Multiple (N=739) No.	Pct.
3. Job-Related Consequences										
Experienced	377	13.5	4	1.4	246	52.2	80	6.2	47	6.4
Not Experienced	2,368	85.0	275	97.9	219	46.5	1,191	92.0	683	92.4
No Response	41	1.5	2	0.7	6	1.3	24	1.8	9	1.2
(a) Got into Trouble at Work Because of Drinking										
Yes	370	13.3	4	1.4	233	49.5	81	6.2	52	7.0
No	2,377	85.3	275	97.9	231	49.0	1,195	92.3	676	91.5
No Response	39	1.4	2	0.7	7	1.5	19	1.5	11	1.5
(b) Lost a Job Because of Drinking										
Yes	240	8.6	0	0	151	32.1	58	4.5	31	4.2
No	2,511	90.1	280	99.6	317	67.3	1,214	93.7	700	94.7
No Response	35	1.3	1	0.4	3	0.6	23	1.8	8	1.1
(c) Neglected Obligations at Work for Two or More Days in a Row										
Yes	382	13.7	0	0	263	55.8	81	6.2	38	5.2
No	2,364	84.8	280	99.6	205	43.5	1,187	91.7	692	93.6
No Response	40	1.5	1	0.4	3	0.7	27	2.1	9	1.2

Continued on next page

Table C.2--Continued

Drinking History	Total (N=2,786)		1st Time DUI (N=281)		DUI Recidivist (N=471)		DUI+ Traffic (N=1,295)		Mixed Multiple (N=739)	
	No.	Pct.	No.	Pct.	No.	Pct.	No.	Pct.	No.	Pct.
4. Non-Job-Related Consequences										
Experienced	1,685	60.5	4	1.4	351	74.5	711	54.9	619	83.8
Not Experienced	1,055	37.9	275	98.2	109	23.2	563	43.5	108	14.6
No Response	46	1.6	2	0.4	11	2.3	21	1.6	12	1.6
(a) Got into Fights When Drinking										
Yes	1,253	45.0	4	1.4	123	26.1	499	38.5	627	84.8
No	1,487	53.4	276	98.2	343	72.8	769	59.4	99	13.4
No Response	46	1.6	1	0.4	5	1.1	27	2.1	13	1.8
(b) Lost Friends or Boyfriends/Girlfriends Because of Drinking										
Yes	626	22.5	2	0.7	218	46.3	288	22.2	118	16
No	2,119	76.0	278	98.9	246	52.2	986	76.2	609	82.4
No Response	41	1.5	1	0.4	7	1.5	21	1.6	12	1.6
(c) Had Liver Trouble Because of Drinking										
Yes	139	5.0	0	0	103	21.9	36	2.8	0	0
No	2,610	93.6	280	99.6	355	75.4	1,240	95.7	735	99.5
No Response	41	1.4	1	0.4	13	2.7	19	1.5	4	0.5

Continued on next page

Table C.2--Continued

Drinking History	Total (N=2,786)		1st Time DUI (N=281)		DUI Recidivist (N=471)		DUI+ Traffic (N=1,295)		Mixed Multiple (N=739)	
	No.	Pct.	No.	Pct.	No.	Pct.	No.	Pct.	No.	Pct.
(d) Had Been Arrested for Drunk Behavior										
Yes	1,213	43.5	6	2.1	338	71.8	709	54.8	160	21.7
No	1,535	55.1	273	97.2	130	27.6	565	43.6	567	76.7
No Response	38	1.4	2	0.7	3	0.6	21	1.6	12	1.6
(e) Had Been Arrested for Drunk Driving or Driving After Drinking										
Yes	2,463	88.4	0	0	463	98.3	1,274	98.4	726	98.2
No	281	10.1	281	100	0	0	0	0	0	0
No Response	42	1.5	0	0	8	1.7	21	1.6	13	1.8

References

Akers, R. L. (1994). *Theoretical Criminology*. Los Angeles: Roxbury.

Argeriou, M., McCarty D. & Blacker, E. (1985). Criminality Among Individuals Arraigned for Drinking and Driving in Massachusetts. *Journal of Studies on Alcohol* , 46, 525-530.

Arstein-Kerslake, G. W. & Peck, R. C. (1985). *A Typological Analysis of California DUI Offenders and DUI Recidivism Correlates*. Sacramento: California Department of Motor Vehicles.

Atkin, C. K., DeJong, W. & Wallack, L. (1992). *The Influence of Responsible Drinking TV Spots and Automobile Commercials on Young Drivers*. Washington, D. C.: AAA Foundation for Traffic Safety.

Baker, E. A. (1990). *Calvert County Study: A Program Evaluation of DWI Probationers Use of an In-Car Alcohol Breath Analyzer Ignition Interlock System*. Ph.D. Dissertation. College Park: University of Maryland.

Bankston, W., Jenkins, Q., Thayer-Doyle, C. & Thompson, C. (1986, March). Fear of the Drunk Driver: Analysis of an Emergent Social Problem. Paper presented at the annual meetings of the Southwestern Sociological Association, Austin, Texas.

Barnes, G. & Welte, J. (1988). Predictors of Driving While Intoxicated Among Teenagers. *Journal of Drug Issues* 18, 367-384.

Bartol, C. R. (1991). Origins of Criminal Behavior. *Criminal Behavior: A Psychosocial Approach*, 3rd edition, pp. 26-57. Englewood Cliffs, NJ: Prentice Hall.

Beerman, K. A., Smith, M. M. & Hall, R. L. (1988). Predictors of Recidivism in DUIs. *Journal of Studies on Alcohol* , 49, 443-449.

Berger, D. E. & Snortum, J. R. (1986). A Structural Model of Drinking and Driving: Alcohol Consumption, Social Norms, and Moral Commitments. *Criminology* , 24, 139-152.

Berger, P. L. & Luckman, T. (1966). *The Social Construction Reality: A Treatise in the Sociology of Knowledge*. New York: Doubleday.

Best, J. E. & Luckenbill, D. F. (1994). *Organizing Deviance.* 2nd edition. Englewood Cliffs, NJ: Prentice Hall.

Blumer, H. (1962). Society as Symbolic Interaction. In *Human Behavior and Social Processes*, edited by A. Rose, pp. 179-192. Boston: Houghton Mifflin.

————. (1969). *Symbolic Interactionism: Perspective and Method.* Englewood Cliffs, NJ: Prentice-Hall.

————. (1975). Symbolic Interaction and the Idea of Social System. *Revue Internationale de Sociologie*, 11, 3-12.

Blumstein, A., Cohen, J. & Farrington, D. (1988). Criminal Career Research: Its Value for Criminology. *Criminology*, 26, 1-35.

Borkenstein, R. F. (1980). Problems of Enforcement. In *Alcohol, Drugs and Traffic Safety: Proceedings of the Eighth International Conference, Vol. 2*, pp. 818-837. Toronto: Addiction Research Foundation.

————. (1985). Historical Perspective: North American Traditional and Experimental Response. *Journal of Forensic Sciences*, 5, 395-444.

Borkenstein, R. F., Crowther, R. F., Shumate, R. P. , Ziel, W .P. & Zylman, R. (1974). The Role of the Drinking Driver in Traffic Accidents (the Grand Rapids Study). In *Blutalkohol: Alcohol, Drugs, and Behavior. Vol.11, Suppl.1.* 2nd edition. Hamburg: Steintor.

Cahalan, D., Cisin, I. H. & Crossley, H. (1970). *American Drinking Practices.* New Brunswick, NJ: Rutgers University Center for Alcohol Studies, 1970.

Cash, W. J. (1941). *The Mind of the South.* New York: Knopf.

Caspi, A., Moffitt, T. E., Silva, P. A., Stouthamer-Loeber, M., Krueger, R. F. & Schmutte, P. S. (1994). Are Some People Crime-prone? Replications of the Personality-Crime Relationship Across Countries, Genders, Races, and Methods. *Criminology*, 32, 163-195.

Cavan, S. (1966). *Liquor License: An Ethnography of Bar Behavior.* Chicago: Aldine.

Chalfant, P. H., Beckley, R. E. & Palmer, C. E. (1994). *Religion in Contemporary Society.* 3rd edition. Springfield, Il: Peacock.

Clinard, M. B. & Meier, R. F. (1979). *Sociology of Deviant Behavior.* 5th edition. New York: Holt, Rinehart and Winston.

Cohen, R. L. (1992). Drunk Driving. *Bureau of Justice Statistics Special Report*. Washington, D. C.: U. S. Department of Justice.

Coser, L. A. (1977). *Masters of Sociological Thought: Ideas in Historical and Social Context*. New York: Harcourt.

Cox, D. J., Gressard, C. F., Quillian, W. C., Westerman, P. & Gonder-Frederick, L. (1992). *The Effects of Blood Alcohol Levels on Driving Simulator, Coordination, and Reaction Time Tests in a High Risk Population: Objective and Subjective Measures*. Washington, D. C.: AAA Foundation for Traffic Safety.

Cox, W. M. (1987). Personality Theory and Research. In *Psychological Theories of Drinking and Alcoholism*, edited by H. T. Blane and K. E. Leonard, pp. 59-89. New York: Guilford Press.

Curtis, L. A. (1975). *Violence, Race, and Culture*. Lexington, MA: Heath.

Denzin, N. K. (1973). Self and Society. In *Introduction to Sociology: Situations and Structures*, edited by J. D. Douglas, pp. 209-226. New York: The Free Press.

———. (1978). *The Research Act: A Theoretical Introduction to Sociological Methods*, 2nd edition. New York: McGraw-Hill.

———. (1987a). *The Alcoholic Self*. Newbury Park, CA: Sage.

———. (1987b). *The Recovering Alcoholic*. Newbury Park, CA: Sage.

———. (1987c). *Treating Alcoholism: An Alcoholics Anonymous Approach*. Newbury Park, CA: Sage.

Doerner, W. G. (1978). The Index of Southernness Revisited: The Influence of Wherefrom Upon Whodunnit. *Criminology*, 16, 47-66.

———. (1979, Spring). The Violent World of Johnny Reb: An Attitudinal Analysis of the 'Regional Culture of Violence' Thesis. *Sociological Forum*, 61-71.

Donelson, A. C., Beirness, D. J. & Mayhew, D. R. (1985). Characteristics of Drinking Drivers. *Impaired Driving. Report No.1*. Ottawa, Canada: Department of Justice.

Donnelly, P. G. (1978). Alcohol Problems and Sales in the Counties of Pennsylvania: A Social Area Investigation. *Journal of Studies on Alcohol*, 39, 848-858.

Donovan, D. M. (1989, September). Driving While Intoxicated: Different Roads to and from the Problem. *Criminal Justice and Behavior*, 16, 270-298.

Donovan, D. M. & Marlatt, G. A. (1982). Personality Subtypes Among Driving-While-Intoxicated Offenders: Relationship to Drinking Behavior and Driving Risk. *Journal of Consulting and Clinical Psychology*, 50, 241-249.

Donovan, D. M., Marlatt, G. A. & Salzberg, P. M. (1983). Drinking Behavior, Personality Factors and High-Risk Driving. *Journal of Studies on Alcohol*, 44, 395-428.

Donovan, D. M., Queisser, H. R., Salzberg, P. M. & Umlauf, R. L. (1985). Intoxicated and Bad Drivers: Subgroups Within the Same Population of High-Risk Men Drivers. *Journal of Studies on Alcohol*, 46, 375-382.

Donovan, D. M., Umlauf, R. L. & Salzberg, P. M. (1991). Bad Drivers: Identification of a Target Group for Alcohol-Related Prevention and Early Intervention. *Journal of Studies on Alcohol*, 51, 136-141.

Donovan, D. M., Umlauf, R. L., Queisser, H. R. & Salzberg, P. M. (1986). Personality Subtypes Among Driving-While-Intoxicated Offenders: Follow-up of Subsequent Driving Records. *Journal of Consulting and Clinical Psychology*, 54, 563-565.

Donovan, J. E. (1993). Young Adult Drinking-Driving: Behavioral and Psychosocial Correlates. *Journal of Studies on Alcohol*, 54, 600-613.

Ehrlich, N. J. & Selzer, M. L. (1967). A Screening Procedure to Detect Alcoholism. In *Traffic Offenders in the Prevention of Highway Injury*, edited by M. L. Selzer, P.W. Gikas & F. F. Hueke. Ann Arbor: Highway Safety Research Institute, University of Michigan.

Elliott, D. S. & Morse, B. J. (1993). *In-vehicle BAC Test Devices as a Deterrent to DUI*, NIAAA Final Report.

Eysenck, H. J. (1984). Crime and Personality. In *Personality Theory, Moral Development, and Criminal Behavior*, edited by D. J. Miller, D. E. Blackman & A. J. Chapman. Lexington, MA: Lexington Books.

Farrow, J. A. (1987). Young Driver Risk Taking: A Description of Dangerous Driving Situations Among 16-to 19-Year-Old Drivers. *International Journal of Addiction,* 22, 1255-1267.

Farrow, J. A. & Brissing, P. (1990). Risk for DWI: A New Look at Gender Differences in Drinking and Driving Influences, Experiences, and Attitudes among New Adolescent Drivers. *Health Education Quarterly,* 17, 213-331.

Federal Bureau of Investigation. (1992) *Uniform Crime Reports.* Washington, D. C.: Government Printing Office.

Fell, J. C. (1990). Drinking and Driving in America: Disturbing Facts--Encouraging Reductions. *Alcohol Health and Research World,* 14, 18-25.

Fillmore, M. T. & Vogel-Sprott, M. (1995). Expectancies About Alcohol-Induced Motor Impairment Predict Individual Differences in Responses to Alcohol and Placebo. *Journal of Studies on Alcohol,* 56, 90-97.

Friel, C. M., Vaughn, J. B. & del Carmen, R. C. (1987). *Electronic Monitoring and Correctional Policy: The Technology and Its Applications.* Washington, D. C.: National Institute of Justice.

Gastil, R. D. (1971). Homicide and a Regional Culture of Violence. *American Sociological Review,* 36, 412-437.

———. (1975). *Cultural Regions of the United States.* Seattle: University of Washington Press.

Goffman, E. (1959). *The Presentation of Self in Everyday Life.* Garden City, NY: Doubleday.

———. (1963). *Stigma.* Englewood Cliffs, NJ: Prentice-Hall.

Goode, E. (1994). *Deviant Behavior,* 4th edition. Englewood Cliffs, NJ: Prentice Hall .

Gottfredson, M. R. & Hirschi, T. (1990). *A General Theory of Crime.* Stanford, CA: Stanford University Press.

Gould, L. A. (1989). Criminality and Drinking While Intoxicated: A Comparison of DWI's and a Random Sample of Licensed Drivers. *Journal of Contemporary Criminal Justice,* 5, 114-126.

Gould, L. A. & Gould, K. H. (1992). First-time and Multiple DWI Offenders: A Comparison of Criminal History Records and BAC Level. *Journal of Criminal Justice ,* 20, 527-539.

Gould, L. A. & McKenzie, D. L. (1990). DWI: An Isolated Incident or a Continuous Pattern of Criminal Activity? In

Drugs, Crime and the Criminal Justice System, edited by R. A. Weisheit, pp. 257-272, Cincinnati, OH: Anderson.

Grasmick, H. G., Bursik Jr., R. J. & Arneklev, B. J. (1993). Reduction in Drunk Driving as a Response to Increased Threats of Shame, Embarrassment, and Legal Sanctions. *Criminology,* 31, 41-67.

Green, D. E. (1991). Inhibition, Motivation, and Self-Reported Involvement in Drinking and Driving Behavior. *Criminal Justice Review,* 16, 1-16.

Greenfeld, L. A. (1988). Drunk Driving, *Bureau of Justice Statistics Special Report.* Washington, D. C.: U.S. Department of Justice.

Gruenewald, P. J. (1991). Loss of Control Drinking Among First Offender Drunk Drivers. *Alcoholism: Clinical and Experimental Research ,* 15, 634-639.

Guardian Interlock Responsible Driver Program. (1993). *Finally, A Real Weapon Against DWI.* Fort Worth, TX: Texas Commission on Alcohol and Drug Abuse.

Gusfield, J. (1976). The Literary Rhetoric of Science: Comedy and Pathos in Drinking Driver Research. *American Sociological Review,* 41, 16-34.

————. (1981). *The Culture of Public Problems: Drinking-Driving and the Symbolic Order.* Chicago: University of Chicago Press.

Gusfield, J., Rasmussen, P. & Kotarba, J. (1984). The Social Control of Drinking-Driving: An Ethnographic Study of Bar Settings. *Law and Policy,* 6, 45-66.

Hackney, S. (1969). Southern Violence. *American Historical Review,* 74, 906-925.

Haight, F. (1985). Current Problems in Drinking Driving: Research and Intervention. *Journal of Studies in Alcohol,* Supplement No. 10.

Henslin, J. M. (1977). *Deviant Life-Styles.* New Brunswick, NJ: Transaction.

Hingson, R. & Howland, J. (1986). Prevention of Drunk Driving Crashes Involving Young Drivers: An Overview of Legislative Countermeasures. In *Proceedings of International Symposium on Young Drivers Impaired by Alcohol and Other Drugs,* edited by T. Benjamin, pp. 337-348. London: Royal Society of Medicine Services.

Hingson, R. & Howland, J. (1990) Use of Laws to Deter Drinking and Driving. *Alcohol Health and Research World*, 14, 36-43.

Homel, R. (1988). *Policing and Punishing the Drinking Driver: A Study of General and Specific Deterrence.* Secaucus, NJ: Springer-Verlag.

Hunt, D. (1971). *Matching Models in Education.* Toronto: Ontario Institute for Studies in Education.

Jacobs, J. B. (1988). Drinking and Crime. *Crime File: Study Guide.* Washington, D.C.: National Institute of Justice.

————. (1989). *Drunk Driving: An American Dilemma.* Chicago: The University of Chicago Press.

Jesness, C. & Wedge, R. (1983). *Manual for Youth Counselors.* Sacramento: California Youth Authority, 1983.

Johnson, V. & White, H. R. (1989). An Investigation of Factors Related to Intoxicated Driving Behaviors Among Youth. *Journal of Studies on Alcohol*, 50, 320-330.

Joksch, H. C. (1985). Review of the Major Risk Factors. *Journal of Studies on Alcohol* , 10, 47-53.

Jonah, B. A. & Wilson, R. J. (1986). Impaired Drivers Who Have Never Been Caught: Are They Different from Convicted Impaired Drivers? In *Alcohol, Accidents, and Injuries*, P-173. SAE Technical Paper Series 860195. Warrendale, PA: SAE Engineering Resource for Advancing Mobility.

Jonah, B. A. & Dawson, N. E. (1987). Youth and Risk: Age Difference in Risky Driving, Risk Perception, and Risk Utility. *Alcohol, Drugs, and Driving* , 3, 13-29.

Jung, J. (1994). *Under the Influence: Alcohol and Human Behavior.* Pacific Grove, CA: Brooks/Cole.

Keane, C., Maxim, P. S. & Teevan, J. T. (1993). Drinking and Driving, Self-control and Gender: Testing a General Theory of Crime." *Journal of Research in Crime and Delinquency*, 30, 30-46.

Keith, B. H. (1973). The Effects of Ethyl Alcohol on Men. In *Drug Use in America: Problem in Perspective.* pp. 6-59. Washington, D. C.: Commission on Marijuana and Drug Abuse.

Keith, R. (1992). *House Arrest Perfected: Monitor Offenders Electronically.* Marietta, GA: The Security Guild International.

Kelley, B. (1994, June 2). Drunken Driver Detectors. *The New York Times*.

Kenkel, D. S. (1993, October). Drinking, Driving and Deterrence: The Social Costs of Alternative Policies. *Journal of Law and Economics*, 877-913.

Kennedy, R. S., Turnage, J., Rugotzke, G. & Dunlap, W. P. (1994). Indexing Cognitive Tests to Alcohol Dosage and Comparison to Standardized Field Sobriety Tests. *Journal of Studies on Alcohol*, 55, 615-628.

Kent, C. S. (1990). Ignition Interlocks Help Deter Drunk Drivers. *The Police Chief*, 1, 54-55.

Kingsnorth, R. F., Alvis, L. & Gavia, G. (1993). Specific Deterrence and the DUI Offender: The Impact of a Decade of Reform. *Justice Quarterly*, 10, 265-288.

Krippendorff, K. (1980). *Content Analysis: An Introduction to its Methodology*. Beverly Hills: Sage.

Landrum, J. W., Windham, G. O. & Roebuck, J. B. (1981). *Criminal Behavior of DUI Offenders. Research Report No. 74.* Starkville, MS: Social Science Research Center, Mississippi State University.

Lane, R. F. (1992). *The Unauthorized Version: Truth and Fiction in the Bible*. New York, NY: Alfred A. Knopf.

Laurence, M. D., Snortum, J. R. & Zimring, F. E. (1988). *Social Control of Drinking Behavior*. Chicago, IL: The University of Chicago Press.

Light, R. (1994). *Criminalizing the Drunk-Driver*. Brookfield, Vermont: Dartmouth.

Lilly, J. R., Ball, R. A., Curry, G. D. & McMullen, J. (1993). Electronic Monitoring of the Drunk Driver: A Seven-Year Study of the Home Confinement Alternative. *Crime and Delinquency*. 39, 462-484.

Linnell, R. H. & Mook, S. J. (1991). *Ignition Interlock Devices: An Assessment of Their Application to Reduce DUI*. Tollhouse, CA: Harmony Institute, Inc.

Loftin, C. & Hill, R. H. (1974). Regional Subculture and Homicide: An Examination of the Gastil-Hackney Thesis. *American Sociological Review*, 39, 714-724.

Lucker, G. W. D., Kruzich, M., Holt, M. & Gold, J. (1991). The Prevalence of Antisocial Behavior Among U. S. Army DWI Offenders. *Journal of Studies on Alcohol*, 52, 318-320.

Lund, A. K. (1992, July/August). How Effective is Administrative License Revocation? *Traffic Safety*, p. 9.

Lund, A. K. & Wolfe, A. C. (1991). Changes in the Incidence of Alcohol-Impaired Driving in the United States, 1973-1986. *Journal of Studies on Alcohol* , 52, 293-301.

Lyman, S. & Scott, M. B. (1970). *A Sociology of the Absurd*. New York: Appleton-Century-Crafts.

McClelland, D. C., Davis, W. N., Kalin, R & Wanner, E. (1972). *The Drinking Man: Alcohol and Human Motivation*, New York: The Free Press.

McCord, J. (1984). Drunken Drivers in Longitudinal Perspective. *Journal of Studies on Alcohol*, 45, 316-320.

McWhiney, G. (1988). *Cracker Culture: Celtic Ways in the Old South*. Tuscaloosa: The University of Alabama Press.

Malone, B. C. (1989). Honky-Tonk Music. In *Encyclopedia of Southern Culture* , edited by C. R. Wilson & W. Farris, pp. 104-106. Chapel Hill: University of North Carolina Press.

Marlatt, G. A. & Rohsenow, D. J. (1980). Cognitive Processes in Alcohol Use: Expectancy and the Balanced Placebo Design. In *Advances in Substance Abuse: Behavioral and Biological Research*, edited by N. K. Mello, pp. 159-199. Greenwich, CT: JAI Press.

Maxfield, M. G. & Baumer, T. L. (1990). Home Detention with Electronic Monitoring. *Crime and Delinquency*, 36, 521-536.

Mead, G. H. (1934). *Mind, Self and Society*. Chicago, IL: The University of Chicago Press.

Megargee, E., Bohn, M. Jr. & Sink, F. (1979). *Classifying Criminal Offenders: A New System Based on the MMPI*. Beverly Hills, CA: Sage.

Metzger, D. S. & Platt, J. J. (1987). Problem Drinker Drivers: Client and Service Involvement Correlates of Treatment Outcome. *International Journal of Addictions*, 22, 181-186.

Miller, W. B. (1958). Lower Class Culture as a Generating Milieu of Gang Delinquency. *Journal of Social Issues* 14, 5-19.

Miller, W. R. & Windle, M. (1990). Alcoholism, Problem Drinking and Driving While Impaired. In *Drinking and*

Driving: *Advances in Research and Prevention*, edited by R. J. Wilson & R. E. Mann, pp. 68-95. New York: Guilford.

Morse, B. J. & Elliott, D. S. (1990). *Hamilton County Drinking and Driving Study: 30 Month Report*. Boulder, Denver: Institute of Behavioral Sciences, University of Colarado.

Morse, B. J. & Elliott, D. S. (1992). Effects of Ignition Interlock-Devices on DUI Recidivism: Findings from a Longitudinal Study in Hamilton County, Ohio. *Crime and Delinquency*, 38, 131-157.

Moskowitz, J. M. (1989). The Primary Prevention of Alcohol Problems: A Critical Review of the Research Literature. *Journal of Studies on Alcohol*, 50, 54-88.

Mullahy, J. & Sindelar, J. L. (1994). Do Drinkers Know When to Say When? An Empirical Analysis of Drunk Driving. *Economic Inquiry*, 32, 383-394.

Murty, K. S. (1989). *The Effects of Georgia's Driver Improvement Courses: An Evaluative Intervention with DUI Offenders.* Prepared for the Governor's Office of Highway Safety. Report No. 89-04-C-308-305, Atlanta, Georgia.

Murty, K. S. & Roebuck, J. B. (1991). The DUI Offender as a Social Type. *Deviant Behavior: An Interdisciplinary Journal*, 12, 451-470.

Murty, K. S., Ugenyi, V. & Roebuck, J. B. (1989). A Comparison of Crime Reportage in Two Nigerian Newspapers: Daily Times and New Nigerian. *International Journal of Comparative and Applied Criminal Justice*, 13, 97-108.

Nagin, D. S. & Paternoster, R. (1994). Personal Capital and Social Control: The Deterrence Implications of a Theory of Individual Deterrence in Criminal Offending. *Criminology*, 32, 581-601.

Nathen, P. E. & Lisman, S. A. (1976). Behavior and Motivational Patterns. In *Alcoholism: Interdisciplinary Approaches to an Enduring Problem*, edited by R. E. Tarter & A. A. Sugerman, pp. 13-33. Reading, MA: Addison-Wesley.

National Institute of Justice. (1984). Jailing Drunk Drivers: Impact of the Criminal Justice System. *Research in Brief*. Washington D. C.: U.S. Department of Justice.

Nichols, J. L. (1990). Treatment Versus Deterrence. *Alcohol Health and Research World*, 14, 44-51.

Nichols, J. L. & Ross, H. L. (1990). The Effectiveness of Legal Sanctions in Dealing with Drinking Drivers. *Alcohol, Drugs, and Driving*, 6, 33-60.

Nochajski, T. H., Miller, B. A., Wieczorek, W.F. & Whitney, R. (1993). The Effects of a Drinker-Driver Treatment Program: Does Criminal History Make a Difference? *Criminal Justice and Behavior.* 20, 174-189.

Official Code of Georgia Annotated. (1989). Charlottesville, Virginia: The Michie Company Law Publishers.

Osgood, W. D., Johnston, L. D., O'Malley, P. M. & Bachman, J. G. (1988). The Generality of Deviance in Late Adolescence and Early Adulthood. *American Sociological Review*, 53, 81-93.

Palmer, T. (1974). The Youth Authority's Community Treatment Project. *Federal Probation*, 38, 3-14.

———. (1984). Treatment and the Role of Classification: A Review of Basics. *Crime and Delinquency*, 30, 245-267.

———. (1992). *The Re-Emergence of Correctional Intervention.* Newbury Park, CA: Sage.

———. (1994). *A Profile of Correctional Effectiveness and New Directions for Research.* Albany: State University of New York Press.

Perrine, M. W. (1970). Identification of Personality, Attitudinal, and Biographical Characteristics of Drinking Drivers. *Behavioral Research in Highway Safety* , 2, 207-225.

———. (1990). Who Are the Drinking Drivers? The Spectrum of Drinking Drivers Revisited. *Alcohol Health and Research World*, 14, 26-35.

Perrine, M. W., Peck, R. C. & Fell, J. C. (1989). Epidemiological Perspectives on Drunk Driving. In *Surgeon General's Workshop on Drunk Driving. Background Papers*, pp. 35-76, Rockville, MD: Office of the Surgeon General, U. S. Department of Health and Human Services.

Petersilia, J. (1986). Exploring the Option of House Arrest. *Federal Probation*, 50, 50-55.

———. (1987). *Expanding Options for Criminal Sentencing.* Santa Monica, CA: RAND.

Petersilia, J., Greenwood, P. & Lavin, M. (1977). *Criminal Careers of Habitual Felons.* Prepared for The National Institute of Law Enforcement and Criminal Justice, Grant number R-2144-

DOJ. Washington, D. C.: National Institute of Law Enforcement and Criminal Justice.

Pfuhl, Jr., E. H. (1986). *The Deviance Process.* 2nd edition. Belmont, CA: Wadsworth.

Pollack, S. (1969). *The Drinking Driver and Traffic Safety Project.* Springfield, Va.: National Technical Information Service.

Preusser, D. F., Blomberg, R. P. & Ulmer, R. (1988). *Follow-up Evaluation of Wisconsin's 1982 Drinking and Driving Law. Final Report.* Washington, D.C.: National Highway Traffic Safety Administration.

Pruis, R. (1984). Anthropological and Sociological Approaches to Deviance: An Ethnographic Prospect. Paper presented at Deviance in a Cross-Cultural Context, Waterloo, Ontario.

Quay, H. & Parsons, L. (1971). *The Differential Behavior Classification of the Juvenile Offender.* Washington, D. C.: U. S. Bureau of Prisons.

Reynolds, J. R., Kunce, J. T. & Cope, C. S. (1991). Personality Differences of First-time and Repeated Offenders Arrested for Driving While Intoxicated. *Journal of Counseling Psychology,* 38, 289-295.

Roebuck, J. B. (1967). *Criminal Typology: The Legalistic, Physical, Constitutional, Hereditary Psychological-Psychiatric and Sociological Approaches.* Springfield, Il: Charles C. Thomas.

———. (1986). Sociability in a Black Outdoor Drinking Place. In *Studies in Symbolic Interaction, Vol. 7,* edited by Norman K. Denzin, pp. 161-197. Greenwich, Conn.: JAI Press.

Roebuck, J. B. & Frese, W. (1976). *The Rendezvous: A Case Study of An After-Hours Club.* New York: The Free Press.

Roebuck, J. B. & Hickson, M. (1984). *The Southern Redneck: A Phenomenological Study of Social Class.* 2nd edition. New York: Praeger.

Roebuck, J. B. & Kessler. R. G. (1972). *The Etiology of Alcoholism: Constitutional, Psychological, and Sociological Approaches.* Springfield, Il.: Charles C. Thomas, 139-235.

Roebuck, J. B., Murty, K. S. & Smith, R. A. (1993). Marielitos, Cuban Detainees, and the Atlanta Riot: A Study in Identity and Stigma Management. In *Studies in Symbolic Interaction, Vol.14,* edited by Norman K. Denzin, pp.239-268. Greenwich, Connecticut: JAI Press.

Roizen, J. & Schneberk, D. (1977). Alcohol and Crime. In *Alcohol, Casualties and Crime*, edited by M. Aarens, T. Cameron, J. Roizen, R. Roizen, R. Room, D. Schneberk & D. Wingard. Berkeley, CA: Social Research Group.

Rosenberg, H. & Davis L. (1994). Acceptance of Moderate Drinking by Alcohol Treatment Services in the United States. *Journal of Studies on Alcohol*, 55, 167-172.

Ross, H. L. (1990). Drinking and Driving: Beyond the Criminal Justice Approach. *Alcohol Health and Research World*, 14, 58-62.

————. (1991, Spring). Decriminalizing Drunk Driving: A Means to Effective Punishment. *Applied Behavior Analysis*, 1, 89-91.

————. (1992). *Confronting Drunk Driving: Social Policy for Saving Lives*. New Haven, Connecticut: Yale University Press, 1992.

Ross, H. L. & Foley, J. P. (1987). Judicial Disobedience of the Mandate to Imprison Drunk Driver. *Law and Society Review*, 21, 315-323.

Ross, H. L., McCleary, R. & LaFree, G. (1990). Can Mandatory Jail Laws Deter Driving? The Arizona Case. *Journal of Criminal Law and Criminology*, 81, 156-170.

Scoles, P., Fine, E. W. & Steer, E. W. (1984). Personality Characteristics and Drinking Patterns of High-Risk Drivers Never Apprehended for Driving While Intoxicated. *Journal of Studies on Alcohol* , 45, 411-416.

Scribner, R. A., MacKinnon, D. P. & Dwyer, J. H. (1994). Alcohol Outlet Density and Motor Vehicle Crashes in Los Angeles County Cities. *Journal of Studies on Alcohol*, 55, 447-453.

Selzer, M. L. (1971). The Michigan Alcoholism Screening Test: The Quest for a New Diagnostic Instrument. *American Journal of Psychiatry* , 127, 1653-1658.

Selzer, M. L. & Barton, E. (1977). The Drunken Driver: A Psychological Study. *Drug Alcohol Dependency*, 2, 239-247.

Selzer, M. L., Vinokur, A. & Wilson, T. D. (1977). A Psychological Comparison of Drunken Drivers and Alcoholics. *Journal of Studies on Alcohol*, 38, 1294-1300.

Sheingold, S. (1974). *The Politics of Rights*. New Haven: Yale University Press.

Simpson, H. M. (1985). Human-related Risk Factors in Traffic Crashes: Research Needs and Opportunities. *Journal of Studies on Alcohol,* Supplement No. 10, 32-39.

Smart, R. G., Adlaf E. M. & Knoke, D. (1991). Use of the CAGE Scale in a Population Survey of Drinking, *Journal of Studies on Alcohol* , 52, 593-596.

Snortum, J. R. (1984). Alcohol-impaired Driving in Norway and Sweden: Another Look at the Scandinavian Myth. *Law and Society,* 6, 5-37.

———. (1988). Deterrence of Alcohol Impaired Driving: An Effect in Search of a Cause. In *Social Control of the Drinking Driver,* edited by M. D. Laurence, J. R. Snortum & F. E. Zimring. Chicago: University of Chicago Press.

Snortum, J. R., Riva, P. R. & Burger, D. E. (1990). Police Documentation of Drunk-Driving Arrests: Jury Verdicts and Guilty Pleas as a Function of Quality and Quality of Evidence. *Journal of Criminal Justice,* 18, 99-116.

Snow, R. W. & Landrum, J. W. (1986). Drinking Locations and Frequency of Drunkenness Among Mississippi DUI Offenders. *American Journal of Drug Alcohol Abuse,* 12, 389-402.

Snow, R. W. & Wells-Parker, E. (1986). Drinking Reasons, Alcohol Consumption Levels, and Drinking Locations Among Drunken Drivers. *The International Journal of the Addictions,* 21, 671-689.

Snowden, L. R., Nelson, L. S. & Campbell, D. (1986). An Empirical Typology of Problem Drinkers from the Michigan Alcoholism Screening Test. *Addictive Behaviors,* 11, 37-48.

Sobell, M. B. & Sobell L. C. (1973). Individualized Behavior Therapy for Alcoholics. *Behavior Therapy,* 4, 49-72.

Sobell, L. C., Sobell M. B. & Toneatto, B. (1991). Recovery from Alcohol Problems Without Treatment. In *Self-Control and Addictive Behaviors,* edited by N. Heather, W. R. Miller & J. Oneeley, pp. 198-242. Elmsford, NY: Pergamon.

Stacy, A. W., Newcomb, M. D. & Bentler, P. M. (1991). Personality, Problem Drinking, and Drunk Driving: Mediating, Moderating, and Direct Effect Models. *Journal of Personality and Social Psychology,* 60, 795-811.

Stacy, A. W., Widerman, K. F. & Marlatt, G. A. (1990). Expectancy Models of Alcohol Use. *Journal of Personality and Social Psychology*, 58, 918-928.

Steer, R. A., Fine, E. W. & Scoles, P. E. (1979). Classification of Men Arrested for Drinking While Intoxicated and Treatment Implications: A Cluster-Anolgistic Study. *Journal of Studies on Alcohol*, 40, 222-229.

Stewart, K. & Gruenewald, P. (1986, October). The Characteristics of Drunk Driving Offenders and the Drunk Driving Offense. Paper presented at the American Society of Criminology, 38th Annual Meeting, Atlanta, Georgia.

Stone, H. P. (1962). Appearance and the Self. In *Human Behavior and Social Pressures*, edited by A. Rose, pp. 86-118. Boston, MA: Houghton Mifflin.

Surgeon General's Office. (1979). *Healthy People, The Surgeon General's Report on Health Promotion and Disease Prevention.* DHEW Publication No. (PHS) 79-55071. Washington, D. C.: Government Printing Office.

Sutker, P. B., Brantley, P. J. & Allain, A. N. (1980). MMPI Response Patterns and Alcohol Consumption in DUI Offenders. *Journal of Consulting and Clinical Psychology*, 48, 350-355.

Tashima, H. & Peck, R. C. (1986). *An Evaluation of the Specific Deterrent Effects of Alternative Sanctions for First and Repeat DUI Offenders.* Sacramento: California Department of Motor Vehicles.

Thornberry, T. P., Lizotte, A. J., Krohn, M. D., Farnworth, M. & Jang, S. J. (1994). Delinquent Peers, Beliefs, and Delinquent Behavior: A Longitudinal Test of Interactional Theory. *Criminology*, 32, 47-83.

Thurman, Q., Jackson, S. & Zhao, J. (1993). Drunk-Driving Research and Innovation: A Factorial Survey Study of Decisions to Drink and Drive. *Social Science Research* , 22, 245-264.

Toplin, R. B. (1975). *Unchallenged Violence: An American Ordeal.* Westport, CN: Greenwood.

U. S. Department of Health and Human Services. (1993). *Eighth Special Report to U. S. Congress on Alcohol and Health.*

Washington, D. C.: National Institute on Alcohol Abuse and Alcoholism.

————. (1990). *Seventh Special Report to the U. S. Congress on Alcohol and Health.* DHHS Publication No. (ADM). Washington, D. C.: National Institute on Alcohol Abuse and Alcoholism.

U. S. Department of Transportation. (1993). *Traffic Safety Facts, 1993,* Washington, D. C.

————. (1992). *Highway Statistics, 1992.* Washington, D. C.

————. (1968). *Alcohol and Highway Safety: Report to the United States Congress.* Washington, D. C.

Van Voorhis, P. (1987). Correctional Effectiveness: The High Cost of Ignoring Success. *Federal Probation,* 51, 56-62.

Veneziano, C., Veneziano, L. & Fichter, M. (1993). Psychological and Sociodemographic Characteristics of DWI Offenders. *Journal of Addictions and Offender Counseling, 14,* 14-24.

Vingilis, E. (1983). Drinking Drivers and Alcoholics: Are They From the Same Population? In *Research Advances in Alcohol and Drug Problems,* Vol. 7, edited by R. J. Smart, F. B. Glaser, Y. Isreal, H. Kalant, R. L. Popham & W. Schmidt, pp. 299-341, New York: Plenum.

Vingilis, E. (1994, Spring). Moderate Drinking and Traffic Crashes: A Case for Health or for Safety? *Contemporary Drug Problems,* 111-121.

Vold, G. B. & Bernard, T. J. (1986). *Theoretical Criminology.* 3rd edition. New York: Oxford University Press.

Votey, Jr., H. L., (1984). The Deterioration of Deterrence Effects of Driving Legislation: Have We Been Giving the Wrong Signals to Policymakers? *Journal of Criminal Justice,* 12, 115-130.

Waller, J. (1967). Identification of Problem Drinking Among Drunken Drivers. *Journal of American Medical Association,* 200, 114-120.

Waller, P. F. (1985). Licensing and Other Controls of the Drinking Driver. *Journal of Studies on Alcohol,* Supplement No. 10, 150-160.

Weed, F. J. (1987). Grass-Roots Activism and the Drunk Driving Issue. *Law and Policy , 9,* 259-278.

Wells-Parker, E., Cosby, P. J. & Landrum, J. W. (1986). A Typology for Drinking Driving Offenders: Methods for Classification and Policy Implications. *Accident Analysis and Prevention*, 18, 443-453.

Wells-Parker, E., Anderson, B., Pang, M. & Timken, D. (1993). An Examination of Cluster-Based Classification Schemes for DUI Offenders. *Journal of Studies on Alcohol*, 19, 209-218.

Whyatt-Brown, B. (1982). *Southern Honor: Ethics and Behavior in the Old South*. NY: Oxford University Press.

Wieczorek, W. F., Miller, B. A. & Nochajski, T. H. (1992). Multiple and Single Location Drinking Among DWI Offenders Referred for Alcoholism Evaluation. *American Journal of Drug Alcohol Abuse*, 18, 103-116.

Wieczorek, W. F., Mirand, A. L. & Callahan, C. P. (1994). Perception of the Risk of Arrest for Drinking and Driving. *Criminal Justice and Behavior*, 21, 312-324.

Wilkinson, J. T. (1987). Reducing Drunken Driving: Which Policies are Most Effective? *Southern Economic Journal*, 54, 322-334.

Willett, T. C. (1964). *Criminals on the Road: A Study of Serious Motoring Offenses and Those Who Commit Them*. London: Tavistock.

————. (1973). *Drivers After Sentence*. London: Heinemann.

Wilson, J. R. & Jonah, B. A. (1985). Identifying Impaired Drivers Among the General Driving Population. *Journal of Studies on Alcohol*, 46, 531-537.

Wolfgang, M. E. & Ferracuti, F. (1982). *The Subculture of Violence*. Beverly Hills, CA: Sage.

Yoder, R. & Moore, R. (1973). Characteristics of Convicted Drunken Drivers. *Quarterly Journal of Studies on Alcohol*, 34, 927-936.

Zelhart, P. F. (1972). Types of Alcoholics and Their Relationship to Traffic Violations. *Quarterly Journal of Studies on Alcohol*, 33, 811-813.

Zelhart, P. F., Schurr, B. C. & Brown, P. A. (1975). The Drinking Driver: Identification of High Risk Alcoholics. In *Alcohol, Drugs, and Traffic Safety: Proceedings of the Sixth International Conference*, edited by S. Isrealstam & S. Lambert, pp. 181-198. Toronto: Addiction Research Foundation.

Zimring, F. E. (1978). Policy Experiments in General Deterrence: 1970-1975. In *Deterrence and Incapacitation: Estimating the Effects of Criminal Sanctions on Crime Rates*, edited by A. Blumstein, J. Cohen & D. Nagin. Washington, D. C.: National Academy of Sciences.

————. (1982). *The Changing Legal World of Adolescence*. New York: Free Press.

Zimring, F. E. & Hawkins, G. (1973). *Deterrence: The Legal Threat in Crime Control*. Chicago: University of Chicago Press.

Zuckerman, M. (1979). *Sensation Seeking: Beyond the Optimal Level of Arousal*. Hillsdale, NJ: Erlbaum.

————. (1989). Personality in the Third Dimension: A Psychological Approach. *Personality and Individual Differences*, 10, 391-418.

Index